INTERNATIONAL VEGETARIAN COOKERY

SONYA RICHMOND

ARCO PUBLISHING COMPANY, INC.

NEW YORK

To My Yoga Pupils

Published by ARCO PUBLISHING COMPANY, Inc.
219 Park Avenue South, New York, N.Y. 10003

Fourth Printing, 1972

Library of Congress Catalog Card Number 66-21124
Paperback ISBN 0-668-01483-0
Library Binding ISBN 0-668-01510-1

Printed in the United States of America

CONTENTS

EDITORIAL NOTE

The majority of the cheeses mentioned in this book are readily available in delicatessens and many of the better supermarkets throughout the country. Some, however, can be purchased only in their home country, but they have been included for the interest and information of the vegetarian and any cheese-lover abroad.

TO ALL WOULD-BE VEGETARIANS

Many people would like, for health reasons and many others, to become vegetarians but often quail before that one great stumbling block—what on earth to eat in place of meat, fish and poultry. The sight of a mere plate of two vegetables without the familiar meat or fish would depress even the most determined would-be vegetarian, particularly the one with the healthy appetite. And so, in this book, I shall solve the problem of how to eat well, nay handsomely, and how to have appetising, well-balanced meals without eating meat, fish or poultry.

My book concentrates mainly on the heart of the problem, that is the soup and the entrée, those two courses with which the new vegetarian has the most difficulty. You will find hitherto unimagined hors d'oeuvres too, and a number of salads which you may not have heard of before, but you will find only the occasional dessert recipe, the one too good, or too unusual, to leave out. The pudding or dessert, not containing meat or fish anyway, is no problem to the vegetarian and you can look up recipes for them in other cookery books. My aim is to fill that vital gap in the middle of the meal.

Taking each country in turn, from A through the alphabet, I have started each chapter, wherever appropriate, with a section on that most valuable source of protein—cheese. And in describing the best cheeses of each country I hope to persuade my readers that cheese, as well as being a concentrated and valuable source of protein, is a connoisseur's delight and a source of endless fascination to those holidaying abroad. As it would take a whole book to mention all the world's cheeses, I have restricted myself to the best known, the most easily obtainable and one or two lesser known ones which are too delectable to leave out.

I have included recipes for eggs, milk, butter and cheese, dairy products frowned upon by vegans, those highly dedicated and totally strict vegetarians who live on a raw diet of fruit, nuts and vegetables. But I would say to them, this book is not for you who have already worked out your raw food diet but for the ordinary hearty eater who likes delicious and appetising meals without overburdening his system.

On my travels I have collected a vast number of exotic recipes from vegetarians throughout the world. Each country has its own colourful specialities and on reading this book you will find that vegetarian cookery, far from being dull, stodgy, and unexciting to prepare, can open up a completely new and delightful vista of the gentle arts of haute cuisine and good eating.

SONYA RICHMOND

9

USEFUL INFORMATION

STANDARD MEASURES

1 cup	breadcrumbs, toasted	2½ oz.
"	breadcrumbs, fresh	3 oz.
"	cheese, grated	3½-4 oz.
"	flour	5 oz.
"	butter	8 oz.
"	margarine	8 oz.
"	cooking fat	8 oz.
"	rice, raw	9 oz.
"	rolled oats	4 oz.
"	sugar, granulated	8 oz.
"	sultanas, currants, raisins	6-6½ oz.
"	maple syrup, molasses, honey	16 oz.
"	icing sugar	5-5½ oz.

N.B. *Cup measures according to the British Standards Institution Measuring Cup = ½ pint.*

Ingredients	Tablespoons per oz.	British Measuring Cup	American Measuring Cup
Fresh breadcrumbs	5	3 oz.	2¼ oz.
Butter	2	8 oz.	6 oz.
Grated cheese	4	4 oz.	3 oz.
Cornstarch	3	5 oz.	4 oz.
Flour	3	5 oz.	4 oz.
Margarine, cooking fat and lard	2	8 oz.	6 oz.
Brown sugar	2½	7 oz.	5½ oz.
Granulated sugar	2	8 oz.	6 oz.
Sifted icing sugar	3½	4 oz.	3 oz.
Water	—	10 oz.	8 oz.

N.B. *Brown sugar should be packed into the cup.*

1	tblsp.	flour	½ oz.
1	"	granulated sugar	1 oz.
1	"	syrup, molasses, honey	1¼ oz.
4	"	breadcrumbs	1 oz.
2	"	butter	1 oz.
2½	"	brown sugar	2 oz.
1	"	jam, marmalade	1 oz.
2½	"	cornstarch	1 oz.
10	"	melted butter	5 oz. (¼ pint)
20	"	melted butter	10 oz. (1 cup)
1 pint		melted butter	20 oz.

N.B. *Unless otherwise stated, 1 tblsp.=a rounded tablespoon throughout.*

OVEN TEMPERATURES

Heat required	Gas	Electric
Very slow	0 - ½	93-121°C. or 200-250°F.
Slow	1 - 2	121-149°C. or 250-300°F.
Very moderate	2 - 3	149-177°C. or 300-350°F.
Moderate	3 - 4	177-190°C. or 350-375°F.
Moderately hot	4 - 5	190-218°C. or 375-425°F.
Hot	6 - 7	218-232°C. or 425-450°F.
Very hot	8 - 9	232-245°C. or 450-475°F.

A Dictionary of Vegetables

Artichoke, globe Prized for the succulence of its flower bud scales and incomparable when dipped in melted butter or margarine. Another variety is known as the Chinese artichoke.

Artichoke, Jerusalem Surprisingly a native of Canada and not of Israel, these oddly shaped, nodular tubers are quite a different plant from the above. A brown mouse of a vegetable to look at, but extremely good when properly cooked.

Asparagus Expensive, succulent, quite without peer, asparagus asks nothing but a little respect and lots of melted butter or margarine.

Beans, broad These need a little help with herbs and seasonings but otherwise make excellent eating.

Beans, butter Added to soups they add flavour, thickening, and substance, but should be used with discretion as they can overpower with sheer bulk.

Beans, French These thin, green, delicate beans are good to look at, easy to cook, and perhaps the most flavourful of all the beans.

Beans, haricot Nutty flavoured and flaky textured when cooked properly, they are perfect for the big stews.

Beetroot The possibilities of the beetroot are seemingly endless. One of the most useful, versatile and economical of vegetables, it can be eaten cooked or raw, young, old or middle-aged. Whatever the season, the beetroot will give faithful service to the ingenious cook. It will see you through from the hors d'oeuvres to the dessert.

Borecole Known also as kale. This is a member of the cabbage family and available in several varieties.

Broccoli This is one of my personal favourites. It needs a careful hand to bring out the exceptionally delicate and fine flavour but it is well worth your time and patience. Buy plenty of it when it is in season for it never stays long in the shops. Also try Calabrese which is a delicious Italian sprouting broccoli.

Brussels Sprouts One of the most unjustly abused vegetables I know, both while being cooked and while being eaten. Most people *boil* them in far too much water and then, when they are reduced to a mass of yellowish sog, the liquid is poured down the sink and the residue placed before the protesting family. Before you attempt to cook them again, try them my way. You will find them under Great Britain and Belgium.

Cabbage The Cinderella of the vegetables. It is usually regarded as being rather unexciting but I have included some ways of preparing it which will send you flying to the nearest greengrocer to buy the biggest one you can find. Don't forget that as well as the familiar green variety there are also to be found, if you search the more adventurous greengrocers' shops, Chinese cabbage (Pe-Tsai), Portuguese cabbage, and the absolutely indispensable hard red cabbage.

Carrots Not everyone's taste when cooked perhaps, but eaten raw when young and fresh, grated or sliced into salads and hors d'oeuvres, they add not only a delicious bite but also a dash of bright colour.

Cauliflower This can be a most attractive vegetable both to look at and to eat, but again much abused and drowned in too much water. Have you ever tried cauliflower chopped up raw in green and tossed salads?

Celeriac Many people wonder just what this is and whether it is merely another spelling for celery. It is indeed a species of celery but with thick swollen roots rather like turnips which are eaten instead of the blanched stems. Celeriac is not only useful as a vegetable in soups and salads but also as a flavouring.

Celery One of the aristocrats of the kitchen garden. It has a delicious and distinctive flavour and adds a touch of haute cuisine to the most mundane salad, soup or stew. Delightful in appearance, flavour and texture.

Chard This is a variety of seakale beet, rich in iron. Colourwise it is quite splendid with its bright red stems, midribs and veins.

Chicory A fine salad vegetable and also good when braised. The slightly bitter flavour is an acquired taste but beloved of good cooks the world over.

Chilli peppers These are used in highly flavoured Asiatic dishes. Green or red they are very fierce, so use them sparingly.

Chives The babies of the onion family, they are easy to grow and impart that indispensable onion taste and bouquet to salads and omelettes without clouding the breath.

Coleworts Cabbages really, so don't be puzzled by the name if you see it at your local greengrocers. They are small hardy cabbages with hard green hearts, but again must not be drowned in water.

Corn on the Cob Always a treat, these golden, succulent cobs are best cooked quickly in a pressure cooker, or in fast boiling water in a heavy pan with a tight-fitting lid, and then smothered in melted butter. Tins of corn cobs, corn taken off the cob, or creamed corn, are also delicious in soups, stews and as omelette fillings.

Courgettes These have become more popular in recent years and are tiny marrows. When young they can be eaten without peeling and are best cooked in butter or margarine with a little salt and served sprinkled with finely grated cheese.

Cress Sharp and tangy, its flavour is unmistakable in a salad and it is also useful as a garnish for sandwiches and vegetable dishes of contrasting colour.

Cucumber Surprisingly this is a native of India. Incomparably elegant in every dish it graces, it can also be cooked and sprinkled with grated cheese, stuffed with a nut mixture and baked, or (in the case of gherkins) can be pickled in a variety of different ways.

Endive This looks like a lettuce with a permanent wave. It can prove cheaper than lettuce for autumn and winter salads, for lettuce is cheap only in summer and late spring. It has a slightly different flavour from lettuce, but is wholly delightful in taste and texture.

Gourds or **Squash** These are of the pumpkin family, are of tropical origin, and can be used in exactly the same way as pumpkins, i.e stuffed and baked or made into jams and preserves.

Horse-radish For a really pungent sauce or garnish this one is a necessity. It is also used as a flavouring agent and, left in the ground when not in use, it will keep indefinitely.

Kohl-rabi A substitute for turnips with a rather exotic name, but the flavour is somewhat milder. Don't buy them if they are larger than tennis balls, and eat the leaves also, either raw in a salad or cooked in butter or margarine.

Leeks These succulent members of the onion family can be cooked in a variety of ways and deserve every bit of their great popularity. Use the white parts only and cook very slowly to bring out the exceptionally delicate flavour.

Lettuce Needs no introduction from anyone. It has just about everything to earn it the title of the perfect vegetable. It looks good, whichever variety you choose, it tastes even better, it has a wonderful texture, and it is packed with vitamins.

Mint Spearmint and Apple mint—this is more useful as a flavouring and a garnish rather than as a vegetable, and it makes quite extraordinary drinks.

Okra This unusual vegetable is called Ladies Fingers in England and other Western countries. A native of Abyssinia, it is a member of the cotton family, and can be bought fresh in many Continental delicatessen shops, but is also available in tins. It is less interesting in texture, which is rather mushy, than in taste, which is not unlike that of ripe gooseberries. The taste is greatly enhanced by the addition of well fried onions and plenty of seasoning.

Onions Cooking without onions is like dancing with only one leg. Choose the big sweet juicy Spanish ones every time. They are more expensive than some other varieties but they are worth it.

Parsley If you are already a cook you will have anticipated my feelings about parsley. Indispensable as a seasoning and without peer as a garnish for absolutely any savoury dish.

Parsnips Not everyone's taste but eaten faithfully by its devotees.

Peas There are few vegetables more pleasing than succulent, fresh garden peas. Treat them gently, a touch of salt, a breath of fresh mint, and serve with a piece of butter. Look out for asparagus peas which are a native of Southern Europe. They have the best of both worlds, a flavour which is half asparagus and half green pea, but in fact they are not of the pea family.

Potatoes These are not nearly as fattening as bread or cakes, and there are literally hundreds of delicious ways of preparing and serving them. They are economical and extremely versatile and can be made into soups, puddings, fritters, salads, cakes, scones, or even whisky! Historical note—potatoes were cultivated in South and Central America as early as A.D. 200.

Radishes These little red vegetables have a crunchy texture and an interesting peppery taste. Sliced thinly they are perfect for salads and hors d'oeuvres.

Salsify This is an unusual one which is called the vegetable oyster. It needs careful preparation but it is worth your patience for it has a subtle and exotic flavour.

Savoy The grand-daddy of the cabbage tribe, this one has a wrinkled face and a mature sort of flavour. Slice thinly and don't drown it in too much water.

Scorzonera Maybe you haven't heard of this one but you might even have bought some thinking they were parsnips. They are cooked in much the same way but have a rather different flavour.

Seakale A marvellous vegetable. Don't be afraid to buy it if you are lucky enough to see it. Treat it like young cabbage.

Swedes or **Rutabagas** Pleasant and earthy, use when no larger than a tennis ball. Add to stews of all kinds, soups and a little grated raw into a salad.

Sweet Peppers or **Capsicums** Beautiful in their luscious skins of shiny green or pillar-box red, sweet peppers have a pungent and mysterious taste and a wonderful crunchy texture. Once they have graced your kitchen and your cooking, I am sure you will never want to be without them again.

Sweet Potatoes Another vegetable which I can describe only in superlatives. Baked in their jackets in the oven and served with butter they are quite delicious. If you can imagine a potato which tastes like a chestnut, there you have the sweet potato, dry, floury and so different.

Tomato This is a native of South America and was first brought to Europe by the Spaniards. There is little the versatile tomato cannot do. In this book you will find some ways of incorporating them into food that you may not have heard of before.

Turnips Use when no larger than billard balls. Add to stews, salads or soups to impart a strong, solid flavour.

Vegetable Marrow This has little flavour of its own but makes an ideal case for a really tasty stuffing. It can also be made into marrow and ginger jam, chutney and marmalade. Look out also for custard marrows and Argentine marrows.

Austria

Here is a list of some of the most delicious of the many cheeses made in Austria. Too numerous to mention them all, I list here my personal favourites.

Bergkäse (Mountain Cheese) A hard cheese in various shades of gold, with holes of all sizes. The flavour varies from the very mild to the pungent.

Mischlingkäse (Blended Cheese) A hard cheese, pale yellow in colour, sometimes turning to green. Sharp flavoured with an aggressive bouquet.

Schlosskäse (Castle Cheese) A small soft cheese, made in the shape of a little sand-castle. Usually full cream but sometimes three-quarter, it has a sharp taste, and comes in a bright red wax wrapping.

Edelpilzkäse Perhaps my favourite Austrian cheese, and the most unusual of that country. It is a full cream cheese, looking, when you cut a piece from it, rather like a good English Stilton. It is a creamy white or a delicate yellow in colour with slight blue veining which is very evenly distributed. In flavour it is quite distinctive, very sharp with a curiously mouldy element, but don't let this description put you off, for it is quite marvellous.

Mondseer Schlosskäse and **Mondseer Schachtelkäse** (Castle Mondseer and Chalet Mondseer) This hails from the Mond Lake (Mondsee) district and is not made anywhere else in Austria. The former is the better one, being whole cream, but both taste good and sharp.

Butter and Salami Cheese, named according to whether it is shaped like a loaf or a sausage, both being soft cheese, mild, unsalted, buttery looking with a slightly sour taste and bouquet.

Quargel Cheese For this you need a stout heart and a strong devotion to cheese for it is one of the most aggressive, both in taste and smell. Made of sour milk, it is a pale bright yellow outside and a creamy white in the centre. Innocuous it seems, until you go near it! It has a covering of rust coloured or buttercup wax.

Of the dozens of other varieties which I have not mentioned many are farm-made cream and soft cheeses which are never sold commercially; others are rather more European than strictly Austrian in character, thus many Swiss born-and-bred cheeses appear with Austrian names. This is also true of Dutch, German and French cheeses.

BERGKÄSE SOUP

The original recipe calls for Austrian Bergkäse, but as this is not always easy to find, a good substitute would be Parmesan. To every pint of a good, strong, vegetable stock take one full teacup of grated strong cheese. Heat the stock but do not boil. Add the cheese a little at a time and stir until the cheese has melted. Beat 2 or 3 eggs, according to size, and put them into a heated tureen. Pour the hot, but not boiling soup over them, a little at a time, stirring with a wooden spoon. Serve at once.

SAUTÉ MUSHROOMS WITH CHEESE AND COGNAC

This is a delicious recipe combining mushrooms with cheese.

1 lb. mushrooms
2 slices toasted black bread per serving
3 tblsp. corn oil

3 tblsp. grated cheese
  (Mondseer or Parmesan)
1 tblsp. cognac
salt and black pepper

Sauté the mushrooms, thinly sliced, in the oil for 10 minutes. Add cheese and seasoning, and just before serving add the cognac. Serve on hot buttered toast.

TYROLEAN CHEESE SOUP

You don't have to spend hours in order to get a really good soup. This one can be made in 25 minutes from start to finish.

¼ lb. grated Swiss or Parmesan cheese
4 tblsp. chopped spring onions or chives
salt and black pepper

½ cup margarine
½ cup flour (wholewheat is best)
1 pint hot water

Melt the butter, take the saucepan off the heat and blend in the flour and seasoning. Very gradually add the hot water, mixing with a wooden spoon until very smooth. If you wish you can use half hot milk and half water. Put on a close-fitting lid and cook very very slowly for exactly 20 minutes. An occasional stir with a wooden spoon is all that is required. Just before serving add the grated cheese and garnish each soup bowl with chopped spring onions or chives. Serve with chunks of good dark bread.

CABBAGE SOUP WITH CHEESE

1 pint milk
1 pint water
1 large potato, grated

2 tblsp. margarine
½ lb. shredded white cabbage
¼ lb. Gruyère or Parmesan, grated

Melt some of the margarine in a heavy-bottomed saucepan with a tight-fitting lid. Cook the cabbage and the grated potato in it until soft. Mash with milk and the rest of the margarine, and gradually add all the liquid. Cook very slowly with the lid on for 15 minutes, stirring occasionally with a wooden spoon. Just before serving add the grated cheese. Serve with ·coarse wholewheat bread.

MUSHROOM AND CHEESE SAUCE (for spaghetti or noodles)

1 cup corn oil	3 cloves of garlic, crushed and chopped
1 lb. mushrooms	2 oz. grated hard cheese
	salt and black pepper

Heat oil, add sliced mushrooms and garlic, and brown slowly. Season and add grated cheese. Simmer for 10 minutes, then serve.

KING OF MUSHROOM SOUP

This delightful and highly unusual haute cuisine soup truly lives up to its name. We have all enjoyed cream of mushroom soup (the recipe for which follows this one) but for mushroom soup par excellence try this one.

1 lb. mushrooms	1 cup cream or tinned milk
1 pint milk	¼ cup cognac
1 oz. flour	⅛ tsp. powdered ginger
1 oz. butter	olives as required
	salt and black pepper

Make a roux of butter and flour, i.e. cook flour in melted butter for a few minutes, add salt and a grate of black pepper and the ginger. Very gradually add the heated milk, stirring all the time with a wooden spoon to keep the mixture velvet smooth. Add the very thinly sliced mushrooms, put the lid on the pan and simmer for 20 minutes. Add the cream or tinned milk and reheat. Just before serving add the cognac and sprinkle with finely chopped olives. The green ones are best for this purpose.

AUSTRIAN CREAM OF MUSHROOM SOUP

½ lb. mushrooms	1 pint scalded milk
½ cup thick cream	1 small onion
1 oz. butter	2 saltsp. powdered nutmeg
1 oz. flour	salt and black pepper

Cook the flour in the melted butter for a few minutes, add 1 saltspoonful of nutmeg, and season. Very gradually add the scalded milk and stir constantly. Add finely sliced mushrooms and cook with the lid on for 15 minutes. Pour in cream, stirring all the time, bring up to just below boiling, sprinkle with remaining nutmeg and serve.

AUSTRIAN POTATO SALAD

1 lb. waxy potatoes	1½ tblsp. tarragon vinegar
1 small onion, minced	1 tblsp. olive oil
1 clove garlic	1 tblsp. parsley
salt and black pepper	½ tsp. French mustard

Boil the potatoes in their jackets and peel them while they are still warm. Slice, and arrange them in salad bowl with the onion, garlic, salt, pepper and chopped parsley. Bring the oil, vinegar and mustard to the boil, pour over the salad and serve cold.

After that highly unusual potato salad, here is one of the most surprising of all salads:

HOT LENTIL SALAD

½ lb. lentils	1 small onion, chopped
½ pint well-flavoured stock or vegetable water	3 tblsp. chopped parsley

Soak the lentils in enough water to cover them for 2 hours. Drain, then cook them in the stock until tender. Mix with parsley and onion, then pour over the following dressing:

2 tblsp. tarragon vinegar	1 egg yolk, beaten
1 tblsp. chopped onion	1 breakfast cup sour cream
freshly grated black pepper	

Mix all together until well blended. Serve the salad warm.

CHEESE, RICE AND TOMATO SOUP

½ lb. ripe tomatoes	2 pints water
¼ lb. Parmesan cheese	1 cup rice
1 oz. butter	1 small onion, minced
salt and black pepper	

Cook the minced onion in the butter until soft, add the tomatoes, the uncooked rice and the water. Stir well, then bring to the boil and simmer very gently for 30 minutes. Add seasoning to taste and just before serving add the Parmesan cheese.

MARROW SOUP

If, like me, you have some enthusiastic gardening friends who present you year after year with an outsize vegetable marrow, you will appreciate the problem it can cause. You can serve it stuffed one day, turn a few pounds of it into jam, add some to the mixed steamed vegetables, and still have a large piece of it left. What to do with this remaining piece has occupied my idle thoughts from time to time, so that when I was in Austria last year I was delighted to find the answer. The following unusual soup was made for me.

½ lb. peeled and chopped marrow	2 oz. butter or margarine
1 medium-sized onion, minced	2 tblsp. wholewheat flour
1½ pints stock	1 tblsp. chopped parsley
1 cup cream or tinned milk	salt and black pepper

Melt the butter in a heavy-bottomed saucepan, add the marrow, onion, and parsley and cook until tender. Add the flour and blend. Take the pan off the heat and add the cream or tinned milk, the stock (which should be boiling) and the seasoning. Serve at once.

While we are on the subject of unusual soups, and where better to find them than in Austria, this one will appeal to all lovers of nuts. To those who have never heard of a nut soup, let me assure them that this one is very easy to make and is quite delicious.

NUT SOUP

½ cup chopped almonds (blanched)	1 tblsp. cornstarch
½ lb. confectioner's sugar	¼ tsp. cinnamon
3 or 4 egg yolks	2 pints milk
1 small carton double cream	

Boil the milk and the finely chopped blanched almonds together, then turn down the heat and simmer gently. Put the cream, egg yolks, sugar and cinnamon in a mixer and blend. Blend the cornstarch with a little cold milk and add the boiling milk to it, stirring with a wooden spoon. Add the egg mixture to the cornstarch and milk and stir, off the heat, until thick and creamy. Serve with savoury biscuits.

BEER SOUP

This last soup is good for keeping out the cold.

2 pints light ale	½ lb. sugar (or less, according to taste)
1 small carton of cream (single)	5 or 6 medium egg yolks
cinnamon powder as required	

This soup must not boil or it will be spoiled, so use a double boiler. Have the water in the lower half boiling, heat the beer in the top half and when warm add the blended cream, egg and sugar. Stir with a wooden spoon, gradually increasing the heat of the soup until it begins to thicken slightly. The soup is now ready. Season with cinnamon and serve at once.

POTATO CAKES

8 oz. mashed potatoes	1 oz. butter or margarine
2 oz. flour	2 beaten eggs
1 oz. semolina	salt and pepper

Beat the eggs with the melted butter. Mix with the other ingredients and form into a dry dough. Add more flour if the eggs are large. Roll on to a floured board and cut into triangles. Brush with melted butter and bake in a fast oven.

These are delicious if split open and spread with butter while still hot.

PAN FRIED POTATO CAKES

8 oz. hot mashed potatoes	oil for cooking
1 oz. butter	nutmeg to taste
3 large eggs	salt and black pepper

Mix all ingredients, except oil, into a dough. Roll out on to floured board and cut into triangles. Heat oil in large pan, and brown cakes on both sides. Serve very hot with butter and grated cheese.

SWEET OMELETTE

The following unusual omelette is a very economical and satisfying supper dish. It would double equally well as a solid dessert after a light meal.

1 large apple, peeled and minced	2 oz. chopped raisins
1 large egg	3 tblsp. butter for frying
4 thick slices of bread with crusts	1 tblsp. confectioner's sugar
½ pint milk	a pinch of salt

Cube bread, mix remaining ingredients, and add to the bread, mixing well. Allow to stand for 20 minutes. Heat butter in a frying pan, pour in the mixture, fry steadily until brown on both sides. Divide into 2 pieces and serve sprinkled with sugar.

FRIED POTATO SAVOURY

This is a good way to serve left-over mashed potatoes, especially if you are in a hurry but also have an appetite.

½ lb. mashed potatoes	1 medium-sized onion, minced
2 oz. butter or margarine	1 large egg
salt and black pepper	

Melt the butter in a frying pan and brown the onion in it. Beat the potatoes with the egg and seasoning and add the fried onion, mixing well. Melt some more butter and brown the mixture in it on both sides. Serve on heated plates.

Here are two excellent cabbage recipes from Vienna. The first is one of the best ways of serving this much abused vegetable.

RED CABBAGE WITH CHESTNUTS

1 medium-sized red cabbage	1 dessertsp. dark brown sugar
10 boiled and peeled chestnuts	½ pint vegetable stock
1 carton single cream	

Trim the cabbage of its outer leaves and cook whole for 15 minutes in boiling, salted water. Scoop out enough of the heart to take the chestnuts which should be sprinkled with the sugar. Simmer the cabbage in the stock until tender and just before serving add the cream.

CABBAGE IN BUTTER SAUCE

1 large white cabbage	2 oz. butter
1 large onion, chopped	1 oz. dark brown sugar
1 cup chopped nuts	1 cup stock
salt and black pepper	

Make the sauce first by making a roux with 1 tablespoonful butter and 3 tablespoonfuls flour, add 2 cups of hot milk and stir with wooden spoon until creamy. Season with salt and black pepper and keep the sauce hot while you prepare the cabbage thus:

Clean and shred the cabbage coarsely, plunge it into boiling water, strain, and plunge into cold. Drain again. Melt the butter and brown the onion in it and then add the sugar and the chopped nuts. Add the stock, bring to the boil, add the cabbage and simmer until tender, with lid on. Pour the sauce over the cabbage and serve.

ONION AND POTATO CASSEROLE

A simple dish for a quick and tasty supper. For best results you should oil the whole dish including the lid. I have tried it with and without oiling the lid and I must confess that the oiled lid method is the better one.

1 medium potato per person	butter as required
1 large sweet Spanish onion per person	hot milk as required
salt and black pepper	

Peel and slice potatoes and onions and arrange in layers in oiled casserole. Dot each layer with butter and sprinkle with salt and freshly ground black pepper. Add hot milk until the casserole is just over half full. Cover and bake in a slow oven (300 degrees maximum) for 2 hours.

LITTLE CAULIFLOWER PIES

Cauliflower is good whichever way you cook it, or even if you eat it raw chopped up into a green or tossed salad. For cooks who want to be different with cauliflower, this is a most unusual way of cooking it.

1 cauliflower	4 egg whites, stiffly beaten
½ lb. flour	grated cheese (Parmesan is best)
½ cup light ale	oil for frying
1 tblsp. melted butter	a pinch of salt

Put the cauliflower on to cook in a small amount of salted water. Keep the lid on tightly and have it on a low heat. While it is cooking make the following pastry. Mix together the flour, melted butter, beer and salt and make into a dough. Add the beaten egg whites. Now coat the partly cooked cauliflower with this pastry and fry in smoking hot oil. Drain and serve with plenty of grated cheese.

CREAM CHEESE SAVOURIES

Start these the day before for best results.

½ lb. flour	¼ lb. butter or margarine
a pinch of salt	¼ lb. cream cheese

Sift the flour, add salt, and using a knife, add the cream cheese and the butter, cutting it into small pieces. Make into a dough and then wrap it in grease-proof paper and leave it in the fridge overnight. Roll it out next day on the paper until it is as thin as a penny and then cut into shapes or rounds. Bake in a hot oven for 10 to 15 minutes. Serve very hot.

This is a lovely Austrian salad which is always a favourite. Green and red peppers are used for a really colourful effect, though the taste is the same whichever the colour.

GREEN AND RED PEPPER SALAD

Green and red peppers   corn oil
1 large onion, coarsely minced   lemon juice
salt and black pepper

Scald the peppers in boiling water and then plunge them into cold. Remove stalk and all the seeds and pith inside. Slice the peppers into very thin rounds. Mix together the onion, salt, black pepper, oil and lemon juice and add the peppers. Set aside in a cool place for several hours before using.

MUSHROOM AND POTATO PANCAKES

This is an economical way of using mushrooms because they are minced and therefore the stalks only can be used. The following quantities are sufficient for a satisfying meal for four hungry Alpine climbers.

1 lb. mushroom stalks   1 tblsp. wholewheat flour
½ lb. potatoes mashed with a little milk   ¼ tsp. nutmeg
¼ lb. grated hard cheese   corn oil for frying
½ cup hot milk   salt and black pepper

Mix together the mushroom stalks, potatoes and cheese in a pan, add the milk and simmer very slowly for 8 minutes, stirring all the time with a wooden spoon. Add the nutmeg and season with salt and freshly grated black pepper. Add the flour and mix well with the pan off the heat. Allow to cool a little before proceeding. Heat some oil until a blue smoke rises and drop spoonfuls of the mixture into it, browning well on both sides. Serve very hot.

MUSHROOM AND EGG SCRAMBLE

We like scrambles in our house and eat all kinds of exotic combinations. This is a simplified version of one we all enjoyed in the Tyrol.

1 lb. mushrooms   4 large eggs, beaten until frothy
1 medium-sized Spanish onion, chopped   1 small tin green peas (½ lb. cooked
¼ lb. grated hard cheese   fresh or frozen)
2 oz. margarine   toast as required (brown or white)
salt and black pepper

Brown the onion in the butter, add thinly sliced mushrooms and cook for 10 minutes. Turn up the heat until most of the liquid has evaporated, add the peas and turn the heat down again for a few minutes until peas are well heated. Add beaten eggs, mixing well, and lastly add the cheese and seasoning. Stir once more and pile the mixture on to hot buttered toast. Garnish with parsley.

PARTY DIP

Yet another way to serve cream cheese, this time with a festive flavour suitable for unexpected guests or late night snacks.

12 green olives	garlic salt as required
12 black olives	paprika
½ lb. cream or curd cheese	salt and black pepper

Chop the olives finely and mix with the cream or curd cheese. Add paprika for colour and salt and black pepper for seasoning. Lastly add a good shake of garlic salt and a touch of thick cream, and beat the mixture vigorously. Serve with large potato crisps as a dip.

I did say in my introduction that the dessert course posed no problems to the vegetarian and therefore would receive little space in my book save in exceptional cases. This is an exceptional dessert in a whole galaxy of delicious desserts known in Austria as **Torten**. A cross between a tart and a cake and a soft, sticky biscuit, the Torte is indescribable. It is typically Viennese and having made every one in existence, the following remains well above the others in my estimation, not only because it is so delectable but also because it is astonishingly easy to make. It is an absolute boon when you are in a hurry but want to stun your party guests.

PISCHINGER TORTE

2-3 cups melted *unsalted* butter	1 cup melted cooking chocolate
2-3 cups confectioner's sugar	4 egg yolks
2-3 cups ground almonds	chocolate icing
rice paper	

With the exception of the chocolate icing and the rice paper, mix all ingredients together. Line a shallow spring tin with rice paper, pressing it flat on to the bottom and spread on some of the mixture with a palette knife. Add a layer of rice paper and continue thus until all the mixture is used up. The top layer should be the chocolate mixture. Open the tin and lift out the torte (no cooking you see) and chill it in the fridge. Ice with chocolate icing and decorate with walnuts. Simple, but very effective.

The Balkans

Bulgaria, a country which breeds fine sheep, has two famous cheeses which surpass all others in the country.

White Cheese in Brine is a ewe's milk cheese, semi-hard, smooth and cream coloured with a bright shine on it. A slightly sour though mild flavoured cheese, it matures fairly quickly and when ripe has a rather salty taste.

Kashkaval is a fairly soft, creamy cheese with a smooth, very firm crust. Also made from ewe's milk it is dark yellow in colour, mild in flavour and bouquet, and like the White Cheese in Brine, is slightly salty. It is also made in Rumania, another of the Balkan countries.

Katschkawalj is another ewe's milk cheese which hails not only from Bulgaria but also from Rumania and Serbia. A close textured, plastic curd cheese, it is cooked and salted and has a somewhat strong though smooth taste. It is similar in flavour to the Italian Caciocavallo.

The cheeses of the other Balkan countries, Turkey and Yugoslavia, are also ewe's milk cheeses. The best of the Turkish cheeses are **Edirne** and **Kaser**. The former is a white, soft textured cheese of high quality. The latter is a semi-hard, closed textured, chewy cheese.

Look out also for **Gravyer** which is Turkey's answer to Swiss Gruyère.

STUFFED MUSHROOMS WITH OLIVES

A typical Balkan dish and a glorious way to serve the biggest, most succulent mushrooms you can find.

20 large mushrooms	4 oz. wholewheat breadcrumbs
20 green olives, finely chopped or minced	2 oz. butter or margarine
1 breakfast cup stock	salt and black pepper

Remove mushroom stems and a little of the insides and mince with the olives. Cook in half the stock for 4 minutes, add the butter, seasoning and breadcrumbs and make into a fairly stiff paste. Fill the mushroom caps with this, then lay them in a shallow baking dish with the other half of the stock, dot with butter and bake in a fairly slow oven for 30 minutes. If liquid reduces too much add more. These quantities make 4 good helpings.

MUSHROOMS IN YOGHOURT

20 large mushrooms	2 oz. butter or margarine
1 medium-sized Spanish onion	¼ tsp. nutmeg
1 carton natural yoghourt	toast as required
salt and black pepper	

As in previous recipe, remove mushroom stems and part of the insides. Mince these with the onion and fill the mushroom caps with this mixture.

Add a nut of butter to each filled cap. Lay them in a shallow casserole, sprinkle with salt and a good grate of black pepper, pour over the yoghourt and bake for 30 minutes in a fairly slow oven. Serve on toast. Alternatively, for a more substantial meal you could serve these with spaghetti. A tip to remember when serving spaghetti. When you take it out of the pan, drain it well in a colander, put it back in the still-hot saucepan, add a good-sized nut of butter and toss with two forks until every strand of spaghetti is coated. Much easier to serve and eat, and imparts a nice gloss.

CHEESE AND OLIVES ON TOAST

You will find olives everywhere when you visit the Balkans. We like all kinds but my favourites are Greek olives which are treated with olive oil and garlic and coriander seeds. The cheese in this recipe can be any hard, rather salty cheese, but when I first tasted this dish it was done with Bulgarian White Cheese in Brine. I have since made it with absolute success with Dutch Edam.

2 slices of cheese per person	prepared mustard as required
12 olives	slices of dark brown bread as required

Begin by toasting the bread on one side and spreading the other with the mustard. Allow 2 slices of bread per serving. Chop the olives and place on top of the mustard. Cover with the cheese slices and brown gently under the grill. Garnish with parsley and chopped chives.

STUFFED TOMATOES

An elegant Eastern dish combining the sweet and the savoury.

12 very large ripe tomatoes	1 cup cooked long grain rice
1 large Spanish onion, minced	1 cup olive oil
2 large cloves garlic, minced	4 oz. chopped nuts
salt and black pepper	2 oz. currants

Cut a lid off each tomato and scoop out the pulp. Mix this with all the ingredients, except the oil, and season well with salt and freshly grated black pepper. Stuff the tomato shells with the mixture. Heat the oil in a casserole and when well heated arrange the tomatoes in it and bake, covered, in a moderate oven for 25 minutes.

GREEK SALAD WITH SOUR CREAM

Slice a large sweet Spanish onion and two unpeeled cucumbers. In a bowl mix the following dressing:

1 cup thick sour or cultured cream	1 tsp. fresh or dried dill leaves
2 tblsp. lemon or lime juice	1 tsp. chopped parsley
¼ tsp. freshly grated black pepper	salt

Line the bowl with lettuce or very young spinach. Arrange a layer of cucumber on this, then a layer of onion rings and then some dressing. Repeat the layers, topping with the dressing. Keep in the fridge for at least 1 hour before using to marry the flavours. Serve with pumpernickel or very dark rye bread.

Sometimes, for variation, I use pickled gherkins instead of fresh cucumbers, also when I find fresh dill difficult to obtain I use finely ground dill seeds. Yet another variation is to use caraway instead of dill seeds.

GREEK CABBAGE SALAD

½ lb. finely shredded white cabbage   12 black olives
1 small shredded raw beet   ½ dessertsp. capers

Mix the ingredients and pour over the following dressing:

8 tblsp. red wine vinegar   1 heaped tsp. prepared mustard
4 tblsp. olive oil   1 clove of garlic, crushed
salt and freshly ground black pepper

Mix together and chill the salad in the fridge before serving.

RUMANIAN VEGETABLE SOUP

2 lb. mixed root vegetables, diced   1 tblsp. sour cream
2 large Spanish onions   1 tblsp. olive oil or butter
1 egg yolk   1 pint water
salt and black pepper

Melt the fat in a saucepan, add the vegetables and steam for 15 minutes. Add the water and simmer for 1 hour. If necessary add a little more water. Mix the egg yolk with the cream and just before serving, stir into the soup. Season to taste. Serve with rough brown bread.

TURKISH AUBERGINES

This is one of the best known Balkan dishes and tastes equally good served hot or cold. Allow 1 aubergine per person. This recipe serves six.

6 aubergines   1 tblsp. fresh lemon juice
1 lb. tomatoes   1 tblsp. chopped parsley
1 lb. Spanish onions   4 cloves garlic, minced
1 cup wholewheat breadcrumbs   a touch of brown sugar
1 cup melted butter   salt and black pepper

Wash, dry, split and seed the aubergines. Scoop out a little of the pulp and sprinkle with plenty of salt. Lay the halves cut side down in a large dish, cover with another dish and leave for about 1 hour, then drain them and wash well. This removes any slight bitterness. Fry the aubergines in the butter until they are quite soft, then lay them in a baking dish with any of the butter left in the pan. Fry together the onions, half the tomatoes, parsley and garlic, season with salt, freshly grated black pepper and the brown sugar. Stuff the aubergines with the mixture and use any left over to surround the aubergines. Add the rest of the tomatoes, sliced, cover with the breadcrumbs and a little more melted butter, sprinkle with the lemon juice and bake in a moderate oven for 20 minutes.

AUBERGINES IN POTATO SAUCE

Allow 1 aubergine per person. The following quantities are sufficient for 4 servings.

4 large aubergines	¾ pint melted butter
4 cloves garlic	½ cup mashed potatoes
flour seasoned with onion salt	½ cup tarragon vinegar
salt and black pepper	

As in the previous recipe leave the aubergines in salt for 1 hour to remove any bitterness. While they are salting, make the sauce as follows. Crush the garlic, and add to the well mashed potatoes. Add the oil and vinegar alternately, a little at a time, stirring well with a wooden spoon. When aubergines are ready, wash and drain them well, dip them into the seasoned flour, fry in melted butter and serve with the sauce.

In writing about food from the Balkans I could go on indefinitely describing recipes using the aubergine. However, I shall confine myself to just two more because they are too good to leave out. Aubergines are quite reasonably priced when in season and can be bought very cheaply in any vegetable market. Many people have told me they have seen aubergines but haven't bought them because they had not the faintest idea what to do with them. The following recipe is a never-failed-yet one for the absolute newcomer to both kitchens and aubergines.

BALKAN STEW

4 large aubergines	½ lb. fresh green or red peppers
½ pint olive oil	½ lb. ripe tomatoes
¼ lb. black olives	½ lb. celery
	garlic salt

Simply cut all the vegetables into small pieces and simmer all together in the olive oil, slightly flavoured with garlic salt, until tender but not mushy. Just before serving add the chopped olives.

The original recipe calls for okra. These can be bought in Continental delicatessen and greengrocers, but if you have no such shop in your vicinity, then the celery is just as good. Okra are delicious if you can get them. They are native to Abyssinia and are used extensively in Indian dishes.

PEPPERS STUFFED WITH AUBERGINES

4 red or green peppers	½ lb. cottage (or similar) cheese
2 aubergines	2 large eggs
1 sweet Spanish onion	salt and black peppers

Wash and peel the aubergines and cook them slowly to a pulp in a little olive oil. Meanwhile prepare the peppers by scooping out the seeds and the pith. Mix together the cheese, minced onion, aubergine pulp and the beaten eggs and season with salt and black pepper. Stuff the peppers with this mixture and bake in a moderate oven for 30 to 35 minutes.

Here are two simple and very savoury recipes using tomatoes.

TOMATO TIGER

4 large ripe tomatoes	olive oil as required
½ lb. grated sharp cheese	toast as required
½ tsp. curry powder	salt and black pepper

Slice the tomatoes and fry them in olive oil. When soft, season lightly as the curry powder has still to be sprinkled on top. Pile the tomatoes on toasted bread (dark brown is good for this recipe), be sparing with the curry powder but as lavish as you can with the grated cheese and then put everything under a fast grill until bubbly and golden and aromatic. You will see the reason for the name of this dish as soon as you taste it.

The following is a good recipe when you have very little in the house and have to provide a meal for 2 or 3 hungry people. It sounds impossible but as long as you can find 1 pound of tomatoes (a large tin would do) and a little cheese, then your worries are over.

SAVOURY BAKE

1 lb. ripe tomatoes	1 egg, beaten
½ lb. raw rice	breadcrumbs as required
¼ lb. any grated cheese	parsley for garnishing
1 tblsp. butter or oil	salt and black pepper

Cook the rice until it is only just done, drain well, rinse with hot water and return it to the pan. Add the butter or oil and stir. Add chopped parsley, salt and pepper and place in an oiled casserole. Cover with sliced tomatoes, add the beaten egg to the cheese and place this on top of the tomatoes. Add a thick layer of breadcrumbs and dot with butter. Bake in a moderate oven until a nice golden brown. Serve at once, garnished with parsley.

TURKISH RICE

This is one of those big comforting Balkan dishes known as a pilaf. It is a good dish for using up left-over bits and pieces and making them taste like something which only a skilled cook can achieve.

Mushrooms in Sour Cream

½ lb. long grain rice
3 oz. chopped nuts
2 oz. currants
1 oz. brown sugar
2 large sweet Spanish onions
1 or 2 large ripe tomatoes

2 pints vegetable water or stock
4 tblsp. olive oil
1 tsp. mixed spice
1 tsp. each chopped sage and parsley
1 tsp. black pepper
salt to taste

eel and slice the onions and cook in the oil until soft. Add the nuts and
e uncooked rice and fry for 6 minutes, stirring all the time with a wooden
oon. Add currants, tomatoes (sliced), the boiling stock or water, and season
ith black pepper and salt. Put the lid on the pan (make sure it fits very
ghtly) and cook over a very low heat until all the liquid has been absorbed.
emove from the heat and, keeping the lid on, let the pan stand for 15
inutes after adding the herbs and spice.

MUSHROOMS IN SOUR CREAM

2 lb. mushrooms
2 oz. butter or olive oil
1 cup sour or cultured cream
1 medium-sized Spanish onion

2 tsp. flour
½ tsp. fresh or dried dill
fresh parsley
salt and black pepper

ry the chopped onion in the butter and then add the chopped mushrooms.
eason. Cook on a low heat for 10 minutes, keeping the lid on the pan; add
e dill (either chopped or if dill seeds are used grind them very finely)
ad the chopped parsley and keep the pan covered while preparing the flour.
ut the flour into a basin and very gradually mix in the cream and then add
e mixture to the mushrooms, cook for 5 minutes longer and serve at once,
iping hot, garnished with a sprig of parsley. This dish is often served on
lain boiled rice or noodles and hails from Rumania.

TURKISH YOGHOURT

his most unusual dish is simple to make and provides an excellent first
ourse to a meal instead of soup. An impressive dinner party recipe, if your
uests are at all adventurous in their eating habits.

6 cartons natural yoghourt
4 cloves garlic

1 medium-sized fresh cucumber
1 tblsp. wine vinegar

salt and black pepper

rush the garlic to a pulp, add the salt and a grate of black pepper, then the
inegar. Gradually add the yoghourt to this mixture. Peel and chop the
ucumber finely, and add it to the yoghourt mixture. Chill well for at least
hour before serving. These quantities make 6 servings.
I have devised a number of variations on the above authentic Turkish
neme, and the most successful of them has been to make the dish in the way
escribed but, just before putting it into the fridge to chill, I added a good
ablespoonful of either thick tomato juice or tinned tomatoes.

GREEK PIMENTOS

4 large green or red peppers (or pimentos)
1 medium-sized Spanish onion
½ lb. cooked long grain rice
¼ lb. chopped nuts
salt and black pepper

5 tblsp. olive oil
2 tblsp. currants
2 tblsp. tomato purée
1 clove garlic

Remove the stalks, seeds and pith from the peppers, and wash thoroughl᷈
The seeds are fiercely hot so be careful not to let any remain. Mix a᷈
irgredients, except the oil, with the finely chopped onion, and stuff tl᷈
peppers. Place in a baking dish, pour over the oil, cover tightly and bake i᷈
a fairly slow oven for 35 minutes.

BALKAN SPAGHETTI

There are a hundred and one ways to serve spaghetti, but perhaps you ha᷈
never tried this one.

½ lb. spaghetti
3 oz. olive oil
3 tblsp. tomato paste
1 tblsp. butter

2½ pints water
2 cartons natural yoghourt
2 cloves garlic
salt and black pepper

Spaghetti should always be cooked thus. Throw it into fast boiling wate᷈
to which a teaspoonful of salt has been added. Boil until it is tender on th᷈
outside but has a slight bite inside. Never cook it until it is absolutely so᷈
right through. Drain in a colander and then run hot water through it unt᷈
the water runs clear. Return the spaghetti to the still-hot saucepan and tos᷈
it, with two forks, with a tablespoonful of butter. See that every strand c᷈
spaghetti is coated with the butter. Melt the oil and fry the chopped garli᷈
in it for a minute or two, then add the tomato paste, and season with sa᷈
and a good grate of black pepper. Take the pan off the heat, add th᷈
yoghourt and pour the mixture over the hot spaghetti.

BULGARIAN PEPPERS WITH CHEESE

This is yet another tasty way to serve cottage cheese. The original recip᷈
calls for ewe's milk cream cheese, but as this may well be hard to come b᷈
away from its native country I find that ordinary cottage cheese is an excellen᷈
substitute.

6 large green or red peppers
3 medium-sized eggs
2 oz. butter

¾ cup cottage cheese
paprika
salt to taste

Wash the peppers and remove fiery seeds and the pith. Shred them finel᷈
and fry them in the butter for 2 minutes. Season with salt. Place in a casserole
add a layer of cheese, then the beaten eggs, sprinkle with plenty of paprik᷈
and bake for 15 minutes in a very moderate oven.

Belgium

elgium is a one-cheese country, that is to say, of the many cheeses made
Belgium only one has international star quality and that is the **Limburger.**
ailing from the province of Liège it was first marketed in Limbourg but,
rangely, it is now made more in Austria and Germany and the United
tates than in its mother country. Limburger can be made with whole,
immed or partly skimmed milk, but always cow's milk, and its chief
iaracteristics are its soft waxy texture and its violently aggressive smell.

I must mention a typically Belgian cheese which has not achieved any
eat popularity outside Belgium but which I found to be extremely good.
his was **Herve** cheese which is made according to a technique peculiar
the district of Herve. A soft textured, fermented cheese, it is washed and
en pressed into a 2½ inch cube. An acquired taste perhaps, but well worth
ltivating.

Similar to the Herve cheese, but twice its size is the salty and bright
avoured **Remoudou**, made from cow's milk, as is Herve. Here is a recipe
r cooking with Remoudou cheese. Those who find it difficult to obtain
utside Belgium will get excellent results with Dutch Edam.

CELERIAC WITH CHEESE

1 lb. celeriac, sliced	2 oz. butter
¼ lb. shredded cheese	1 teacup hot milk
salt and black pepper	

utter a casserole, line it with celeriac, then sprinkle with a layer of cheese.
dd alternate layers of celeriac and cheese until all is used up. Pour over
he hot milk, season, dot with butter and bake in a moderate oven for 40
inutes.

SCRAMBLED EGGS WITH CHEESE

2 eggs per serving	2 tblsp. warm milk per serving
2 oz. grated cheese per serving	salt and black pepper

Melt the cheese in the milk very slowly, add the beaten eggs, cook slowly in
double saucepan, and season. Serve piled on to toast. Garnish with parsley
nd sprinkle with paprika.

Frontiers are ill-defined in Continental cuisine and the following soup
an be obtained in almost any country. I place it in my chapter on Belgian
ooking because it was here that I first encountered this unique way of
avouring.

31

CREAM OF MUSHROOM SOUP

1¼ pints scalded milk	1 level tblsp. flour
1 cup thick cream	1 level tblsp. butter
½ lb. mushrooms, minced finely	green or black olives as required
¼ cup cognac	a pinch of powdered nutmeg
⅛ tsp. powdered ginger	croutons of toasted bread
salt and black pepper	

Make a roux of the flour and butter, add nutmeg, salt and pepper and coo
for 1 minute. Add the ginger and then gradually add the scalded milk an
stir all the time with a wooden spoon. Add minced mushrooms and simme
for 15 to 20 minutes. Take pan off the heat, add cream, bring up to ju
below boiling and stir in the cognac. Place a crouton or slice of brow
toast in the bottom of each soup bowl, pour over the soup and sprinkle eac
serving with finely chopped olives.

BRUSSELS SPROUT SOUP

As I have already said, sprouts are nearly always spoiled by bad cooking
When properly cooked to bring out their delicate flavour they should b
freshly green and nutty, with not a drain of water in sight, and served wit
melted butter. To do this, first remove any coarse outer leaves, and cu
the sprouts in half, Belgian style. Melt some butter, toss in the sprouts an
a little salt, and stir until the sprouts are coated with the butter. Cover an
cook on a low heat for 5 minutes. Add 1 tablespoonful of very hot stock
replace the lid and cook for a further 10 minutes. Turn them out on to
heated plate and sprinkle with grated cheese.

Here is the soup, and again, you will see, the sprouts are not overcooked

2 lb. Brussels sprouts	1 cup thick cream
2 medium-sized egg yolks	1 tblsp. butter
2 pints hot milk	½ oz. flour
nutmeg to taste	salt and black pepper

Cook the sprouts as described above. No moisture should be left after cook
ing by this method. Chop them coarsely and toss them in the melted butter
add the flour and stir. Very gradually add the hot milk and cook for
minutes. Mix the egg yolks well with the cream in a large bowl and add th
soup to it very gradually, stirring all the time. Season with salt, a good grat
of black pepper, and nutmeg. Return to the pan and reheat but do not let i
boil. Serve with croutons.

If you are a salad addict, Belgium is your country. I found severa
unique salads there and the following is one I am sure that many peopl
will not have heard of before.

RAW MUSHROOM SALAD

1 lb. mushroom caps	1 tblsp. sweet pepper, shredded
1 head of lettuce	1 tblsp. capers
3 hard-boiled eggs	1 tblsp. green olives
½ cup corn oil	a touch of cayenne
¼ cup wine vinegar	salt and black pepper

Thinly slice the mushrooms and soak them in a marinade of the vinegar, oil and the seasonings. Be sparing with the cayenne for it is fiery. Cover the mushrooms and keep them in the fridge for at least 1 hour. Wash the lettuce and also chill it well before using. Arrange the lettuce leaves in your salad bowl, pile the mushrooms in the middle, sprinkle with the peppers, capers and olives and decorate with sliced hard-boiled eggs.

ARTICHOKES ROYALE

2 hard-boiled eggs per serving	2 oz. minced mushrooms per serving
1 globe artichoke per serving	2 tblsp. breadcrumbs per serving
1 small onion, minced, per serving	grated cheese

Cook the artichokes in a very little water with the lid on tightly. Remove centre leaves and lift out the choke. Keep hot while making the stuffing. Combine all ingredients, and mash well. If a little more moisture is needed add a very little hot milk or stock. Stuff the artichokes with the mixture, pop them into a slow oven to reheat and serve with plenty of grated cheese which is handed round separately.

CREAMED JERUSALEM ARTICHOKES

This delicious dish is the best way I know of serving Jerusalem artichokes.

1 lb. Jerusalem artichokes	1 large sweet Spanish onion
4 oz. grated cheese	wholewheat breadcrumbs
3 oz. butter	salt and black pepper

Steam the artichokes in a little salted water until tender. When cool enough to handle, rub off the skins and slice them into a shallow oven-proof dish. Cover with sliced onion, which has been previously sauté in butter, add a layer of grated cheese, then a layer of breadcrumbs, dot with plenty of butter and brown in a hot oven for 10 or 15 minutes.

The following is a most unusual sandwich filling. It is remarkably goo
yet is simple to make.

TOMATO AND AUBERGINE SAVOURY FILLING

6 large aubergines	2 tblsp. butter
3 Spanish onions	1½ lb. tomatoes
2 cloves garlic	

Bake the aubergines in a moderate oven and when quite soft scoop out th
pulpy insides with a wooden spoon as metal spoons discolour this vegetabl
Chop the skinned tomatoes, onions and garlic and add to the aubergin
pulp. Heat the butter in a frying pan until really hot and fry the mixtur
in it until well heated (about 10 or 15 minutes), and then season with sa
and grated black pepper. Allow to cool before using.

Not only is this a sandwich filling but it can also be served in tiny vol-au
vent cases, warmed in the oven, and used as hors d'oeuvres. Another ide
would be to bake it in shortcrust pastry and serve cold for a packed lunc
or a picnic.

BEANY BAKE

The Belgian name for this highly nutritious and savoury dish I have lon
since forgotten, so we always call it Beany Bake.

1½ lb. cooked haricot beans	white sauce as required
3 large tomatoes	butter as required
3 hard-boiled eggs	wholewheat breadcrumbs
chopped parsley	paprika
salt and black pepper	

Slice the tomatoes in a greased casserole, and pour over enough white sauc
to cover. Sprinkle with plenty of chopped fresh parsley. Add a layer o
breadcrumbs, then the chopped eggs, then the beans. Cover with the res
of the sauce, add the rest of the breadcrumbs, dot with butter and brown ir
a moderate oven. Be careful with the salt in this recipe if you have cooked
the haricots in salted water, and only a small amount of black pepper is
required; also be judicious with the paprika. The flavour of this dish should
be delicate.

BELGIAN SAVOURY PUDDING

1 lb. broccoli	½ pint warm milk
4 oz. grated hard cheese	butter
2 eggs	salt to taste

Wash the broccoli and remove any tough stalks. Put it in a pudding basin
and sprinkle with salt. Mix together the beaten eggs, the cheese, the milk
and a tablespoonful of butter. Season, then pour over the broccoli. Cover
the basin with greaseproof paper and steam for 1 hour. Serve at once.

VITAMIN PUDDING

This nutritious dish is easy to make and shows how vitamin-rich wheat germ can be used to enhance the flavour of food.

6 oz. noodles	2 cups vegetable stock
¼ lb. cottage cheese	½ cup sour cream or yoghourt
1 tblsp. raw sugar	½ cup wheat germ
1 tsp. salt	½ pint milk
1 or 2 eggs	paprika and black pepper

Add the noodles to the boiling stock, throw in the salt and cover the pan. Simmer for 10 minutes until most of the liquid has evaporated. Add the beaten egg or eggs to the milk and mix with the cottage cheese, sugar, cream or yoghourt, and season with paprika and freshly ground black pepper. Put the noodles and the cheese mixture into a casserole, sprinkle with the wheat germ and bake in a very moderate oven for 10 to 15 minutes until well heated. Serve at once.

BELGIAN BAKED POTATOES

4 large potatoes	4 tblsp. thin cream
1 cup shredded Cheddar cheese	2 or 3 tblsp. parsley
½ tsp. salt	1 tblsp. thick mayonnaise
black pepper	1 tblsp. chopped olives
	paprika

Bake the potatoes in a hot oven until soft. Cut off a lid from each one and scoop out the pulp. Mix with all the other ingredients and pack the mixture into the potato jackets. Put the lids back on the potatoes and return them to the oven to get throughly hot before serving. This is a delicious TV supper for you can serve the potatoes in napkins and save any washing-up.

35

Canada

Think of Canadian cheese and one word springs to mind—**Cheddar**. The best known of all Canadian cheeses, it is known more usually in its own country as Canadian cheese, and is also called Store cheese or Bulk cheese. White or yellow in colour it is made by traditional English cheddaring techniques, of unpasteurised milk. In flavour it varies from mild to very sharp according to how long it has been allowed to mature. When very young it is mild and milky, when mature it is full bodied and rich. Of the really mature Canadian cheddars the best are Black Diamond and Cherry Hill which are matured under different conditions from those of standard cheddar cheeses. The former is quite superlative in quality.

Oka cheese and French Port Salut are first cousins, the first starting life as an imitation of its French relative. Oka now, though, is wholly Canadian and is made at Oka in Quebec.

Stirred Curd or **Colby-Type** cheese gets its name from the technique of continually stirring the curd during draining to produce an open textured cheese.

Two quasi-French cheeses are **Bluefort** and **Eremite**, blue cheeses similar to the French Roquefort but made, not of ewe's milk, but of cow's.

Here is a simple and nourishing dish which can be made from Canadian Cheddar cheese.

CHEESE AND POTATO BAKE

7 oz. Canadian Cheddar	2 lb. potatoes
1 medium-sized onion	½ cup milk
celery salt	black pepper

Cook the potatoes in their jackets and when cool enough to handle skin and slice them. Slice the onion very thinly and line a buttered casserole with it. Add a layer of sliced potato, more onion, and season with celery salt and black pepper. Add the milk and lastly add the grated cheese. Put the lid in place and bake at 400 degrees for 30 minutes. Remove lid for last 10 minutes for a brown top.

CANADIAN SANDWICH

½ lb. curd cheese	1 small gherkin, pickled and chopped
4 oz. chopped walnuts	thick cream as required
2 tsp. paprika	mustard and cress to garnish
1 tblsp. chopped dates	salt and black pepper

Mix all the ingredients into a paste, adding thick cream to obtain the right consistency. Spread on buttered, untoasted rye bread, and make into double deckers. Toast sandwiches under a hot grill until brown on both sides. Veil with mustard and cress and serve as hot as possible.

And now for the first of my special favourites among Canadian soups.

CHEESE AND ONION SOUP

4 oz. grated Canadian Cheddar	2 tblsp. butter
2 large Spanish onions	2 tblsp. wholewheat flour
1 pint milk	salt and black pepper

Scald the milk first. Peel and chop the onions very finely, and brown them in the butter. Add the flour, blend, and then begin pouring on the heated milk, a little at a time, stirring with a wooden spoon to keep it creamy and free from lumps. Season to taste, add the cheese and serve at once. Hand round chunks of dark rye bread with it.

VERY THICK ONION SOUP

This soup is a meal in itself and if made carefully and served with a good rough wholewheat bread, it can fill the most ravenous family.

6 large Spanish onions	1½ oz. butter
4 large potatoes	1 oz. flour
2 tblsp. wholewheat breadcrumbs	chopped chives
½ pint milk	paprika
thick cream	salt and black pepper

Peel and slice the onions thinly and brown them in the butter. Add the flour and the breadcrumbs and blend. Add seasoning and then the milk, a little at a time, stirring constantly. Cook in the top half of a double boiler for 30 minutes. Meanwhile boil 4 large potatoes in their skins and when cooked and cool enough to handle, skin and mash them with a little milk and butter. Add them to the onion mixture and thin to the right consistency with thick cream. Garnish with paprika and chopped chives.

SPICY TOMATO SOUP

1 small onion, chopped	2 tblsp. noodles
1 oz. red or green pepper, chopped	1 tblsp. butter
½ lb. ripe tomatoes	1 tblsp. flour
1 pint vegetable water	3 tsp. horse-radish sauce
tabasco sauce (optional)	1 tsp. tarragon vinegar
salt and black pepper	

Cook the chopped onion and pepper in the butter for 6 minutes. Add the flour and blend, then add the heated vegetable water very slowly, stirring all the time with a wooden spoon. Slice the tomatoes and add to the soup, and simmer very slowly for 15 minutes. Season with plenty of grated black pepper, salt and if you like it, a dash of tabasco sauce. Cook the noodles separately in boiling, salted water, drain and add to the soup just before serving. Lastly add the horse-radish sauce and vinegar, and serve piping hot.

BARLEY SOUP WITH MUSHROOMS

The previous soup is one for the palate which likes high seasoning. For a more delicate flavoured soup try the following which incorporates wheat germ, rich in protein.

½ lb. mushrooms	2 tblsp. wheat germ
4 oz. pearl barley	1 tblsp. julienned carrot
3 pints vegetable water	1 tblsp. julienned celery
a touch of grated nutmeg	1 tblsp. julienned green pepper
toast as required	salt and black pepper

Wash the barley well and cook it in half the vegetable water until soft. Cook the remaining ingredients, except the toast, in the remaining water for 20 minutes. Add both mixtures together and season with salt, black pepper and nutmeg. Put a slice of brown toast in the bottom of each soup plate and pour over the soup.

For those who like peas, this soup is enhanced by the addition of 4 or 5 tablespoonfuls of cooked green peas.

As Jerusalem artichokes are native to Canada, here is a number of different ways of cooking them. You might like to know that they belong to the sunflower family.

CREAMED ARTICHOKE CHOWDER

1 lb. Jerusalem artichokes	1 pint milk
1 large Spanish onion	1 pint water
1 small turnip	2 egg yolks
2 sticks celery	2 oz. butter
2 tblsp. thick cream	salt and black pepper

Peel and slice the onion and sauté in the butter for 3 minutes. Scrub the artichokes, slice fairly thinly and add to the onion. Julienne the turnip and the celery and add to the artichokes. Add the water and cook for 20 minutes. Pass through a sieve, add the milk and season. Take the pan off the heat and add the egg yolks beaten with the cream. Reheat but do not boil, and serve with croutons.

ARTICHOKE AND POTATO SOUP

1 lb. Jerusalem artichokes	3 pints vegetable water
1 lb. potatoes	2 stalks celery
1 Spanish onion	1 tblsp. flour
1 oz. butter	salt and black pepper

Slice all vegetables and sauté them in the butter for a few minutes. Keep the lid on the pan and see that they do not burn. Add the water and bring to the boil, season and then simmer for 30 minutes. Pass the vegetables through a sieve, reheat to boiling point, then mix the flour with a little water and add to the soup. Simmer for another 4 minutes and serve as hot as possible.

ARTICHOKE ALLUMETTES

Chips are always delicious, especially the tiny, sizzling matchstick ones which are called allumettes, and are served in high-class restaurants. Try cooking artichokes this way.

Scrape the artichokes to remove the brown skins, put them through a coarse julienne mincer, and dry the resulting matchsticks in a clean cloth. Drop into smoking hot oil, fry for a few minutes until golden brown, and drain on absorbent paper. Make lots of these for the family are sure to shout for more.

ARTICHOKE SAUTÉ

1 pound of Jerusalem artichokes serves 3 people. Parboil the artichokes in a very little salted water and when cool enough to handle, skin and slice them. Dust with a little wholewheat flour and fry in shallow corn oil until golden brown. These could be termed Canada's answer to French fries.

CANADIAN ARTICHOKE SALAD

To end this short sequence of artichoke recipes from Canada here is a simple and quite delicious salad.

¼ lb. cooked artichokes	1 tblsp. grated horse-radish
1 bunch watercress	1 tblsp. chopped green olives
home-made salad cream	1 tblsp. chopped capers
grated raw beetroot to garnish	

Dice the artichokes, and sprinkle with the horse-radish, capers and olives. Add enough salad cream to moisten and put the mixture in a salad bowl surrounded with watercress and sprinkled with grated raw beetroot. Chill well before serving.

CANADIAN APPLE SALAD

This is an elegant party salad.

4 large sweet apples	1 cup cooked green peas
1 head lettuce	½ cup shredded celery
2 tblsp. chopped walnuts	corn oil
home-made salad cream	tarragon vinegar
salt and black pepper	

Cut the tops off the apples and scoop out the centres being careful not to break the skins. Immediately brush the insides of the apple cups with oil and a little vinegar. Chop the apple pulp and mix with the peas, the celery and the chopped nuts. Add enough salad cream to moisten and pile the mixture back into the hollowed-out apples. Wash and separate the leaves of the lettuce, line a salad bowl with them, sprinkle with salt and arrange the apples on them. Chill before serving.

CANADIAN TOMATOES ON TOAST

½ lb. large ripe tomatoes	1 tblsp. butter
1 Spanish onion	½ tblsp. flour
1 green or red pepper	2 tsp. raw or Barbados sugar
½ cup (approx.) thick cream	1 tsp. sweet basil leaves
grated black pepper	½ tsp. salt
paprika	toast as required

Chop the onion, the seeded peppers, and slice the tomatoes. Cook in the butter until tender, with the lid on the pan and at a very low heat. This takes approximately 15 to 20 minutes. Season with salt, black pepper, paprika and brown sugar. Add the basil leaves. In a separate pan blend the flour with the cream and then cook it slowly until it is thick. Add the vegetable mixture, bring to the boil and serve. If the mixture seems slightly too dry add more cream. Serve piled up on toasted dark rye bread. Garnish with parsley.

JELLIED EGG SALAD

6 large hard-boiled eggs	2 teacups thick cream
1½ lb. tomatoes	½ pint mayonnaise
1 lettuce	1 heaped tblsp. powdered gelatine
green and black olives	sweet basil leaves
salt and black pepper	

Let the gelatine dissolve in a little hot water and while it is cooling chop the eggs very finely and stir them into the mayonnaise. When the gelatine is cool, fold it into the egg mixture and then add the cream, salt and a good grate of black pepper. Pour the mixture into a ring mould, put it in the fridge, and when it is quite set turn it out on to a bed of lettuce leaves. Pile the sliced tomatoes in the centre, sprinkle them with sweet basil leaves and garnish with plenty of finely chopped olives.

SAGE AND ONION POTATOES

1½ lb. potatoes	1 tblsp. dried sage
3 large Spanish onions	1 tblsp. breadcrumbs
butter as required	salt and black pepper

Sauté the chopped onions in butter, add breadcrumbs, sage, salt and pepper. Peel and slice the potatoes into a greased casserole, season, and smother them with sage and onions. Dot with plenty of butter, cover the casserole with a greased lid, and bake in a moderate oven for 1 hour.

ONION BATTER PUDDING

This is one of those meal out of nothing recipes, so useful in an emergency.

1 sweet Spanish onion	4 tblsp. flour
1 large egg	1 tblsp. water
2 oz. butter	½ pint milk
salt and black pepper	

Season the flour with salt and a good grate of black pepper and mix with the egg and milk until a smooth batter is obtained. Add the water, cover, and allow it to stand for at least 1 hour. Fry the finely sliced onions in butter until soft but only slightly coloured. Put them into a shallow baking dish or casserole, together with any onion juice or butter left in the frying pan, and bake in a very hot oven for 6 minutes. Pour over the batter, return to the oven, and bake in a hot oven for 15 minutes, then reduce to moderate for another 30 minutes. Serve with 1 large jacket potato per serving.

SPINACH FRITTERS

Spinach being an acquired taste, this is a novel way to serve it which may appeal to those who cannot eat plain cooked spinach.

2½ lb. spinach	breadcrumbs as required
3 eggs	oil for frying
1 dessertsp. butter	grated cheese
salt and black pepper	

Cook the spinach in a little butter with a touch of salt and pepper. When tender, chop finely. Add the beaten eggs, taste for seasoning and add enough breadcrumbs to make a firm mixture. Make into balls the size of small tomatoes and fry in smoking hot oil. Drain on absorbent paper and serve with grated cheese. Parmesan is best for this dish.

ONION AND APPLE FRY-UP

This is an unusual recipe, and one which we first cooked outdoors over an open fire. Maybe hunger is sweet sauce but it seems to me it was one of the best meals I can remember.

4 large sweet Spanish onions	½ cup water
3 large cooking apples	butter as required
2 tblsp. brown sugar	salt to taste

Cook the sliced onions in butter until nearly soft but not quite. Slice the apples and add them to the onions. Pour over the water and sprinkle with salt. Put the lid on the pan and cook for about 15 minutes until apples are soft but not mushy. Remove the lid, sprinkle with brown sugar and drive off any excess moisture by turning up the heat.

Let me finish this chapter on Canadian cooking with something which requires more than just one large pan and some impatient appetites. This one needs particular care, but you will be proud of yourself when you take it out of the oven.

MUSHROOM SOUFFLÉ

4 eggs	2 oz. butter
3 oz. mushroom caps	2 oz. flour
½ pint hot milk	

Make a roux of the butter and flour and cook for 1 minute. Add the hot milk, stirring all the time with a wooden spoon to keep the mixture as smooth as cream. Remove the pan from the heat and allow to cool slightly before adding the finely chopped mushrooms and the beaten egg yolks. Blend well and then fold in the egg whites which have been beaten until stiff and stand up in peaks. Grease a straight-sided soufflé dish and pile the mixture into it. Tie a piece of greaseproof paper all round the dish so that it projects for 2 inches at least above the rim. Bake in a slow oven, 350 degrees only, for 40 minutes. Eat it at once for a soufflé must not wait for guests; they must wait for the soufflé!

The Caribbean

Caribbean food seems to taste better in its natural setting. However I brought home many fabulous dishes from this colourful part of the world and happily I have been able to get most of the necessary ingredients in England and other countries. Here is a selection of them which I hope you will be adventurous enough to try.

A soup to start your Caribbean meal and a typical one of this region is the following:

EGG AND GREEN BANANA SOUP

9 green bananas	¾ pint water
7 large eggs	salt to taste
3 pints vegetable stock	oil for frying

Peel bananas and cut them down the middle, and then again into 4 pieces. Soak in salted water for 10 minutes, then drain and deep fry in hot oil for a further 10 minutes. Mash bananas either with a potato ricer or with a fork. Heat the soup stock and add the bananas to it, mixing well. Beat the eggs and add to the soup while off the heat, swishing the eggs with a fork to make little rags in the soup. Add salt to taste, then bring soup to the boil and serve at once, with toasted bread.

FRIED BANANA SOUP WITH CHEESE

6 firm bananas	1 cup grated hard cheese (try Parmesan)
3 pints well-flavoured vegetable stock oil for frying	salt to taste

Peel bananas and cut into chunks. Fry these in deep hot fat for 10 minutes. Mash very finely and add to the hot stock, stirring well. Cook for 10 minutes over a very low heat and then, just before serving, add the grated cheese and season to taste. Boil up once more and serve with dark bread.

CARIBBEAN FRY-UP

I had this tasty dish many times in the Caribbean but I have forgotten its original name.

6 eggs, separated	2 pints water
2 large Spanish onions	2 cups corn oil
2 lb. potatoes	butter as required
½ lb. tomatoes	salt as required
sweet basil leaves	

Peel potatoes as thinly as possible (the goodness lies just under the skin), then cube them. Heat the oil in a thick saucepan until smoking hot, add the potatoes, cover, and cook slowly for 25 minutes. While the potatoes are cooking, melt a little butter in a small saucepan and fry the sliced tomatoes in this with 1 spoonful of sweet basil leaves, then add ½ teaspoonful of salt. When potatoes are cooked drain them on absorbent paper to remove as much oil as possible. Fry the onions in the remaining oil until golden brown, then add the tomatoes and the potatoes. Beat egg whites until they stand up in peaks, then beat the yolks. Add to the potato mixture and heat through very slowly for 4 minutes. Taste for seasoning and serve very hot.

SWEET AND SAVOURY PANCAKES

4 large eggs	2 cups wholewheat flour
2 oz. butter	2 cups milk
2 tsp. baking powder	1 cup grated hard cheese
melted honey as required	salt as required

Sift together the flour, a pinch of salt and the baking powder in a suitable bowl. Gradually add the milk and whisk well. Stand the mixture aside for 1 hour. Slightly melt the butter and beat it until it is like cream and add it to the milk and flour mixture together with the grated cheese. Beat the eggs and add those as well. Take a well seasoned omelette pan, cover it lightly with frying oil and fry a quarter of the mixture, browning on both sides. Cook the rest of the mixture in this way while keeping everything as hot as possible. Dot the pancakes with butter and serve with melted honey.

ONIONS STUFFED WITH CHESTNUTS

4 large Spanish onions	salt and pepper as required
½ lb. chestnuts	oil as required
a little milk or cream	butter as required

Do not peel the onions. Pour boiling water over them, into which you have dropped 1 teaspoonful of salt and allow them to stand for 10 minutes. When cool enough to handle cut a slice from the top of the onion and take out most of the centre. Now make the stuffing thus: put the chestnuts under a fast grill after cutting each one with a cross-shaped cut. Leave for 5 minutes under the heat when you should be able to peel them quite easily. Cover the shelled nuts with enough boiling water to cover them and cook, with the lid on the pan, for 20 minutes. Make sure they are tender before proceeding. Pass them through a fine sieve and add 1 tablespoonful of butter, salt and black pepper to season, and mix with a little hot milk or cream to moisten. Stuff this mixture, together with the chopped onion centres, into the onion shells, brush with a little milk and bake in a moderate oven in a casserole, with the lid on and a cupful of water added, for 45 minutes to 1 hour. Baste occasionally. Serve in the skins which are peeled at table.

ONIONS STUFFED WITH MIXED VEGETABLES

Try this way of serving stuffed onions when chestnuts are out of season.

4 large sweet Spanish onions	1 teacup wholewheat breadcrumbs
2 tblsp. parsley, minced	¾ cup chopped nuts
1 large stick celery, minced	1 oz. melted butter
½ carrot, minced	cream as required
	salt and black pepper

Prepare the onions for stuffing as in recipe above. Combine all other ingredients and season with salt and plenty of black pepper. Moisten the mixture with enough cream to bind and stuff it into the prepared onion shells. As before, bake the onions in their skins in a covered casserole with a little water, in a moderate oven.

SAVOURY MOCK DUCK

This one comes from Trinidad and is another meal out of nothing recipe.

½ lb. cooked soya beans	3 tblsp. butter
½ lb. cooked lentils	2 tblsp. chopped parsley
1 small onion, chopped	½ tsp. fresh or dry sage
1 cup mashed potatoes	tomato juice as required
sweet basil leaves	salt and pepper

Soya beans are one of the most valuable sources of protein and so I suggest that you use them in place of haricot beans. They are quite easy to obtain in any health food shop or in big stores which have a food department. To cook them, simply soak overnight in cold water and then boil them, with 1 teaspoonful of salt and a little raw sugar, until tender. They will cook in about 30 minutes in a pressure cooker or, if you use the ordinary method, then they will take from 2 to 4 hours. I always cook about a ½ pound at a time and then store them in the fridge until I need them. This way you save time and gas or electricity. Soya beans are cheap, so you save money as well.

Add the cooked soya beans to the lentils and the mashed potatoes. Fry the onion in half the butter, and add the soya bean mixture. Add sage and chopped parsley and season with salt and black pepper. Shape into balls the size of tennis balls, put the ducks on to a greased baking tin, pour over the rest of the butter which has been melted, and bake in a fairly hot oven until deep brown. Serve in a hot tureen with lots of hot, thickened tomato juice.

TWENTY-MINUTE BEAN DISH

1 large Spanish onion	1 tblsp. chopped parsley
½ lb. soya beans	1 tblsp. butter
½ lb. tomatoes	1 tblsp. vegetable extract
1 teacup vegetable water or stock	salt and black pepper

Cook the soya beans as described above. Fry the thinly sliced onion in the butter until golden. Add stock or vegetable water and cook for 10 minutes.

Add the sliced tomatoes, the vegetable extract and seasoning and simmer for another 10 minutes. Mix the tomato mixture with the beans and serve sprinkled with parsley.

ASPARAGUS SOUFFLÉ

For this dish you need a double boiler. Prepare the boiler by having the water hot in the lower half and buttering the upper half. Have a moderate oven ready.

7 eggs	6 tblsp. flour
1 large tin asparagus tips	4 tblsp. butter
1½ cups tepid milk	1 tblsp. lemon juice
salt as required	

Make a roux with the butter and the flour, add salt and gradually stir in the milk. Bring slowly to the boil and stir with a wooden spoon until thickened. Take the pan off the heat and add the drained asparagus tips which have been well chopped. Beat the egg whites until stiff and also beat the yolks separately. Add the yolks to the mixture, then the lemon juice, and lastly the egg whites. Pour the mixture into the greased pan and assemble the double boiler. Bake in the oven for 1 hour and, as with all soufflés, serve at once.

MUSHROOMS WITH CHESTNUTS

1 lb. button mushrooms	2 tblsp. butter
½ lb. chestnuts, boiled and peeled	salt as required
½ cup dry white wine	boiled rice as required

Cook the mushrooms slowly in the butter in a covered pan. This will take about 15 minutes. Add chopped chestnuts and salt to taste. Heat thoroughly, then add the wine, boil up once and serve on a bed of plain boiled rice.

MUSHROOMS WITH MIXED NUTS

1 lb. button mushrooms	1 medium-sized onion, minced
½ lb. mixed nuts	noodles as required
3 oz. butter	nutmeg to taste
salt and black pepper	

Sauté the onion in the butter, add the mushrooms and cook for 10 minutes until golden. Add the nuts, season to taste, and serve on a bed of boiled noodles.

JAMAICA PEPPERS

4 green or red peppers	4 tblsp. flour
2 large Spanish onions	4 tblsp. margarine
¼ lb. sliced cheese	1 tsp. salt
3 oz. butter	2 cups hot milk
black pepper	2 cups white sauce

First make the white sauce: melt the margarine, add the flour, and cook slowly for exactly 3 minutes. Gradually add the hot milk and stir constantly with a wooden spoon. Season with salt and pepper. Now remove the seeds and the pith from the peppers and slice into thin rings. Also peel and slice the onions into thin rings. Sauté the peppers and the onions in the butter, then arrange them in layers in a buttered casserole, alternating with sprinkled breadcrumbs. Top with buttered breadcrumbs and thinly sliced cheese and bake in a hot oven for 10 to 15 minutes.

STEWED OKRA WITH NUTS

I mentioned okra in the Dictionary of Vegetables and if you are able to get them, and most Continental shops have them, then here is your chance to learn how to cook them to bring out their best qualities.

1 lb. okra	2 large tomatoes
3 oz. chopped nuts	2 large potatoes
1 green or red pepper, seeded	2 pints water
1 Spanish onion	2 tblsp. butter
1 chilli pepper	tomato sauce as required
salt to taste	

Soak the okra in salted water for 1 hour. Brown sliced onion and the nuts in the butter, add the drained okra, then the sliced tomatoes, the seeded and sliced green pepper (or red if you prefer) and the chilli pepper, which has also been seeded and sliced. Add 3 breakfast cups of warm water, about 5 tablespoons of tomato sauce, the peeled and diced potatoes and salt to taste. Mix well and bring to the boil. Turn down the heat, clamp on the lid, and cook for 30 minutes or longer until sauce is thick.

CARIBBEAN SALAD

For this recipe you need 1 large avocado pear. They are buttery and marvellous, but away from their native countries they are rather expensive. Sometimes, however, when they are in season I have been able to buy them very cheaply in the market.

1 small white cabbage	1 green or red pepper
1 small cucumber	½ cup corn oil
1 large avocado, peeled	¼ cup tarragon vinegar
2 large radishes	1 tblsp. raw sugar
2 large sweet Spanish onions	½ tsp. lemon juice
salt and black pepper	

Seed and slice the pepper, thinly shred the cabbage and slice all the other vegetables thinly. Mix well with two forks in a deep salad bowl. Mix the oil, vinegar, lemon juice, salt and pepper, and the sugar well together and toss with the sliced vegetables. Chill well in the fridge before serving with hot, buttered bread.

China

EGG AND PEA SOUP

1 lb. raw green peas	3 eggs
¼ tsp. M.S.G. (monosodium glutamate)	1 tsp. cognac
2 pints cold water	1 small piece preserved ginger
	salt and black pepper

Shell the peas, thinly slice the ginger, and simmer them in the water for 30 minutes. Beat the eggs well and add the M.S.G. (obtainable in any delicatessen) and the cognac and add to the soup. Flavour with salt and black pepper according to taste and boil up the soup once more. Serve very hot.

CHINESE BROWN EGGS

6 large eggs	2 oz. butter
3 tblsp. soy sauce	cold water as required

Boil the eggs for 5 minutes, leave them in cold water until cool enough to handle and then shell them. Melt the butter in a small saucepan, add the soy sauce and then the eggs. Cook them for 6 or 7 minutes, basting them all the time until they are evenly browned. Leave them to go cold and serve them, cut in slices, on a bed of fried savoury rice.

FRIED SAVOURY RICE

3 cups cold cooked rice	2 eggs
4 oz. chopped nuts	2 oz. chopped spring onions or chives
1 tblsp. soy sauce	2 oz. butter
1 tblsp. water	1 oz. currants
¼ tsp. salt	1 stick celery, chopped

Heat the butter in a large thick-bottomed saucepan, add the rice and the salt and fry for 8 minutes while stirring with a wooden spoon. Beat the eggs and add to the rice, then add the chopped onions, currants, finely chopped celery, soy sauce and the water. Check the seasoning, and add a touch of black pepper if you wish. Serve very hot.

FRIED RICE WITH BEAN SPROUTS

Bean sprouts can be obtained very easily now. You can buy a tin of them at your local delicatessen. They are delicious and are used in many of the Chinese savoury dishes. I have recently been able to buy them fresh in good fruit shops and greengrocers.

5 cups cold cooked rice	3 tblsp. peanut oil
2 cups bean sprouts	2 eggs, beaten
4 tblsp. soy sauce	1 small onion, chopped
1 level tsp. salt	2 tblsp. chopped spring onions or chives
	grated black pepper

Cook the eggs in the hot oil with the salt until firm. Add the bean sprouts, the single chopped onion, and soy sauce and cook for 2 minutes. Add the rice, and mix well, and heat everything right through thoroughly. Add the chopped spring onions and a good grate of black pepper, check the seasoning, then serve very hot.

SWEET AND SOUR CARROTS

1 tsp. peanut oil	2 tblsp. chopped sweet pickle
1 tsp. tomato sauce	1 tsp. vinegar
1 tsp. cognac	3 tsp. brown sugar
¼ tsp. powdered ginger	2 tsp. cornstarch
1 cup finely sliced raw carrot	¼ pint cold water

Before you begin the preparation of this dish, slice your carrots in the Chinese way, that is not straight across the carrot but on the slant so that each slice is oval rather than round. It gives a much more Oriental look to this dish. Incidentally, the original recipe calls for green ginger but as you may not be able to obtain this, or may not have a jar of preserved ginger just on hand, I find that the powdered variety, though not quite so delicious, makes a good substitute. Fry the chopped pickles and the ginger in the oil for 1 minute. Add together the cornstarch, sugar, vinegar, tomato sauce and cognac to make a paste, and gradually add the water, mixing well. Pour over the fried pickles and ginger and cook until the sauce thickens. Now add the very thinly sliced carrots, heat to boiling point and serve at once.

SOYA BEAN NOODLES

This is a most useful recipe for the vegetarian because it requires soya bean flour. As I have said before soya bean is one of the most valuable sources of protein known to man. It is easy to buy soya beans, both whole and cracked, in health-food shops and delicatessens. It is equally easy to obtain soya bean flour which is yellow in colour. Do not attempt to use it like ordinary flour for it contains no starch and therefore is not a thickening agent. It has to be cooked according to its own nature. This Chinese recipe makes excellent use of it, and this recipe is also extensively used in Japan.

1 lb. soya bean flour	2 egg yolks
1 tsp. salt	cold water as required

Mix the sifted flour, egg yolks and the salt with enough cold water to make a very thick paste. Roll this in a clean cloth and leave it aside for at least 1 hour before proceeding. Roll it out as thinly as possible and then roll it up into a sausage shape. Cut slices off the sausage very thinly, each slice being only ⅛ of an inch wide. Cook these in boiling salted water for 5 minutes and serve. Any savoury dish can be served with soya bean noodles. Try the following for a high protein, low price meal.

STIR-FRY HONEY MUSHROOMS

2 oz. button mushrooms	1 tsp. salt
2 tblsp. peanut oil	1 tsp. M.S.G.
2 tblsp. sherry	1 tsp. cornstarch
1 tblsp. honey	½ cup water
1 tblsp. soy sauce	1 clove garlic

Mix together the soy sauce, honey, M.S.G., sherry and cornstarch. Stir until well blended. Heat the oil and add the salt and the clove of garlic, add the mushrooms, halved, and stir-fry for 5 minutes, using a wooden spoon. Add the water, cover the pan and cook for a further 5 minutes. Add the honey mixture, and stir-fry until boiling. Simmer over a low heat until the gravy becomes quite translucent. Serve very hot with soya bean noodles (as above).

PINEAPPLE CHOP SUEY

1 cup sliced pineapple (tinned or fresh)	1 tblsp. peanut oil
1 cup celery, thinly sliced	1 tblsp. cornstarch
3 cups bean sprouts	2 tblsp. sherry
1 cup shredded white cabbage	1 tsp. brown sugar
1 medium-sized onion, thinly sliced	1 tsp. salt
½ cup vegetable water	1 tsp. M.S.G. (monosodium
1 clove garlic, minced	glutamate)
a few drops sesame oil (optional)	1 tsp. soy sauce
black pepper	

Mix the soy sauce, sherry and sesame oil (if you are using it). Sesame oil is easy to get in any health shop and is very nutritious. Stir well, then mix the cornstarch, M.S.G., sugar and grated black pepper together and add ½ cup cold water. Heat the oil, add the salt, garlic, celery, onion and the cabbage and stir-fry for 3 minutes. Add the sherry preparation and mix well. Add the stock, cover the pan and cook for 3 minutes. Add the cornstarch preparation and heat until gravy thickens. Lastly add the bean sprouts and the pineapple and when very hot serve at once.

Variations:

1. **Green Pepper Chop Suey.** Omit pineapple and substitute 2 seeded and finely shredded green peppers.
2. **Tomato Chop Suey.** Omit pineapple and use instead ½ pound sliced tomatoes. Add these to cabbage before stir-frying.
3. **Mushroom Chop Suey.** Omit pineapple as before and use ½ pound thinly sliced button mushrooms. Add to the cabbage before stir-frying.
4. **Egg Chop Suey.** Instead of the pineapple add 3 or 4 sliced hard-boiled eggs to the mixture at the same time as the bean sprouts. If you want to be really authentic, cook the eggs with soy sauce to make Chinese brown eggs.

EGG FOO YONG

This is one of the easiest Chinese dishes to make. It requires little preparation and, as with a chop suey, there are many variations on the original theme. First the basic recipe.

1 small onion, chopped	1 tblsp. soy sauce
3 large eggs	4 tblsp. chopped spring onions
1 cup bean sprouts	1 tsp. salt
	frying oil

Mix together the chopped onion, bean sprouts (fresh ones are better than tinned), spring onions, soy sauce and the salt and stir the eggs into the mixture until well blended. Deep fry the mixture, a teacupful at a time, and brown lightly on both sides. Keep hot until all the mixture is used up and serve at once with a little soy sauce.

Variations:

1. **Vegetable Foo Yong.** To the above mixture add one more egg, 1 green pepper seeded and thinly sliced, 1 stick celery thinly sliced, and 1 tablespoon finely shredded carrot. Add more salt if necessary.
2. **Mushroom Foo Yong.** To the basic recipe add ¼ pound thinly sliced mushrooms, 2 tablespoonful cooked string beans and extra salt if necessary.
3. **Onion Foo Yong.** To the basic recipe add one large sweet Spanish onion thinly sliced and then chopped, and 1 extra egg (small).

CANTONESE EGG FOO YONG

6 eggs, well beaten	1 tsp. salt
3 cups bean sprouts	1 tsp. garlic or onion salt
¼ lb. mushrooms, shredded	1 tsp. M.S.G.
1 small onion, chopped	½ cup vegetable water
plain boiled rice as required	grated black pepper
	oil for frying

Mix together all ingredients except the rice and stock. Heat oil until very hot and fry the mixture all at once, pressing it well down into the pan. Half-way through the frying add the stock. Stir well before browning the other side. Serve with plain boiled rice.

CHINESE CUSTARD

This is a recipe probably never eaten in any restaurant outside China. Indeed one doesn't usually associate custard with Chinese cookery.

3 large eggs	½ tsp. M.S.G.
1 cup milk	½ tsp. rice wine
a few drops of sesame oil	½ tsp. soy sauce
grated black pepper	½ tsp. salt

Blend all ingredients and then beat well with an egg whisk. Pour into a bowl and place the bowl in a large pan containing 4 inches of boiling water. Cover the bowl containing the egg mixture and steam for 30 minutes. Just before serving add 1 tablespoonful of melted butter.

MUSHROOM EGG CUSTARD

This is a delicious variation of the above. To the mixture add 1 extra egg and 4 ounces very thinly sliced mushrooms. This recipe will serve at least 2 more people.

CHINESE SCRAMBLED EGGS

6 eggs	2 tblsp. peanut oil
1 small tin garden peas or cupful cooked peas (fresh)	1 tsp. soy sauce
1 cup water	1 tsp. M.S.G.
1 clove garlic, minced	1 tsp. salt
grated black pepper	½ tsp. sesame oil

Beat the eggs with the water, add the M.S.G., the minced garlic, the grated black pepper (about 8 grates will be enough), and the soy sauce. Blend thoroughly. Heat the peanut and the sesame oil until very hot and add the salt. Add the peas and heat through, then add the egg mixture and scramble it with a wooden spoon until the eggs are just set. Serve at once on very hot plates.

Variations:

1. Omit peas and substitute ¼ pound cooked broccoli, chopped very fine.
2. Omit peas and instead use 1 large green or red pepper, seeded and sliced very thinly.
3. Use, instead of the peas, 1 medium-sized cucumber cut in ⅛-inch thick slices.
4. Instead of the peas use 1 cupful of bamboo shoots. Do not confuse these with bean sprouts. They are quite another thing. Ask at your local delicatessen; you will find them quite easy to obtain in tins.
5. Use 1 large sweet Spanish onion, very finely chopped, and add a touch of extra salt.
6. String beans, finely shredded before cooking, add a delightful flavour. Use 1 cupful together with 1 tablespoonful finely chopped spring onions.

DUCK EGGS IN SAUCE

One doesn't often come across a recipe using duck eggs, in fact they are often frowned upon by devotees of hens' eggs. However the Chinese have a way with them and here it is.

6 duck eggs, hard-boiled	2 tblsp. honey
1 small cup soy sauce	2 tsp. M.S.G.
1 small onion, finely chopped	1 tsp. salt
2 cloves garlic, minced	1 tsp. cut mixed peel
1¾ pints water	

With the exception of the eggs, mix all other ingredients and bring to the boil. Add the hard-boiled, and shelled, duck eggs and put the lid on the pan. Now go away and leave it all to cook over a low heat for 3 hours. Check after an hour and a half to see if any more water is needed. If so, add hot water, *not* cold. Serve the dish hot or cold with the eggs neatly sliced, and surrounded by sliced tomatoes sprinkled with a little salt.

CHINESE BROCCOLI

Broccoli is delicious whichever way it is cooked, and it appears on our table as often as I can get it, for it is not always in season. The Chinese way with this vegetable is quite extraordinary, and tastes superb.

1½ lbs. broccoli	2 tsp. ginger
4 tblsp. peanut oil	2 tsp. brown sugar
3 tblsp. soy sauce	1½ tsp. salt

Wash the broccoli well under running water, and then slice into thin pieces, diagonally, not more than 2 inches long. Heat the oil and add the broccoli and the salt and cook for 8 minutes. Meanwhile mix together the soy sauce, ginger and sugar and add to the broccoli, stirring well. Add 4 tablespoonfuls of hot water and then put the lid on the pan, bring to the boil and cook quickly for 2 minutes, then serve.

Creole

Creole cookery has a charm of its own which combines the best culinary features of several different countries. There is a delicious **Creole cheese** which is made in Louisiana. If you can imagine a cottage cheese whipped up with an equal quantity of thick rich cream, there you have Creole cheese, soft and succulent, and full of nourishment. A good substitute for the original would be to make it yourself. It is quite easy, particularly if you have an electric blender.

CREOLE CREAMED CORN

1 small tin sweet corn, taken from the cob	2 tsp. brown sugar
3 eggs	½ cup thick cream
3 oz. melted butter	nutmeg to taste
salt and pepper	1 small cup milk

Beat the eggs, and add the butter, sugar, salt and black pepper and blend well. Add the milk and then the drained corn. Mix again, place in a buttered casserole with a pinch of nutmeg, and bake for 25 minutes in a moderate oven. Just before serving stir in the cream.

CORN ON THE COB

The following quantities are for 3 people:

6 corn cobs	1 tsp. salt
black pepper	2 tsp. brown sugar
melted butter	

Boil 1 pint of water and add the salt and the sugar. Remove the husks and the silk from the corn cobs and put the cobs into the boiling water. Then add a good grate of black pepper, close the lid of the pan and simmer for 30 minutes. Serve with plenty of melted butter to which a little salt has been added. The corn cobs are held in the fingers and the succulent buttery corn bitten off until the stem is clean.

CREOLE MACARONI SOUP

2 pints vegetable water	4 oz. cooked macaroni
1 green pepper, seeded and chopped	2 oz. butter
1 small onion, chopped	1½ tblsp. flour
½ lb. ripe tomatoes	½ tsp. tarragon vinegar

Fry the chopped onion and green pepper in the butter until soft. Add the flour, stirring well, then gradually add the vegetable water, the sliced tomatoes, salt and grated black pepper to taste and simmer for 15 minutes. Add the macaroni and the vinegar, taste for seasoning and serve very hot.

ONION AND GREEN PEPPER SOUP

2 large Spanish onions	3 tblsp. flour
1 small green pepper	½ cup thick cream
1 pint vegetable water	parsley to garnish
4 oz. butter	salt and black pepper

Thinly slice the onions and fry in 2 ounces of the butter until golden. Fry the flour in the other half of the butter and gradually blend in the vegetable water until the mixture is creamy. Add the onions and the seeded, finely chopped pepper, and cook for a few minutes at boiling point. Just before serving add the cream and the seasoning. Garnish with sprigs of parsley.

MUSHROOM AND TOMATO SOUP

¼ lb. mushrooms, minced	1 oz. butter
1 small onion, chopped	1 oz. flour
2 cups tomato juice	nutmeg to taste
2 cups milk	paprika
½ cup thick cream	toast as required
sour cream	salt and black pepper

Fry onion in the butter for a few minutes, add the flour, and very gradually add the hot milk, thick cream and the hot tomato juice, stirring all the time with a wooden spoon. Season with nutmeg, salt and paprika. Add the mushrooms and cook the soup in the top of a double boiler for 30 minutes. Put a slice of toast in each soup bowl, top with one tablespoonful sour cream sprinkled with paprika, and pour the soup over it.

CREOLE OMELETTE

This is a splendid omelette with a very special filling. The following quantities make 1 serving.

3 medium eggs	3 tblsp. warm milk
2 oz. mushrooms, thinly sliced	½ cup thick cream
1 small sweet onion	salt and black pepper
corn oil for frying	

Beat the eggs with a fork, add the milk and a shake of salt and grated black pepper. Leave to stand while you fry the thinly sliced onion and mushrooms together until soft, season with salt and black pepper, and stir in the cream. Keep this filling hot while you are making the omelette. Allow a very little oil to become very hot in your omelette pan, add the egg and milk mixture and stir with a fork. When egg is only just set add the filling, fold over the omelette and serve on a hot plate.

Creole cooking abounds with exciting soups. Here is an iced one for midsummer meals and picnics.

ICED PEA SOUP

1 tin thick pea soup	1 small carton thick cream (garnish)
½ pint cold milk	1 small sweet onion (garnish)
½ tsp. garlic salt	parsley (garnish)
¼ tsp. curry powder	paprika to taste
	salt and black pepper

Mix all ingredients, except garnishes, carefully together, pour into a suitable container and heat through without boiling. Put the soup in the fridge to get thoroughly chilled before serving. Finely mince the onion, add it to the thick cream and allow to stand for at least 1 hour in the fridge before using. When the soup is well chilled, serve it with a good tablespoonful thick, onion-flavoured cream floating on top, and garnished with a sprig of parsley.

RICE AND NUT PUDDING

1½ pints milk	4 oz. chopped nuts
¼ pint water	4 oz. brown sugar
1 tblsp. ground rice	2 oz. long grain rice
	1 tsp. cinnamon

Boil the milk and the water together, add the rice and simmer for 10 to 15 minutes. Take a little milk from the pan to make a paste of the ground rice, add this to the cooked rice and simmer for a further 10 minutes. Add a teaspoonful cinnamon and stir well. Leave to go cold before serving sprinkled with the chopped nuts.

COLD HONEY SOUFFLÉ

Both this and the previous recipe come under the heading of desserts, and are rich in proteins.

7 tblsp. honey	¼ pint thick cream
4 eggs, separated	

Whip the egg whites until they stand up in peaks. Beat the egg yolks with the honey, heat in the top of a double boiler until thick, then when cool fold in the egg whites and the cream. Do not allow the mixture to boil at any stage of the proceedings. Place in the fridge and serve as cold as possible.

CREOLE FRIED POTATOES

2 lb. small potatoes	2 cups corn oil
2 tblsp. salt	flour as required
	water as required

Scrub the potatoes and boil them in their jackets for 30 minutes in salted water. Drain and peel them. Meanwhile heat the oil until a blue smoke rises from it and brown the potatoes in it. Put the potatoes between layers of absorbent paper, and flatten each one with the palm of the hand. Reheat the oil until the blue smoke rises again, dust the potatoes with a little flour, and fry them again until golden all over. Drain, sprinkle them with salt and serve. You could serve them with corn on the cob for a really satisfying meal.

SWEET POTATO PUDDING

We like sweet potatoes any way in our house, and this novel way of serving them is often on the menu. They are very easy to obtain and are reasonably cheap.

¾ lb. sweet potatoes	1 cup milk
½ lb. raw sugar	1 pint boiling water
½ cup flour	4 medium eggs, beaten
½ cup brown sugar	4 tblsp. butter
1 dessertsp. salt	

Scrub potatoes and boil in salted water for 30 minutes. To cook them more quickly cut them in fairly small pieces. Melt the brown sugar in a baking pan until golden, and make sure the pan is well coated with the sugar. Drain and mash the potatoes with the warmed milk, add the eggs, the raw sugar and a pinch of salt, and blend well. Add the melted butter and mix once more, then add the flour. Place mixture in sugar-coated baking pan, place the pan in another containing 1½ inches of boiling water and bake in a moderate oven for 50 minutes, then reduce heat and bake for a further 30 minutes. Serve cold.

France

France has long been associated with many fine cheeses, so many in fact that it is difficult to know where to begin. But as I am not writing a book solely about cheeses I shall have to confine myself to mentioning my own personal favourites together with the very best known ones.

Brie This is made of renneted cow's whole milk, slightly salted. Reddish-brown crust and heavy cream coloured inside, it must be tasted to be believed. It has a superlative flavour and an aggressive bouquet.

Camembert Perhaps the best known of the French cheeses, this one bears the name of a village in Normandy where it is reputed to have first been made. It seems somewhat inadequate to describe it as a soft paste made of cow's milk with a white mouldy crust, which traditionally should come in a little round wooden box, as this would hardly suffice to make anyone rush to the nearest delicatessen to buy one. Buy a good ripe one, lift the lid, smell, taste, and decide for yourself.

Neufchatel This is a whole milk cheese made of renneted cow's milk which has been slightly salted. It has a white, velvety down on it, something like **Camembert**. It can be eaten when young, with a creamy and innocuous taste, and in fact many unadventurous people prefer it this way. But this isn't doing justice to the Neufchatel for when it matures it acquires a firmer texture, a pungent taste and a bouquet all its own. If you want to try the matured one, ask for Neufchatel affiné. If you must eat it when it is young, ask for Neufchatel fleuri.

Port-Du-Salut and **Port Salut** is a mild flavoured cheese, the former name being the original cheese made by the Trappists of the Abbey of Notre Dame du Port du Salut in Entrammes, south of Laval, and the latter name being that of the carbon copies. The copy, I must add, is as good, and often better than the original. In appearance this cheese has a russet surface with a creamy inside. It is semi-hard, and is excellent with thickly buttered dark bread.

Gerome is not so well known as those which I have just mentioned but it deserves a place in this short list of French cheeses for its highly unusual flavour. It is a cylindrical, whole milk cheese, rather soft in texture, and fermented. The most delightful are flavoured with fennel, cumin or aniseed. They are brick red in colour on the outside and yellow inside. It is strong to aggressive and is a real connoisseur's cheese.

Saint-Paulin is a cow's milk cheese, semi-hard, slightly salted, and rather similar in taste and texture to a Dutch Gouda.

Roquefort is one of those cheeses that can be described only in superlatives. So let it suffice to say that it is the only ewe's milk cheese to have won international fame and it is also the only French cheese which has dared to challenge the right of Brie to be called the King of Cheeses. Made from the morning and evening milks mixed, it is salted and mixed with mouldy breadcrumbs, and eventually, wherever it is made in France, it is brought to the famous Roquefort caves to mature. Conditions in these caves make it impossible for Roquefort to be made anywhere else. When you buy it, it is foil-wrapped and has green mould veins inside. In texture it is semi-hard and crumbly, in flavour creamily piquant. Genuine Roquefort is marked with the single name. Otherwise it is marked Roquefort-France.

The list of French cheeses is almost without end, so I will mention only one or two more which stand out from the rest, if only for the fact that it is difficult to live with them unless you are a real devotee. If you have a stout heart and a strong desire to savour the bite of an aggressive but wonderful cheese then try **Le Dauphin**, one of the Maroilles cheeses. It is half-moon shaped and flavoured with tarragon and powdered cloves. A rindless version of the above is known as **Gris de Lille** or sometimes Le Maroilles Gris.

EGG AND CHEESE SAVOURY

2 eggs per person	melted butter
2 slices of bread per person	grated cheese (Gruyère or Parmesan)
2 thin slices of cheese per person (preferably Gruyère)	salt and black pepper to taste

Take a large, flat baking dish and oil it   Dip the bread, both sides, in the melted butter, and cover each slice with a slice of cheese. Put the bread and cheese in the dish and put it under a fast grill until the cheese melts into the bread. Do not brown the cheese. Remove the dish from the grill, break an egg on to each slice of bread and cheese, sprinkle with salt and a good grate of black pepper, pop it back under the grill until the egg whites are just set and serve sprinkled with grated cheese. This is a very good breakfast dish.

CHEESE SOUFFLÉ

This is an excellent recipe for using Swiss Emmentaler cheese, but Gruyère is equally good.

¼ lb. grated cheese	2 tblsp. flour
4 separated eggs	2 tblsp. butter or margarine
1½ cups cold milk	salt and pepper to taste

Using a thick-bottomed saucepan melt the butter, add the flour and blend thoroughly. Add the milk a little at a time, and keep stirring until the mixture is smooth. Add salt to taste and a grate of black pepper, and take off the heat. Beat the egg yolks and add, with the grated cheese, to the mixture. Whisk the egg whites until they stand up in peaks and then fold them into the mixture, and turn it into an 8-inch diameter soufflé dish which has been well buttered. Bake in a moderate oven for 15 minutes and serve at once. These quantities are sufficient for 4 large helpings, or 6 modest ones.

COURGETTES AU BÉCHAMEL

This is one of the most interesting ways to serve young marrows. Use any good flavoured cheese you like. My favourite is Parmesan, but Canadian Cheddar is also excellent.

First make the Béchamel sauce as follows:

Melt 1 ounce of butter in a pan, add 1 tablespoonful of flour or cornstarch, and make a roux by cooking it for 30 seconds. Add ½ pint boiling vegetable stock, stirring all the time, then gradually add ½ pint boiling milk. Add a good sized bunch of parsley, which is removed later, also salt to taste and a grate of pepper and nutmeg.

Prepare the courgettes by peeling, cutting into rounds ¼ inch thick and boiling for 2 minutes in a very little salted water. Drain thoroughly and then brown in butter on both sides. Place in small casserole lid, cover with the Béchamel sauce (don't forget to remove the parsley), and sprinkle with plenty of grated cheese. Dot with butter or margarine and brown quickly under the grill. Serve in the casserole lid. I always use an unbreakable glass one which looks nice on the table.

GRILLED SALSIFY WITH PARMESAN

In the Dictionary of Vegetables I mentioned salsify as one of the more unusual vegetables. If you manage to get it, and you may well, for it is becoming increasingly popular, here is one of the very best ways to serve it.

1 lb. salsify	grated Parmesan
1 tblsp. lemon juice	wholewheat breadcrumbs
1 tblsp. butter or margarine	white sauce or Béchamel sauce

Wash or scrape the salsify under a running cold water tap and plunge them, after cutting into 4-inch lengths, into boiling salted water to which you have added 1 tablespoonful of lemon juice. This stops the salsify from discolouring. Vinegar will do if you have no lemons. Boil until the salsify are nearly tender, lift them out of the water and dry with a cloth. Arrange in a buttered baking dish or casserole lid, add the white sauce or Béchamel sauce, also plenty of grated Parmesan mixed with wholewheat breadcrumbs, and dot with butter or margarine. Put under a very hot grill until brown. Serve at once.

ROQUEFORT MOUSSE

This is an excellent way to serve this incomparable cheese, and I once committed the sacrilege of using a good, creamy Gorgonzola with equally astonishing results. Blue Stilton can also be used, but Roquefort or Gorgonzola are best.

½ lb. Roquefort	5 tblsp. cream, unwhipped
½ cup thick whipped cream	1 tblsp. gelatine
4 egg yolks	2 tblsp. cold water
3 egg whites, beaten into a froth	½ tsp. powdered saffron (optional)

The egg yolks should be beaten until thick and then the 5 tablespoonfuls of unwhipped cream added. Add the melted gelatine. Mash the cheese well with fork and add to the mixture, mixing well. At this stage add the saffron if you want a yellow colour, though personally I prefer it without. Beat the egg whites once more and add them, with the ½ cup of thick whipped cream, to the mixture. Turn into a greased mould and chill. Serve with a salad.

The previous recipe being a luxury item with no expense spared, here is an example of Haute Cuisine on a shoestring. It shows how to make a succulent dish from an unusual vegetable.

CHEESE AND ARTICHOKE PIE

1½ lb. Jerusalem artichokes
2½ oz. grated cheese (strong Cheddar is best)
½ lb. sweet Spanish onions

½ oz. butter or margarine
plenty of wholewheat breadcrumbs
salt and black pepper

Cook artichokes and onions, thinly sliced, in a little butter or margarine, in a pan with a close-fitting lid. When very tender mash them finely and season with salt and freshly milled black pepper. Grease a glass casserole and put a layer of the mashed vegetable in the bottom. Sprinkle with grated cheese, repeat these layers until everything is used up. The top layer is breadcrumbs mixed with grated cheese. Dot with butter or margarine and brown in a fast oven, approximately 25 to 30 minutes. Serve in casserole.

FRENCH ONION SOUP

The French claim to make the best onion soup in the world and I quite agree. After trying out this time-honoured recipe for yourselves I am sure you will too.

2 lb. sweet Spanish onions
2 pints vegetable water
2 tblsp. flour
salt and black pepper

4 oz. butter
4 oz. grated Parmesan
toast or croutons as required

The secret is to start the day before you need the soup, for it improves greatly with reheating. Peel and slice the onions thinly and cut each slice into four pieces. Sauté the onions in the butter but be careful not to brown them as you will spoil the look of the soup. Cover the pan, turn down the heat *very* low, and leave it for at least 30 minutes. When the onions are quite soft, sprinkle the flour over them and gradually add the hot vegetable water, stirring with a wooden spoon. Add salt and a good grate of black pepper. Put back the lid and simmer for another hour. Leave the lid on and leave the soup to go quite cold. Let it stand overnight and the next day, when you want it, heat it slowly to boiling point and serve with croutons or toast and plenty of Parmesan. Needless to say you eat it with warmed French bread.

CREAM OF CELERY SOUP

This is what I call a big soup. It is so filling that the course following it should be comparatively slight.

1 large head of celery (or 2 small ones)	1 tblsp. flour
2 large sweet Spanish onions	1 tblsp. butter
2 large floury potatoes	½ pint milk
1 carton thick cream	salt and black pepper

Fry the thinly sliced onions in the butter. Scrape the celery and shred it very finely, then add it to the softened onions. Slice the potatoes very thinly, add them to the onions and celery, then add 2 pints of water and simmer until vegetables are tender. Pass them through a sieve, and return them to the pan, add the heated milk and reheat being careful not to boil. Lastly stir in the cream, season and serve.

Now for two tomato soups, the first most definitely a party dish to impress your guests, the other a good plain family soup.

NO EXPENSE SPARED TOMATO SOUP

2 lb. ripe tomatoes	3 tblsp. cognac
1 large Spanish onion	1 tsp. brown sugar
1 pint cream	2 oz. butter
1 pint milk	sweet basil leaves
salt and black pepper	

Hold each tomato with a skewer under the grill for a few moments. You will then be able to peel them quite easily. Mash the peeled tomatoes to a pulp, and mix them with the minced onion and 1 teaspoonful of sweet basil leaves. Cook very slowly for 10 minutes, then pass through a sieve and after returning to the pan, add the heated milk, the melted butter, the heated cream and the sugar. Reheat the soup but do not boil it, add the cognac and season with salt and black pepper. Serve at once in heated plates.

ECONOMICAL TOMATO SOUP

¾ lb. ripe tomatoes	2 tblsp. sago
1 small sweet onion	2 tblsp. chopped parsley
1 medium carrot	1 tblsp. flour
2½ pints vegetable (or plain) water	1 tsp. brown sugar
sweet basil leaves	2 oz. margarine
salt and black pepper	

Peel and thinly slice the onion and the carrot and brown them in the margarine. Add the sliced tomatoes, the vegetable water or plain water (heated), season with salt, black pepper, sweet basil leaves and a little of the brown sugar. Simmer with the lid on for 1 hour, then rub through a sieve. Return to saucepan and add the rest of the teaspoonful of brown sugar and the flour which has been well mixed with a little cold water. Bring to boiling point, add the sago and cook for a further 20 minutes over a low heat, stirring occasionally with a wooden spoon. Check the seasoning, adding more sweet basil leaves if liked. Serve garnished with chopped parsley.

FRENCH SUMMER SOUP

3 pints vegetable water	½ cup of each of the following:
1 tsp. parsley	diced carrots, turnips,
1 tsp. brown sugar	fresh green peas, French beans,
1 tsp. chopped mint	tomatoes
a pinch of powdered clove	6 spring onions, chopped
salt and black pepper	

This is a very easy soup to make and can be served hot or cold. Simmer all the ingredients together for 45 minutes. Serve hot, garnished with sprigs of parsley. If you like iced soup chill it well in the fridge before using and serve with a spoonful of thick cream in each plate.

GOLDEN SOUP

1 large sweet Spanish onion	3 tblsp. butter
½ lb. ripe tomatoes	½ tsp. oregano or marjoram
1½ pints vegetable water	4 oz. grated Parmesan
salt and black pepper	

Cook the peeled and sliced onion in the butter until golden. Add the sliced tomatoes and cook for 6 minutes, then add oregano or marjoram, salt and a good grate of black pepper. Simmer very slowly for 15 minutes. Pass soup through a sieve, return to pan and reheat. Serve with plenty of Parmesan and French bread.

STUFFED GREEN PEPPERS

Thrifty French housewives find this an excellent way of using up mushroom stems when the caps have been used for another dish.

4 large green peppers	½ lb. mushroom stems
4 slices French bread	¼ lb. butter
1 medium onion, minced	¼ lb. black olives
½ pint vegetable stock	buttered breadcrumbs
salt and cayenne pepper	

Seed the green peppers and scoop out the pith. This is best done with a spoon rather than a knife. Now make the stuffing as follows. Soak the bread in the stock while you sauté the coarsely chopped mushroom stems in the butter. Add the squeezed out bread and mix well. Add a touch of cayenne pepper, salt, the minced onion and the chopped olives and mix well. If the mixture seems too dry moisten it with stock. Fill the peppers with the mixture, sprinkle with buttered breadcrumbs, and bake them, standing in 1 inch of stock, for 30 minutes in a moderate oven.

HARICOTS A LA FRANCAISE

Soak the haricots and soya beans overnight before preparing this dish, and cook them in boiling salted water until tender. If you use a pressure cooker you will save time and fuel. Cook the soya beans with the haricots.

1½ lb. cooked haricots	2 tblsp. chopped parsley
½ lb. cooked soya beans	white sauce as required
3 hard-boiled eggs	breadcrumbs as required
4 large tomatoes	salt and black pepper

Grease a casserole, and arrange the ingredients in layers as follows. A layer of tomato slices, then white sauce sprinkled with chopped parsley, breadcrumbs, chopped hard-boiled eggs, haricot and soya beans mixed, white sauce, chopped parsley, and lastly breadcrumbs. Sprinkle a little salt and black pepper between the layers. Bake in a fairly hot oven until nicely browned. This is a high-protein and very filling meal. The above quantities are sufficient for 6 good servings.

CHESTNUT AND BRUSSELS SPROUTS SALAD

This is a really delicious salad and is a useful method of serving Brussels sprouts for people who normally do not like them.

1 lb. hard Brussels sprouts	as many chestnuts as sprouts
1 large cooking apple	mayonnaise as required
	parsley sprigs as required

Boil the chestnuts in salted water until tender. When cool enough to handle, shell them and chop them finely. Wash the sprouts in salted water and discard any withered outer leaves. Chop them finely too. Peel the apple, take out the core and chop the pulp. Mix the apple with the chestnuts and the sprouts, moisten very thoroughly with mayonnaise, and serve garnished with parsley sprigs.

HOW TO COOK CELERIAC

This very useful and tasty vegetable is sadly neglected because too many people do not know how to cook it. It really is quite easy, and it can, as all vegetables can, be served chopped up in a salad. The following is the French country style celeriac.

The bulbous roots are the parts to eat. Scrub them well, slice them fairly thinly, and cook in salted water until tender. Test with a silver fork to avoid causing discoloration. While the celeriac is cooking, fry a medium-sized thinly sliced Spanish onion until golden. Now lay the cooked slices of celeriac in your serving dish, add the golden onions, and pour over enough white sauce to just cover and no more. Make the sauce with the water in which you boiled the celeriac. Season with salt and black pepper, cover with grated sharp cheese and brown quickly under the grill.

TOMATO ASPIC SALAD

2 large cans tomato juice	1 oz. gelatine crystals
2 cups shredded white cabbage	2 tsp. salt
1 medium-sized Spanish onion	1 tsp. caraway seeds
endive or lettuce	mayonnaise as required
grated black pepper	

Open both cans of juice. You should have at least four large breakfast cups. Mix the gelatine with one cupful of the juice and heat the rest to just under boiling point. Add the finely grated onion, the salt, and the gelatine mixture, stirring until all the crystals have dissolved. Pour into a ring mould (one which holds 1 to 1½ pints) and place in the fridge until well set. Meanwhile mix the finely shredded white cabbage with the caraway seeds, salt and grated black pepper, and enough mayonnaise to moisten. Unmould the tomato aspic, fill the centre with the cabbage mixture, and serve on a bed of endive or lettuce.

SAVOURY PEPPERS WITH COURGETTES

Courgettes feature in the Dictionary of Vegetables and are, in fact, very tiny marrows. Try to buy them early in the season, otherwise the skins tend to be rather bitter. In that case peel them before cooking.

2 large Spanish onions	1 oz. butter
3 sweet red or green peppers	½ lb. ripe tomatoes
1 clove garlic	½ lb. courgettes
salt and black pepper	

Peel and thinly slice the onions and fry them in the butter for 5 minutes. Add the sliced tomatoes and simmer for a further 5 minutes. Seed and thinly slice the peppers, thinly slice the courgettes and add to the onions and tomatoes. Add more butter if necessary and cook all together slowly for 10 minutes, the lid firmly on the pan. Season with finely minced garlic, salt and black pepper. Stir well and serve on a bed of plain boiled rice.

Again using green and red peppers here is a delicious sandwich filling which I had frequently in France although I have not seen it anywhere else.

SANDWICH FILLING

2 large green or red peppers	2 tblsp. mayonnaise
3 large eggs, hard-boiled	1 tblsp. butter
salt and black pepper	2 tsp. capers

Seed the peppers and take out all the pith. Chop finely together with the hard-boiled eggs and the capers. If you have a mortar and pestle pound it all together into a paste, otherwise chop it as finely as you possibly can. Add the slightly softened butter, mix well and season with a little black pepper. Add enough mayonnaise to make a soft but not a runny consistency, taste to see if the mixture needs salt and then spread on sandwiches.

Still on the subject of sweet peppers, here is yet another way of serving them.

KEBABS WITH MUSHROOMS AND PEPPERS

1 lb. hard tomatoes	3 sweet peppers
¾ lb. buttom mushrooms	5 tblsp. melted butter
salt and black pepper	

SAUCE

¼ lb. mushroom stalks	1 tblsp. butter
½ cup milk	½ tsp. flour
1 clove garlic	salt and black pepper

Make the kebabs first. Halve the button mushrooms, seed and cut up the peppers into pieces roughly the same size as the mushrooms. Cut up the tomatoes likewise. Fix the mushrooms, peppers, and tomatoes on skewers alternately until all is used up. Brush with melted butter, and grill for 10 minutes, turning the skewers every few minutes and basting with melted butter. While they are grilling, make the sauce. Cook the chopped mushroom stalks, the finely minced garlic and the milk all together over a very low heat for 10 minutes. Cream the butter with the flour, season with salt and black pepper and to it add 3 tablespoonfuls of the mushroom mixture, blending well. Pour all into a pan, stirring all the time, and when boiling pour over the kebabs.

COUNTRY EGGS

6 large eggs	1 cup grated sharp cheese
1 large Spanish onion	3 tblsp. butter
salt and black pepper	

Peel and mince the onion and sauté it in 2 tablespoonfuls of butter for 6 minutes. Butter a baking dish and put the onions in the bottom of it. Sprinkle lightly with cheese and salt and black pepper. Break the eggs carefully and place them on top of the onions. Add more seasoning, dot with the remaining tablespoonful of butter, add a thick layer of cheese, and bake in a very moderate oven for 15 minutes.

SAGE AND ONION BAKE

It was in France that I first learned that sage and onions can be used other than as a stuffing for marrows and nut roasts. This recipe can be eaten hot with noodles or, used cold, it makes a wonderful sandwich filling.

2 large sweet Spanish onions	1 tblsp. fresh or dried sage
2 oz. butter	1 tblsp. tarragon vinegar
hot water as required	3 tsp. brown sugar
salt and black pepper	

Fry the thinly sliced onions in the butter until brown. Season with salt and black pepper, add the vinegar, brown sugar, sage and 2 tablespoonfuls of hot water and simmer very slowly for 15 minutes. Add a little more hot water when necessary.

FRENCH CROQUETTES

2 large potatoes	½ cup white sauce
2 eggs	sweet basil leaves
1 shallot	wholewheat breadcrumbs
½ lb. ripe tomatoes	salt and black pepper
4 oz. chopped mixed nuts	deep frying oil

Scrub the potatoes, boil them in their jackets, and when cool enough to handle, rub the skin off. Put them through a ricer or a sieve and mix them thoroughly with the finely chopped nuts. Make the white sauce with the potato water. Separate the eggs and mix the yolks into the nut and potato mixture. Add the finely minced shallot, season with salt and black pepper. Add enough white sauce to make a workable mixture. Put it in the fridge to get quite cold before proceeding. Flour your hands and form the mixture into croquettes, brush well with whipped egg white and roll in the breadcrumbs. Fry in deep hot oil until golden brown on both sides. While your croquettes are frying, slice the tomatoes, sprinkle with sweet basil leaves, salt and black pepper. Drain the croquettes well on absorbent paper and serve with the tomatoes.

TIPSY SANDWICH

This is a most unusual *baked* sandwich and the following ingredients will make 4 generous helpings.

¼ lb. Swiss cheese	4 tblsp. flour
¼ lb. butter, melted	bread as required (stale will do)
1 cup milk	white wine as required
1 large egg yolk	cognac as required
salt and black pepper	

Blend together the flour, melted butter, salt and pepper, and very gradually add the warm milk. Cook over a gentle heat, stirring with a wooden spoon, until very thick. Take the pan off the heat, blend in the diced cheese and the egg yolk and mix well. Clut thick slices of bread, dip them quickly in the wine, and spread them with the cheese mixture. Grease a baking sheet and place the slices on it. Bake in a hot oven for 10 minutes and just before serving, sprinkle a teaspoonful of cognac over each slice.

POMME ANNA

1 large potato per person	cold water as required
melted butter as required	salt and black pepper

Peel the potatoes as thinly as possible so that you will not waste the nutritious part just under the skin. Slice them thinly and soak them in cold water for 15 minutes. Drain and dry thoroughly with a cloth. Butter a casserole and arrange the potato slices in layers, sprinkling each layer with salt and black pepper and adding a few tablespoonfuls of melted butter. When all is used up, cover the casserole with greaseproof paper, put on the lid, and bake in a moderate oven for at least 1 hour. Then remove the lid and the paper and cook for a further 25 minutes to brown the top. Serve on a hot dish garnished with sprigs of parsley.

FRENCH MUSHROOM BAKE

½ lb. mushrooms	2 oz. butter
1 large sweet Spanish onion	½ cup thick cream
1 large egg	1 tblsp. fresh chervil, chopped
2 cups cooked long grain rice	salt and black pepper

Chop the mushrooms and the onion finely and fry in the butter until golden. Place in the bottom of a well greased casserole. Mix the well beaten egg with the rice and season with salt and black pepper. Spread the rice mixture on top of the mushroom mixture, dot with plenty of butter and bake for 30 minutes. Heat the cream, stir in the chervil and serve with the mushroom bake.

BANANAS AND SPINACH AU GRATIN

This is an unusual combination but well worth trying.

2 lb. spinach	2 tblsp. chopped parsley
5 bananas	1 tblsp. thick cream
1 cup grated cheese	butter as required
breadcrumbs	salt and black pepper

Wash the spinach well. Melt a teaspoonful of butter in a deep saucepan, add the spinach and put on the lid. Turn down the heat to very low and cook the spinach until tender. Rub through a sieve, then flavour with salt and black pepper. Place spinach purée, mixed with the thick cream and 1 tablespoonful melted butter in a greased casserole. Peel and quarter the bananas and sauté them lightly in butter, then lay them on the spinach. Add a thick layer of breadcrumbs, the grated cheese mixed with the parsley, dot with butter and bake in a hot oven until brown on top.

CHAMPIGNONS AU GRATIN

½ lb. button mushrooms	1 cup breadcrumbs
½ lb. ripe tomatoes	1 cup grated cheese
2 eggs, beaten	butter as required

This dish is usually served with jacket potatoes so put these to bake in the oven before you commence the recipe. Sauté the mushrooms in butter until tender. While they are cooking, mix together the breadcrumbs, beaten eggs, cheese, and a little melted butter to make a soft consistency. Place the mushrooms in a deep oven-proof plate, spread with the egg mixture, and brown well in a hot oven. Serve one large or two small jacket potatoes with each serving.

ROQUEFORT WITH FRENCH BEANS

This sounds an unlikely combination but it isn't sacrilege to cook with Roquefort, it is inspired culinary art. You don't have to be a French chef to serve this dish perfectly cooked, so it would be a good party dish to delight your guests.

¼ lb. Roquefort cheese	2 cups cooked French beans
3 tblsp. wholewheat breadcrumbs	¼ cup vegetable water
butter as required	salt and black pepper

Butter a small casserole, and arrange a layer of the French beans on the bottom. Crumble the Roquefort and sprinkle some on the beans. Add a slight shake of salt and a good grate of black pepper. Repeat the layers until all is used up. The top layer should be beans. Pour the vegetable water over the beans, add a thick layer of breadcrumbs and another grate of black pepper. Dot with plenty of butter and brown in a moderate oven.

Here is just one more recipe with Roquefort, and a better late-night snack with a glass of wine was never invented.

¼ lb. Roquefort cheese	butter as required
1 cup chopped salted almonds	dark rye bread as required

Toast the bread on both sides, and butter one side. Spread the Roquefort, which has been mashed with the chopped almonds, on to the buttered side and pop into a moderate oven for 8 minutes. Serve with a mixed green salad.

STUFFED ONIONS

6 large Spanish onions	4 oz. butter
2 eggs	2 oz. chopped walnuts
6 oz. grated sharp cheese	¼ tsp. brown sugar
4 oz. brown breadcrumbs	salt and black pepper

Skin the onions and parboil in a little salted water for 10 minutes, keeping the lid on the pan. Remove the centres, chop these and mix with the cheese, breadcrumbs, nuts and the well beaten eggs. Season with salt and black pepper. Stuff the hollowed-out onions with the mixture, and sprinkle the outsides of the onions with a little more salt and pepper. Melt the butter in a casserole and put in the onions. Baste them with the butter, cover with the casserole lid, which has been greased, and bake in a moderate oven for 1 hour. The onions should be just tender when tested with a silver fork.

CAMEMBERT SALAD

If you had not heard of using Roquefort in cooking before, then probably you will be just as suprised to discover that this recipe contains Camembert. I thoroughly recommend this recipe and as a special treat for the non-dieting members of the family I think it is incomparable.

1 whole box Camembert, very ripe	1 tsp. French mustard
1 cup thick cream	1 tsp. salt
2 egg whites	black pepper
a head of crisp lettuce	a bunch of watercress

Mash the Camembert, rind and all, and blend in the salt, pepper, mustard and cream, mixing well. Fold in the stiffly beaten egg whites and pour into a ring mould. Put in the coldest part of the fridge until fairly solid. Unmould and serve on a bed of lettuce, surrounded by watercress.

Germany

Germany is a country of fine cheeses. The list is formidable so I will mention only a few of the best and most easily found.

Tilsiterkäse needs no introduction from anyone, and is perhaps Germany's most popular cheese both in its native country and abroad. A cow's milk cheese, it is firm textured, pale yellow, with small round eyes. The flavour varies from mild to sharp, and sometimes caraway seeds are added to Tilsiter made with skimmed milk.

Spitzkäse is another German cheese with caraway seeds added. Made from skimmed cow's milk it has an agreeable spicy flavour.

Munster is a tan coloured cheese with a white inside which turns yellow with curing. It is good both for cooking and as a table cheese.

Weisslacker is a white, lustrous cheese made from cow's milk. When fresh it has a mild flavour but when allowed to ripen well it attains a flavour of its own.

Nieheimer Hopfenkäse is a sour milk cheese which is cured between layers of hops, hence its name. It is flavoured with salt and caraway seed, and sometimes beer is added to give that extra pungency beloved of cheese connoisseurs.

If you like cream cheese, then look for a delicious German one called **Mainauer**. It is one of the best of that country.

Having introduced some of Germany's best cheeses here are some ways of serving them. The following is a very economical way of serving the delightful Tilsiterkäse or, as it is sometimes called, Tilsit.

TILSIT SOUFFLÉ

2 oz. Tilsit, grated or cut into small pieces	1 teacup warm milk
1 oz. margarine	2 large eggs (or 3 medium)
1 dessertsp. flour (wholewheat is best)	salt and black pepper to taste

Make a roux by melting the butter and frying the flour in it for a few moments, add the milk slowly and stir until boiling. Take the pan off the heat for 5 minutes and then stir in the yolks of egg. Add the cheese and taste for seasoning. Pepper is essential but the cheese may make the mixture salty enough. Beat the egg whites until stiff and fold carefully into the mixture. Pour into a greased soufflé tin or deep cake tin, sprinkle with the breadcrumbs, dot with margarine and bake in a hot oven for 10 minutes. Serve at once.

MUNSTER POTATOES

The original recipe requires German Munster cheese, that tan coloured cheese with the strong flavour. However, if it is difficult to obtain, you could use as a good substitute, strong Canadian Cheddar. Take 2 large, floury potatoes per person and scrub well. Bake in their jackets in a moderate oven until quite soft. Cut off a lid, scoop out part of the inside, mash this pulp well with salt, pepper, margarine and grated cheese and stuff potato cases with the mixture.

Replace lid and put back into the oven to get thoroughly warm. Serve each one wrapped in a paper napkin.

BARLEY AND CHEESE CAKE

An unusual recipe, combining the chewiness of barley with the richness of tomato and strong cheese.

2 cups cooked pearl barley	1 tblsp. minced parsley
½ cup grated strong cheese (Munster or Canadian Cheddar)	1 small tin tomato purée or ¼ pint tomato sauce
1 tblsp. minced onion	salt and black pepper

Mix all ingredients together, turn into a greased glass dish, and bake in a slow oven for 30 minutes. For variety put in a thick layer of breadcrumbs and grated cheese on top. Serve in baking dish.

MUSHROOM AND TOMATO BAKE

¼ lb. mushrooms	1 tblsp. hot milk
½ lb. tomatoes	sweet basil leaves
½ cup beer	breadcrumbs
1 small onion	butter as required
salt and black pepper	

Slice the onions and mushrooms and fry in the butter for 10 minutes with the lid on the pan. Arrange in a greased casserole and cover with the sliced tomatoes. Sprinkle with sweet basil leaves (about 2 teaspoonfuls), salt and plenty of black pepper. Add a layer of finely chopped onion, then pour over the heated beer and the milk. Add another sprinkling of seasoning and cover with a thick layer of breadcrumbs. Dot with butter and bake in a slow oven for 35 minutes.

GERMAN POTATO SALAD

1 large potato per person	1 dessertsp. tarragon vinegar per person
1 pickled gherkin per person	chopped parsley
1 tblsp. olive oil per person	salt and black pepper

Boil the potatoes in their jackets until tender. When cool enough to handle skin them and cut them into small dice. While still warm, dress them with oil, and then vinegar. Dice the gherkins and mix with the potatoes. Sprinkle with salt and plenty of black pepper, and garnish with chopped parsley.

BEER SOUP

1 pint mild ale	3 tblsp. lemon juice
1 pint milk	1 tsp. brown sugar
3 egg yolks	½ tsp. cinnamon
	salt and black pepper

This is a very simple soup to make. Just heat the ale with the lemon juice and cinnamon. Heat the milk in a separate pan, and add the beaten egg yolks, mixing well. Add to the beer, season with salt and black pepper and add the sugar. Heat to boiling point and serve with toasted rye bread.

LENTIL SOUP WITH SOYA BEANS

½ lb. lentils	4 sticks celery
¼ lb. soya beans	1 tblsp. tarragon vinegar
1 large Spanish onion	½ tsp. brown sugar
	salt and black pepper

Soak the lentils and the soya beans overnight in plenty of salted water. Chop the onion and the celery and cook with the beans and lentils (which have been strained), in enough water to cover, until tender. This takes about 2½ to 3 hours, over a very low heat. Season with plenty of black pepper and the sugar and salt, and just before serving add the vinegar. This soup is a very nice colour which you can complement by garnishing with a sprig of watercress.

SPAGHETTI AND CHEESE WITH A DIFFERENCE

6 oz. spaghetti	½ lb. tomatoes
4 oz. grated sharp cheese	2 tblsp. black olives
2 oz. butter	1 small onion
	salt and black pepper

Boil the spaghetti until tender, drain, rinse with hot water and return to the still-hot pan. Add 1 tablespoonful butter and toss the spaghetti with two forks until each strand is coated. Season with black pepper and add the grated cheese. Taste to see if it needs any salt. Pile the spaghetti on to a serving dish and keep hot in the oven while you fry the onion and the tomatoes together for 10 minutes, then surround the spaghetti with them. Sprinkle with the finely chopped olives and serve very hot.

POTATOES AND ARTICHOKES AU GRATIN

3 large potatoes	¼ pint beer
½ lb. Jerusalem artichokes	¼ pint milk
4 oz. grated sharp cheese	2 tblsp. olive oil
breadcrumbs as required	1 tblsp. flour
butter as required	salt and black pepper

Boil the potatoes and artichokes in their skins and when tender and cool enough to handle, skin and slice them. Put them in a greased casserole. Now make the cheese sauce thus. Fry the flour in the oil for 3 minutes, stirring all the time. Gradually add the heated milk and then the heated beer, and stir once again until quite smooth. Season with pepper, add the grated cheese and add salt if necessary. Pour the sauce over the potatoes and artichokes, add a thick layer of breadcrumbs, dot with plenty of butter and bake in a moderate oven for 30 minutes.

WALNUT SAVOURY

1 lb. cooked potatoes	4 oz. grated sharp cheese
6 tblsp. milk	3 oz. chopped walnuts
2 eggs	salt and black pepper

Mash the potatoes with the chopped nuts, cheese, milk and beaten eggs. Add plenty of freshly grated black pepper and taste for salt. Grease a shallow tin and press the mixture well down into it. Bake in a moderate oven until golden, about 30 minutes. Cut into squares and serve each square with a fried egg on top.

EGG CUTLETS

3 large eggs, hard-boiled	4 tblsp. breadcrumbs
1 large raw egg	4 tblsp. tomato juice
1 fresh lemon	1 tblsp. butter
oil for grilling	1 tblsp. flour
salt and black pepper	½ tsp. curry powder

Make a roux with the melted butter and the flour, cook for 1 minute, then add the curry powder. Very gradually add the heated tomato juice, stirring all the time until the mixture is smooth. Take the pan off the heat, add the chopped hard-boiled eggs, 2 teaspoonfuls of lemon juice, and mix well. Spread out on a plate and leave to go quite cold. Shape into round cutlets and brush with the beaten raw egg and coat well with breadcrumbs. Grill under a high heat until brown each side, basting occasionally with the oil, then turn down the heat and cook for a further 5 to 10 minutes. Serve with slices of fresh lemon.

RICE CUTLETS

½ lb. cooked long grain rice	2 large eggs
¼ lb. mushrooms, chopped	1 oz. butter
4 tblsp. milk	breadcrumbs as required
2 tblsp. flour	oil for grilling
2 tsp. chopped parsley	salt and black pepper

Cook the chopped mushrooms very slowly in the butter until soft, add the flour and blend. Gradually add the heated milk stirring all the time until the sauce is smooth. Take the pan off the heat and add one of the eggs (beaten), the parsley, the rice and the salt and black pepper. Blend well, then leave aside to cool thoroughly. Shape into cutlets, dip into the other well beaten egg, and roll in breadcrumbs. Grill until golden on both sides, basting well with the oil. Drain and serve. These make a filling supper dish when served hot but are equally good served cold for picnics or packed lunches.

RICE WITH CUCUMBER

1 large cucumber	3 oz. grated sharp cheese
1½ cups cooked long grain rice	4 tblsp. milk
½ lb. ripe tomatoes	2 tblsp. butter
1 small sweet onion	1 tblsp. chopped parsley
sweet basil leaves	1 tsp. cornstarch
salt and black pepper	

Fry the sliced tomatoes and the sliced onion for a few minutes until the tomatoes are soft, sprinkle with sweet basil leaves and blend. Add the cooked rice, mix well and season with salt and black pepper. Cover and cook over a low heat while you prepare the cucumber. Peel and cube the cucumber, fry in butter for 3 minutes, then add the milk, salt and pepper. Mix well. Blend the cornstarch with a little cold water and add to the cucumber. Stir until boiling and then add the grated cheese, mixing well. Serve very hot, surrounded by the rice mixture.

BEETS WITH CHEESE

For this dish choose small round baby beets which have been cooked.

8 baby beets, cooked	thick cream as required
2 tblsp. breadcrumbs	butter as required
1 cup grated cheese (Parmesan is best)	salt and black pepper

Scoop out the insides of the beets being careful not to break the outer walls. Mash the part you have scooped out with the cheese and breadcrumbs. Add enough cream to make a firm mixture. Season with black pepper and a very little salt. Remember the cheese is highly flavoured. Stuff the beets with the mixture, add a knob of butter on top of each one and bake in a moderate oven for 20 minutes. Allow 2 baby beets per serving.

STUFFED TOMATOES

For this dish choose the very largest tomatoes you can find.

4 large tomatoes	1 clove garlic, minced
¼ lb. mushrooms	1 cup vegetable water
2 dessertsp. butter	breadcrumbs as required
salt and black pepper	

Cut a lid off the top of each tomato and scoop out the pulp being very careful not to damage the outer walls. Fry the chopped mushrooms very gently in butter with the tomato pulp and garlic for 4 minutes, then add the stock and cook for a further 10 minutes with the lid on the pan. Season with salt and black pepper. Add enough breadcrumbs to make a fairly solid mixture and stuff the tomatoes with this. Sprinkle with more breadcrumbs and bake for 15 minutes in a hot oven with 4 tablespoonfuls of stock or stock mixed with white wine.

MUSHROOM SAUTÉ

1½ lb. mushrooms	3 tblsp. corn oil
1 medium onion	toast as required
4 hard-boiled eggs	salt and black pepper

Sauté the sliced mushrooms in the oil with the onions until golden brown. Allow about 12 minutes for this, then add the chopped hard-boiled eggs and season with salt and black pepper. Heat through thoroughly and serve piled on to hot buttered toast.

HOT POTATO SALAD

The German people are fond of potato salad and this one, served hot, was new to me. I give it to you by permission of my dear friend and fellow potatophile, Hilde Grumer.

6 medium-sized waxy potatoes	¼ lb. chopped mushrooms
3 hard-boiled eggs	3 tblsp. tarragon vinegar
2 large eggs	2 tblsp. butter
1 small sweet onion	1 clove garlic
salt and black pepper	

I stress that this dish is much easier to prepare with waxy potatoes rather than floury ones. Scrub the potatoes and boil them in their jackets until tender. When cool enough to handle, skin them and cut them into dice. Keep them hot while you prepare the rest. Crush the clove of garlic and drop it into the vinegar. Fry the finely chopped mushrooms in the butter until soft, then add the minced onion. Cook for a further 3 minutes, then add the chopped hard-boiled eggs and the beaten raw egg and mix well. Heat the vinegar, discard the garlic, and season with salt and pepper. Mix all together with the potatoes and serve hot.

ONION AND CHEESE BAKE

Make this recipe only with a very sharp cheese, otherwise it will lose its character.

3 large sweet Spanish onions	4 tblsp. wholewheat flour
1 cup sharp cheese	2 tsp. paprika
2 cups milk	1 tsp. French mustard
4 oz. butter	1 stick celery
breadcrumbs	frying oil
salt and black pepper	

Make a roux with the butter, flour and the heated milk. Stir until the sauce is smooth. Season with salt and black pepper, add the cheese and keep hot.

Thinly slice the onions and sauté in the hot oil until golden brown. Place them in a well greased casserole (grease the lid as well), and pour the sauce over them, after adding the mustard and the minced celery. Cover with a thin layer of breadcrumbs, dot with butter and bake in a moderate oven for 20 minutes.

CHESTNUTS AND RICE

This is a very economical and filling supper dish when chestnuts are in season.

1 lb. chestnuts	½ lb. raw rice
2 oz. butter	vegetable water as required
salt and black pepper	paprika

Make cross cuts on the chestnuts with a sharp knife and bake them in a hot oven for 15 minutes. Meanwhile wash the rice several times, put in a pan with enough cold water to cover, add a teaspoonful of salt and bring to the boil. Drain well in a colander or sieve. Grease a casserole, add the rice, add the peeled and chopped chestnuts, the melted butter and pour over enough vegetable water to cover. Add a sprinkling of black pepper and a little salt. Bake in a moderate oven, with the lid on, for at least 30 minutes until all the stock is absorbed. Should stock evaporate too quickly add some more, but make sure that it is boiling first. Serve sprinkled with paprika.

To end this chapter on German cooking, a dessert recipe which is too good to leave out. These are savoury biscuits and are best eaten with coffee for a crunchy end to a meal.

SAVOURY NUT BISCUITS

1 cup chopped nuts	1 tblsp. butter
2 cups flour	1 tsp. baking powder
a pinch of salt	milk for mixing

The original recipe requires chopped, mixed, unsalted nuts, but salted peanuts are equally good. I leave you to try both ways and decide for yourself. Blend together the nuts, the flour, and the salt (if unsalted nuts are used), and the finely shredded spoonful of butter. Add the baking powder and mix thoroughly. Use enough milk to make a firm paste and knead on a floured board for a few moments. Then roll out thinly, cut into circles, squares, triangles or any shape you like, and place on a well buttered baking sheet. Put into a preheated slow oven until golden.

Great Britain

The best of all the many delectable British cheeses is without a doubt the **Stilton**. It is one of the truly great cheeses of the world. Seasonal because it can be made only from May to September in England, it is made from the finest and richest milk obtainable to which has been added the cream of other milk. A semi-hard, double cream, cow's milk cheese, it is distinguished by the blue veining in its creamy inside. The rind is of a brownish colour, crinkled, and with a white velvety fur. This cheese should always be eaten when fully ripe, and once bought, it should on no account be allowed to go dry.

Stilton can also be eaten when it is white, in which case it is a chalky colour and lacks any distinctive taste although it is very nourishing. White Stilton is similar in taste and in appearance to **Caerphilly.**

Double Gloucester is a fairly strong tasting semi-hard cheese which comes in two colours, a delicate pale yellow and a pale red. Single Gloucester is still made but is quite undistinguished and lacks bite, unlike the Double.

Leicestershire is one of my personal favourites of the British cheeses. This is a full and satisfying cheese with a lovely golden red colour, a waxy texture, and a rich flavour. It is a good cheese for people who like a medium flavour which is not too aggressive either in taste or in bouquet, yet is by no means innocuous. This is what I would call a good breakfast cheese.

Lancashire cheese has a rather split personality. When young it is so soft that it can be spread on bread like a double cream cheese, but with maturity it hardens into a crumbly texture, quite different from what it was. Lancashire always has a mild flavour, full and rich tasting, but perhaps rather unexciting. It improves when toasted. Bubbly and delicious it is the perfect cheese for toasting under the grill or for making Welsh Rarebit.

Wensleydale is another blue English cheese, although it is more often seen in the shops in its white state. When there is sufficient demand, the blue Wensleydale will be made in much greater quantities. Tradition has it that this cheese was born over a thousand years ago. It is a medium-strong tasting cheese with a rather close heavy texture. Also a good cooker.

I leave the most widely consumed of British cheeses to the last, **English Cheddar.** Close textured, creamy, nutty and mild, this is a first class all-purpose cheese. It makes sweet eating and cooks to perfection. Whichever way you eat it, you cannot mistake that distinctive taste. There are many Cheddars but perhaps the English one is the most subtle. Here are a few of the best English Cheddar recipes.

CHEESE AND TOMATOES ON TOAST

3 ripe tomatoes	½ tsp. dried basil leaves
2 cups grated Cheddar	1 large clove garlic
½ glass cider or white wine	2 tblsp. butter or margarine
2 slices of toast per serving	grated black pepper

Fry the tomatoes in the butter or margarine, and when quite soft add the garlic and basil leaves. Add the wine or cider and a good grate of black pepper, and stir well. Add the grated Cheddar and when the cheese is melted serve on the toast.

SCOTCH TART

This is a very economical dish, and a filling one too. Again Cheddar cheese is best.

shortcrust pastry	2 oz. margarine
1 teacup grated Cheddar	½ tsp. dry mustard
1 teacup rolled oats	salt and black pepper

Line a greased pie-plate with pastry, mix cheese, oats and seasoning with melted margarine and spread on pastry. Sprinkle with grated cheese and bake in a hot oven for 20 minutes.

WELSH CHEESE SAVOURY

Use 2 round dinner rolls per serving and soak them inside with boiling milk. When the bread inside is thoroughly soft, stuff the rolls with the following mixture. Take a ½ pound of finely grated Wensleydale or strong Cheddar cheese and mix with the beaten yolks of three eggs. To the mixture add the well beaten whites of the eggs, and season with salt and black pepper. Put into a very hot oven and bake for 15 minutes. Serve piping hot in dinner napkins. I find that the easiest way of stuffing the rolls is to slice a lid off the top before soaking the insides and put the lid back after the stuffing is in place.

WELSH RAREBIT WITH A DIFFERENCE

If you have ever wondered if there was any new way of serving rather plain and ordinary cottage or cream cheese, try this one for a tasty breakfast.

2 rounds toasted bread per serving	4 oz. cream or cottage cheese
2 hard-boiled eggs	2 oz. mushrooms fried in butter or margarine
	salt and black pepper

Mash the eggs thoroughly, add to the cheese and season. Add mushrooms, and pile the mixture on the toast. Put into a fast oven for a few minutes until golden.

79

ONION AND CELERY SOUP

1 lb. Spanish onions	6 oz. butter
1 head of celery	2 oz. flour
1 pint milk	½ pint vegetable water
salt and black pepper	

Peel and slice the onions thinly. String and clean the celery and shred finely. Sauté both in 4 ounces hot butter until golden, with the lid on the pan. Make a roux with the rest of the butter and the flour and cook for 1 minute. Gradually add the mixed heated liquids, stirring all the time to keep the mixture smooth. Mix with the onion and celery, put the lid on the pan and simmer for 20 minutes. Season with salt and black pepper.

WELSH LEEK SOUP

6 leeks	1 pint milk
4 tblsp. raw rice	1 cup grated cheese
paprika	1 cup white wine
salt and black pepper	

Clean the leeks and slice them. Wash the rice several times and then put both leeks and rice in a saucepan with just enough water to cover. Simmer until rice is tender, about 25 minutes. Add the milk, bring to the boil and season with salt and black pepper. Add the cheese and the wine and just before serving, sprinkle paprika on the top of each plate.

IRISH TIDDY

This is one of the simplest and most delicious breakfast recipes I know.

4 large ripe tomatoes	1 oz. butter
2 eggs, beaten	¼ tsp. sweet basil leaves
hot buttered toast	salt and black pepper

Slice the tomatoes and fry them in the butter for 3 minutes. Add sweet basil, more or less according to your taste, then add the beaten eggs. Turn the heat to very low, stir the mixture well with a wooden spoon and leave to cook for a further 2 minutes. Season with salt and black pepper. Do not overcook this dish or you will spoil it. Take the pan off the heat while the egg is still slightly runny. The heat of the pan will do the rest. Stir once more, then pile on to hot buttered toast.

TIPSY WELSH RAREBIT

1 egg, large	1 teacup beer
2 oz. butter	1 tsp. French mustard
salt and black pepper	3 full cups grated cheese

Melt the butter, add the cheese and mustard, and cook very slowly until cheese has melted. Stir in the beer and mix well. Season with salt and black pepper, and just before piling on to hot buttered toast stir in the beaten egg.

SOBER WELSH RAREBIT

8 oz. grated sharp cheese	4 tblsp. milk
1 oz. butter	1 tsp. French mustard
hot buttered toast	parsley
salt and black pepper	

Melt the butter in a small saucepan, add the cheese, milk, mustard and pepper and cook over a very gentle heat until the mixture is smooth. Taste to see if salt is needed. Put on to hot buttered toast and put under the grill until the mixture is brown and bubbly. Garnish with sprigs of parsley.

DEVONSHIRE BUBBLY CASSEROLE

6 oz. grated cheese	3 tblsp. flour
3 oz. butter	1 pint milk
¼ lb. salted nuts	a head of celery
salt and black pepper	

Clean and finely shred the celery and place in a well buttered casserole. Sprinkle with the chopped nuts. Make a roux with the butter and the flour, and cook for 1 minute. Gradually add the heated milk stirring all the time. Cook over a very low heat until smooth. Add the grated cheese, mix again and pour over the celery. Bake in a hot oven for 25 minutes until the top is a bubbly golden brown. The celery should be firm rather than soft.

WATERCRESS SOUP

3 very large potatoes	3 pints vegetable stock
2 bunches watercress	1 oz. flour
1 large sweet Spanish onion	salt and black pepper

Cook the peeled and sliced potatoes in the vegetable stock until tender. Add the chopped watercress, reserving a few leaves for garnishing. Put the stalks in the soup as well. *Never* throw them away as they are full of nourishment. When all the vegetables are soft, rub them through a sieve and return them to the pan. Mix the flour with just a little water in a cup. Add some of the hot soup and then stir the contents of the cup into the soup. Stir until boiling, scatter the remaining leaves over the soup and serve with dark rye bread.

CHEESY EGGY TOAST

3 eggs, well beaten	1½ cups milk
6 oz. grated cheese	butter for frying
½ a stale loaf	salt and black pepper

Mix together the beaten eggs, the cheese, milk and pepper. Season with salt (lightly if the cheese is sharp). Cut thick slices of bread, dip them in the mixture so that they are thoroughly coated each side and fry in plenty of butter until brown on each side.

There are three ways of serving Cheesy Eggy Toast.
1. Place each piece in the bottom of a soup bowl and fill the bowl with clear soup.
2. Serve the toast on its own, garnished with chopped olives.
3. Serve with a lightly poached egg on each slice.

WILTSHIRE CUSTARD CHEESE

½ lb. grated cheese	3 beaten eggs
1½ lb. spinach	3 cups hot milk
a dash of Worcester sauce	butter as required
salt and black pepper	

Mix the hot milk with the cheese, season with salt and black pepper. Mix with the beaten eggs and pour into a large pudding basin. Set the basin in a pan of hot water and bake in a very slow oven for 1 hour until custard is set. You can test this by inserting a thin knife into the custard and if it comes out quite clean the custard is ready. Turn the bowl upside down on to a hot plate and surround with the hot spinach which has been cooked in a little butter and salt.

NUTTY SPROUTS WITH CHEESE

1 lb. small tight sprouts	3 oz. butter
1 cup grated cheese (Parmesan is best)	salt and black pepper

Wash the sprouts and discard any shrivelled outer leaves. Without drying them place them in the hot butter in a saucepan. Sprinkle with salt and a grate of black pepper, put on the lid, turn the heat down very low and leave them to cook in their own steam for at least 30 minutes. You can turn them once during the cooking time. After 30 minutes the sprouts are still nutty as they should be and not at all soggy. Pile them into a heated bowl and sprinkle with the grated cheese.

A WELSH MEAL FOR SIX

2 lb. leeks	breadcrumbs as required
¾ lb. grated Cheddar cheese	butter as required
3 cups white sauce	chopped parsley
salt and black pepper	

Wash and slice the leeks and soak in salted water while you make the white sauce. Stir about 4 tablespoonfuls of cheese into the sauce, then pour it into a shallow greased casserole. Place the leeks on top of the sauce and cover them with the rest of the cheese. Sprinkle with freshly grated black pepper and a little salt. Cover with plenty of brown breadcrumbs and dot with butter. Bake for 30 minutes in a slow oven.

MINT TART

½ lb. shortcrust pastry	3 tblsp. chopped fresh mint
2 tsp. marmalade	3 tblsp. currants
1 egg for coating	3 tblsp. very dark brown sugar

Line a tart plate with the pastry and spread one teaspoonful of marmalade over it. Mix the other teaspoonful of marmalade with the currants and then mix with the chopped mint and the brown sugar. Spread the mixture over the pastry, top with another layer of pastry and brush with beaten egg before baking in a moderate oven until golden brown.

BREAD AND BUTTER PUDDING

Like every enthusiastic cook I keep numerous books containing all kinds of recipes, and on looking up my personal recipe for the Mint Tart I found, on the page opposite, a dozen different recipes for that most English of puddings, Bread and Butter pudding.

Here are the best two. Either makes first-class eating.

BREAD AND BUTTER PUDDING (1)

1 small brown loaf (stale will do)	6 oz. raisins and sultanas (mixed)
1 pint milk	4½ tblsp. brown sugar
1 carton thick cream	4 eggs
butter as required	cinnamon as required
	nutmeg to taste

Cut the loaf into thick slices, remove the crusts, and butter both sides. Take a square or oblong oven tin and butter it well, then arrange a layer of the buttered bread on the bottom. Sprinkle with a little of the fruit, and a dusting of cinnamon. Repeat the layers until the bread and fruit are used up, making sure that the top layer is buttered bread. Pour the milk into a bowl, add the 4 beaten eggs, the cream, the brown sugar and a pinch of nutmeg and whisk thoroughly with an egg whisk. If you have an electric blender so much the better. Pour the milk mixture over the bread and leave for 45 minutes before baking. Cover the tin and bake in a slow oven for 1 hour, the last 20 minutes with the lid off to brown the crust.

BREAD AND BUTTER PUDDING (2)

1 small malt or fruit loaf (stale will do)	2 oz. sultanas
1 pint milk	1 oz. brown sugar
2 eggs	1 tsp. grated lemon rind
	butter as required

Butter a square or oblong baking tin, and line with slices of the buttered malt or fruit bread (buttered on both sides). Scatter with the sultanas. Repeat layers until bread and fruit are used up. Beat the eggs with the sugar and the milk. Add the grated lemon rind. Pour over the bread and fruit and allow to stand for 30 minutes. Cover with a lid or greased paper and bake in a slow oven for 1 hour.

SCOTCH BROTH

1 oz. butter	2 tblsp. rolled oats
1 pint milk	2 tblsp. chopped parsley
1 pint vegetable stock	salt and black pepper

Melt the butter in a saucepan, and fry the rolled oats in it for 3 minutes over a very low heat. Gradually add the heated milk and then the heated vegetable stock stirring all the time. Bring to the boil, put on the lid and simmer for 25 minutes over a low heat. Season with salt and black pepper and garnish with chopped parsley.

LITTLE DEVILS

12 hard-boiled eggs	3 tblsp. mayonnaise
½ lb. grated sharp cheese	2 tblsp. butter
salt as required	1 heaped tsp. grated horse-radish
butter as required	½ tsp. dry mustard
sliced bread as required	grated black pepper

Halve the eggs lengthwise and remove the yolks which mash with the butter, mustard, horse-radish and mayonnaise. Add grated black pepper to taste and a little salt if necessary. Stuff this mixture back into the whites. Cut an appropriate number of slices of bread and toast them on one side, then butter them on the other. Put 4 egg halves on each slice, sprinkle liberally with cheese, and brown under the grill. Marvellous on a really cold night.

EGG FRICASSEE

6 hard-boiled eggs	1 small onion
½ pint white sauce	1 oz. butter
2 tblsp. thick cream	a touch of nutmeg
1 tsp. chopped parsley	salt and black pepper

Cut the eggs into 8 pieces each, remove the yolks and mash them. Fry the minced onion in the butter, add the egg yolks, white sauce, nutmeg, salt and pepper and the pieces of egg white. Bring to boiling point, then put the fricassee into individual bowls and sprinkle with chopped parsley. Serve with hot buttered toast.

TOMATO AND CHEESE RAREBIT

4 oz. grated sharp cheese	½ cup milk
1 oz. butter	½ cup tomato purée
½ oz. flour	1 tblsp. chopped parsley
2 eggs	sweet basil leaves
	black pepper

Make a roux with the butter and the flour and stir well. Add the heated milk and the heated tomato purée and bring to boiling point, stirring all the time. Add the cheese, plenty of grated black pepper and a teaspoonful of basil leaves. Lastly add the beaten eggs and stir until just below boiling point. Serve on buttered toast, garnished with chopped parsley.

MOTHER'S CHEESE AND ONION PIE

Here is my mother's recipe for cheese and onion pie, with the exact quantities to make one 8-inch pie.

½ lb. grated sharp cheese	1 egg
½ lb. shortcrust pastry	2 large sweet Spanish onions
1 tsp. salt	grated black pepper

Make the pastry beforehand and leave in the fridge for at least 2 hours. Roll out and line a buttered, deep 8-inch oven plate with it. Add a layer of thinly sliced onions, then sprinkle liberally with grated cheese. Season with salt and black pepper. Repeat the layers until all is used up and then add the top pastry crust and seal well all round with a fork dipped in water. Make 3 cuts in the top crust to let out the steam. Brush with beaten egg and bake in a moderate preheated oven for 45 minutes until golden brown. Serve very hot.

NORMAN'S FAVOURITE PIE

This is my husband's favourite version of the previous recipe. It is a rather more savoury pie.

½ lb. grated sharp cheese	1 egg
½ lb. shortcrust pastry	2 large sweet Spanish onions
¼ lb. ripe tomatoes	1 tsp. salt
2 oz. butter	sweet basil leaves
grated black pepper	

Line a greased 8-inch pie-plate with the pastry. Put the plate in the fridge while you prepare the onions. Peel and slice them and fry them in the butter until golden. Put a layer on to the pastry, add salt and pepper, a layer of tomatoes sprinkled with sweet basil leaves, and then a layer of cheese. Repeat the layers and top with pastry. Make 3 cuts in the top crust as before, brush with egg after sealing the edges and bake as above. Serve steaming hot.

CRUMB CRUST CHEESE AND ONION PIE

½ lb. grated sharp cheese	3 eggs
6 oz. savoury cracker crumbs	2 large Spanish onions
5 tblsp. melted butter	1½ cups hot milk
2 tblsp. solid butter	salt and black pepper

Mix the melted butter with the cracker crumbs and press well down into a buttered pie-dish. Fry the thinly sliced onions in the butter until golden and spread them over the cracker crust. Heat the milk to boiling point, turn off the heat immediately and add the milk to the beaten eggs very slowly, stirring with a wooden spoon. Add the cheese and grated black pepper and salt if necessary. Pour over the onions and bake in a slow oven for about 45 minutes.

CHEESE TART WITH OATMEAL

½ lb. shortcrust pastry	1 teacup rolled oats
6 oz. grated sharp cheese	½ tsp. mustard (made)
2 oz. butter	salt and black pepper

Line a greased pie-plate with thinly rolled out pastry. Mix the cheese, oats and seasoning with the melted butter. Reserve a little of the cheese, say about 2 ounces, for sprinkling on the top. Bake in a hot oven for 20 minutes. Serve at once garnished with parsley.

SCOTCH EGGS

½ lb. nutmeal (obtainable at health-food shops)	3 hard-boiled eggs
corn oil for frying	water as required

Shell the eggs, dry them well and roll in flour. Mash the nutmeal with a little water until the mixture becomes workable. Roll out on a well floured board and wrap each egg well with the mixture, making sure that there are no signs of the egg showing through. Make the oil really hot and see that there is enough for deep frying. Fry the eggs until golden brown, drain well and serve on noodles, rice or spaghetti.

HAZELNUT BAKE

This unusual dish is sure to please all members of the family and is very easily and quickly made.

4 oz. mashed potatoes	½ lb. fried tomatoes
4 oz. ground hazelnuts	1 small onion, grated
1 cup grated cheese	chopped parsley
salt and black pepper	

With the exception of the cheese mix all ingredients and season. Put it into a greased baking tin, sprinkle with the cheese and bake for 25 minutes in a fairly hot oven.

HONEY OMELETTE

4 eggs	2 tblsp. milk
1 small tin sliced peaches	1 tblsp. butter
butter for frying	1 tblsp. honey

Warm the honey and mix it with the beaten eggs and the warmed milk. Heat a small amount of butter in an omelette pan and fry the omelette quickly, stirring at first with a fork and then when the eggs begin to set, add the drained peach slices which you have warmed with the tablespoonful of butter. Fold over the omelette, cut into 2 pieces and serve on warm plates. Sufficient for 2 servings.

CHEESE AND POTATO BAKE

½ lb. sliced boiled potatoes	2 eggs
¼ lb. grated sharp cheese	1 small onion, minced
5 tblsp. milk	butter as required
	salt and black pepper

Grease a pie-dish, and arrange a layer of sliced potatoes on the bottom. Sprinkle with grated cheese, then onion, then add small pieces of butter. Repeat the layers, reserving a little of the cheese for sprinkling on top. Mix the eggs, milk, salt and pepper and pour over the layers. Sprinkle with grated cheese and bake in a fairly moderate oven until well heated through, about 30 minutes.

CAULIFLOWER RICHMOND-STYLE

Fry 2 large Spanish onions in corn oil with plenty of salt and pepper. Make onions *really* brown, then add a touch of dark brown sugar. I use raw sugar which I am able to get easily in any health-food shop or large food store. Now prepare your cauliflower by cutting off the tough stalks, then cut into small sprigs, meanwhile keeping your onions sizzling in the pan. Add the cauliflower to the onions, together with 2 tablespoonfuls of tomato juice, put on the lid of the pan and turn the heat down as low as possible. Leave for at least 30 minutes, then taste for seasoning and turn into a heated serving dish. Sprinkle with plenty of Parmesan and brown quickly under a grill. I stress that the cauliflower must be still nutty, not soft.

To end this chapter on Great Britain here is a nourishing sweet.

MACAROONS

8 oz. dark brown sugar (raw if possible)	2 egg whites
4 oz. ground almonds	1 level tblsp. ground rice
1 oz. confectioner's sugar	⅛ tsp. vanilla extract
a few blanched almonds	rice paper as required

Line 2 baking sheets with rice paper. Mix together brown sugar, confectioner's sugar and ground rice. Add egg whites and vanilla. Beat the mixture vigorously using a wooden spoon, then leave to stand for 10 minutes. Beat again and then spoon the mixture out on to the rice paper in small heaps. Flatten each one with a palette knife which has been dipped in water and stick two almond halves in each one. Bake in a slow oven for 25 to 30 minutes until golden. Leave to cool slightly, then trim the rice paper round each macaroon and leave on a wire tray until quite cold.

Hungary

Much of the cheese eaten in Hungary is made by farmers and cottagers for their own consumption, and is not available commercially. This type of soft cheese is virtually tasteless and is served with various condiments to point up the flavour. Of the many condiments served with the cheese the most popular are butter, paprika, chopped chives, kummel seeds, mustard and of course salt. Of the cheese made for export the most easily obtainable are the following.

Pannonia A hard cheese made from cow's milk, primrose yellow with eyes all over it. It is a cheese with a taste and bouquet all its own.

Bryndza is a ewe's milk cheese with a delicious pungent taste. Eaten with good dark bread it is a very satisfying cheese.

Hungary, like many other countries, has its imitations of the well-known cheeses of Switzerland, Italy, Denmark and France. Among these, and most popular with Hungarians are Emmentaler, Parmesan and Hungary's version of Danish Blue.

BRANDIED CHEESE

Take ½ pound of blue cheese and crumble it into a bowl. Soften 4 ounces of butter and cream it with the cheese and 4 tablespoonfuls of brandy. Keep it in a jar covered with melted butter in a cool place. Serve on plain or salted crackers.

CHEESE AND POTATO SOUP

1½ cups mashed potatoes	1 oz. flour
1 cup grated sharp cheese	1 tblsp. butter
½ pint milk	salt and black pepper

Make a roux with the butter and the flour and very gradually add the heated milk, stirring well until smooth. Simmer very gently until it thickens, then add the potatoes and the salt and pepper. Mix well, bring to boiling point and add the cheese, stirring until melted. This is a very good way to use up left-over mashed potatoes.

CHEESE AND EGG SOUP

This is one of our favourites and goes particularly well with large chunks of sour black bread.

¼ lb. grated sharp cheese	3 tblsp. butter
¾ pint boiling water	3 tblsp. flour
2 egg yolks	paprika (optional)
salt and black pepper	

Fry the flour in the butter until golden, gradually add the boiling water and seasoning, stirring until smooth and well blended. Simmer very gently for 25 minutes, then add the cheese, stir, and remove from the heat. Just before serving add the beaten egg yolks, but be careful not to let the soup boil again or you will spoil it. Taste for salt again before serving. Sprinkle with paprika if liked.

HUNGARIAN LEEK SOUP

6 large leeks	2 oz. butter
1½ lb. potatoes	1 oz. cornstarch
3½ to 4 pints vegetable water	2 tblsp. chopped parsley
salt and black pepper	

Prepare the vegetables in the usual way and dice them. Brown them in the butter, then add the vegetable water and simmer very gently until tender. Rub through a sieve, return to saucepan and heat again gently as you mix the cornstarch with a little water. Add this to the soup and stir all the time until boiling. Add salt and grated black pepper and simmer for a few more minutes before serving. Sprinkle with chopped parsley and serve with croutons.

BUDAPEST ONION SOUP

3 large Spanish onions	3½ pints vegetable water
½ lb. tomatoes	1¼ tsp. paprika
¼ lb. fine vermicelli	2 oz. butter
salt and black pepper	

Peel and slice the onions and brown in the butter. Add paprika, sliced tomatoes and gradually add the vegetable water. Bring to boiling point, turn down the heat and cook for 25 minutes. Rub through a sieve, boil once again and add the cooked and drained vermicelli. Season well with grated black pepper and salt.

THREE COURSE SOUP

This soup got its name simply because after a good plateful of it you need nothing else. It is particularly welcome during the winter.

1 pint vegetable (or plain) water	1½ tblsp. butter
½ pint sour cream	1½ tblsp. rice
1 large onion	1 heaped tblsp. flour
1 carrot	chopped chives for garnish
salt and black pepper	

Wash the rice well and then cook in the vegetable water or plain water with a little salt until tender. Make a roux with the butter and the flour, gradually pour on the rice and its liquid, then add the finely chopped onion and carrot. Simmer for 10 minutes over a low heat, stirring frequently, then taste for seasoning. Add plenty of grated black pepper, then take the pan off the heat and stir in the sour cream. Garnish with chopped chives and serve with toasted dark bread.

Variation:

This soup is even more filling if served sprinkled with grated Parmesan as well as the chives.

HUNGARIAN RED CABBAGE

Each country has its own way of serving cabbage, and the Hungarian way is one of the best I know.

1 medium-sized red cabbage	2 tblsp. butter
1 lb. roasted chestnuts	1 tblsp. sour cream
2 oz. currants and sultanas mixed	1 tsp. brown sugar
¼ cup tarragon vinegar	½ pint water
salt and black pepper	

Cut cabbage in half and take out the white stalk. Discard any withered outer leaves. Shred coarsely, then sauté it in the butter until it is well coated. Add the heated water, vinegar and the sugar and simmer until just tender. The cabbage should always have a bite to it and should never be sloppy or limp. Chop the chestnuts coarsely and add them, with the dried fruit, to the cabbage. Bring to boiling point, then remove from the heat and stir in the sour cream until well blended. Season with salt and pepper and serve.

If you prefer red cabbage to be more sour than sweet and sour, add more vinegar but never omit the teaspoonful of brown sugar.

STUFFED TOMATOES (1)

2 hard-boiled eggs	6 oz. nutmeat or chopped nuts
1 doz. large tomatoes	breadcrumbs
1 medium-sized onion, minced	butter
1 teacup sour cream	boiled rice
salt and black pepper	

Cut a lid off the top of each tomato and scoop out the pulp being careful not to damage the shells. Chop the eggs and mix with the tomato pulp, nutmeat or chopped nuts and cream and season to taste. Stuff the tomatoes with this mixture, scatter breadcrumbs over them and dot with butter. Bake in a medium oven for 20 minutes and serve on a bed of plain boiled rice. Allow three tomatoes to each serving.

STUFFED TOMATOES (2)

1 doz. large tomatoes	3 tblsp. chopped parsley
3 large eggs	breadcrumbs
¾ lb. grated sharp cheese	butter
½ pint sour cream	boiled rice
salt and black pepper	

Prepare the tomatoes as above, scooping out the pulp. Mix this with the cheese, beaten eggs, cream, chopped parsley and enough breadcrumbs to make a soft mixture. Season with salt and black pepper. Stuff tomatoes and bake in a greased casserole for 20 minutes. Serve on a bed of plain boiled rice.

HUNGARIAN SOUFFLÉ

I have to thank my dear friend and Yoga pupil, Magda Eitlel, the Hungarian violinist, for this very unusual recipe.

½ lb. Spanish onions, minced	4 eggs, separated
1 teacup butter	3½ tblsp. flour
1 cup vegetable water	a little paprika
parsley sprigs	salt and black pepper

Sauté the onions in the butter until pale gold. Add the flour and cook for 1 minute, blending well with a wooden spoon. Gradually add the heated vegetable water and cook slowly stirring all the time until smooth. Season with salt and black pepper. Beat the egg yolks and add to the onion mixture. Beat the egg whites until stiff and fold into the mixture. Pour into a straight-sided soufflé tin, then place in a shallow pan of water and bake in a moderate oven for 40 minutes. Test for perfection by inserting a thin knife in the centre of the soufflé. If it comes out clean the soufflé should be served at once. Sprinkle with paprika and garnish with sprigs of parsley.

The following comes under the heading of Memorable Desserts. I tasted it the first time I ever had a meal in a Hungarian restaurant and I have never forgotten it.

CREAMED CHESTNUTS

1 lb. boiled and peeled chestnuts	2 tblsp. rum
2 oz. brown sugar	2 cups thick cream
1 oz. gelatine crystals	1 pint milk
5 egg yolks	

Start by making egg custard. Beat the egg yolks into the milk and cook in the top of a double boiler until thick. Do not let the water boil on any account. Finely chop the chestnuts and mix them, with the sugar, into the egg custard. Dissolve the gelatine crystals in a very little warm water and add it, with the cream and the rum, to the mixture. Put it into individual glass dishes and chill well before serving.

LIPTAUER CHEESE SPREAD

½ lb. cottage cheese	2 tblsp. chopped nuts
¼ lb. softened butter	2 tsp. capers
1 tblsp. chopped dates	1 tsp. French mustard
1 tblsp. chopped olives	lots of paprika
salt and black pepper	

Mash all ingredients well together and make sure it is well seasoned. Serve with pumpernickel.

Variations:

1. Omit capers and substitute finely chopped pickled gherkins.
2. Omit French mustard and substitute sweet pickle.
3. Omit dates and substitute sultanas.
4. Omit chopped nuts and substitute caraway and dill seeds.
5. Omit French mustard and substitute sour cream.
6. Omit sour cream and substitute mayonnaise.
7. Omit cottage cheese and substitute curd cheese.
8. Omit chopped nuts and substitute ground almonds.
9. Add a dash of cognac.

CHESTNUTS WITH RICE

1 lb. boiled chestnuts	½ teacup vegetable water
¼ lb. mushrooms	½ teacup white wine
1 medium-sized onion	1 tsp. flour
boiled rice	butter as required
salt and black pepper	

Sauté the peeled and finely sliced onion and mushrooms in the butter until brown. Add the flour and blend, then gradually add the heated vegetable water, stirring until smooth. Add the peeled and chopped chestnuts and mix well. Then flavour with salt and black pepper. Lastly add the white wine, heat to boiling point and serve on plain boiled rice.

CARROTS IN SOUR CREAM

Many people do not care for cooked carrots, partly because of their soft texture but mostly because of their sweetness which is enhanced by cooking. This Hungarian method of preparing carrots is most impressive and those who dislike cooked carrots may like to try them done this way.

6 large carrots	2 tblsp. finely shredded celery
1 cup sour cream	¾ tsp. dried thyme
butter as required	salt and black pepper

Wash the carrots and scrape off the outer skin. Put them through a coarse Julienne or if you do not have one, shred them coarsely. Melt plenty of butter until it is really hot but do not brown it. Sauté the carrots in this for 3 minutes, then add the celery and the thyme. Heat to boiling point again, then season with salt and black pepper. Lastly add the cream, stirring well, away from the heat. Reheat to just below boiling point and serve. The carrots have a delicious nuttiness and the sauce is excellent.

CABBAGE WITH NUTS

3 lb. white cabbage	1 tblsp. lemon juice
¼ lb. chopped nuts	1 tblsp. sugar
2 oz. butter	salt and black pepper

Cut the cabbage in quarters and take out the hard stem. Discard any coarse outer leaves and then shred it finely. Heat the butter in a heavy-bottomed saucepan and sauté the cabbage in this until it begins to colour slightly. Add the lemon juice, sugar, and seasoning and mix well. When very hot again put on the lid and turn down the heat to very low. The cabbage will then cook in its own steam. Leave it for 20 minutes, then check to make sure that there is a little liquid in the bottom of the pan. If there is not, then add another tablespoonful of butter. Cook in all for 40 minutes, then stir in the chopped nuts and serve. If you like a more pronounced sweet and sour taste, use additional lemon juice and sugar. This is very much a matter of individual taste.

FRIED CAULIFLOWER

1 large cauliflower	salted butter as required
2 eggs	milk as required
4 tblsp. flour	deep oil for frying
salt and black pepper	

First make your batter by mixing the flour with a little milk until well blended. Beat in the eggs and then add enough milk to make a thick batter. flavour with salt and a little black pepper. Leave aside for 1 hour before using. Now cut off all the thick outer stems of the cauliflower and cut it up into fairly small sprigs about the size of a dessertspoon. Now heat plenty of salted butter in a saucepan and when really hot but not brown, toss in the cauliflower sprigs and mix until well coated. Turn down the heat, put on the lid and leave for about 15 minutes. The cauliflower should still be nicely crisp and crunchy. Drain the cauliflower and then dip each sprig into the thick batter and fry in smoking hot, deep oil until golden.

STUFFED AUBERGINES

8 medium-sized aubergines	½ lb. chopped nuts
1 medium-sized onion	¼ lb. fresh breadcrumbs
3 dessertsp. oil	butter as required
2 cloves garlic	salt and black pepper

Wash the aubergines and dry them. Cut them in half lengthways and scoop out the pulp. Chop this well. Chop the onion and the garlic and brown them in the hot oil. Add the nuts and the aubergine pulp and season with salt and grated black pepper. Cook over a low heat with the lid on for 5 minutes. Add enough breadcrumbs to make a suitable mixture for stuffing, then pack this into the hollowed-out aubergines, sprinkle with breadcrumbs, dot with plenty of butter and bake in a greased casserole in a moderate oven for 20 to 25 minutes.

HUNGARIAN BROWN BAKE

1 lb. potatoes	1 large egg
¼ lb. grated cheese	1 clove garlic
½ pint milk	breadcrumbs
butter as required	grated nutmeg
salt and black pepper	

Wash the potatoes and peel them as thinly as you can, then slice them very thinly and put them into cold water. Butter a small casserole, including the lid, and rub it well with a crushed clove of garlic, which you should hold in a pair of kitchen tweezers to prevent the smell adhering to your fingers. Now drain the potato slices and dry them well on a cloth. Lay them in the bottom of the casserole and season with salt, pepper and a sprinkle of grated nutmeg. Beat the egg well, add the milk and some of the cheese and pour over the potatoes. Add another thick layer of cheese, then sprinkle lightly with breadcrumbs, dot with plenty of butter and bake in a moderate oven until darkly golden on top. Serve in the baking dish.

MUSHROOMS, SPINACH AND RICE

2 lb. spinach	3 tblsp. sour cream
1¼ lb. button mushrooms	butter as required
¼ cup vegetable water	boiled rice
salt and black pepper	

Wash the spinach and remove coarse stalks. Shake in a colander and then put it into a saucepan with a well fitting lid just on its own, without water. Cook over a gentle heat until tender. While the spinach is cooking, sauté all the button mushrooms in plenty of butter for 10 minutes. Drain the spinach well, pressing out as much moisture as you can, chop it and season with salt and pepper. Add it to the cooked mushrooms and cook for a further 5 minutes. Then add the heated vegetable water and taste for seasoning. Heat all well together, stir in the cream, and serve on plain boiled rice.

TOMATO CASSEROLE

This dish is very simple and is an ideal one for making quickly when you are short of time. Heat the oven first, a moderate rather than a hot one. Now gather together all the tomatoes you can find in the house and 2 onions and any sort of cheese so long as you have about a ¼ pound. Put 2 or 3 ounces of butter or margarine in a casserole and fry the very thinly sliced onions in it until golden, add a thick layer of sliced tomatoes and season with a little salt and plenty of paprika and black pepper. Top with the grated cheese and put it into the oven for 30 minutes.

MARROW ALLUMETTES

This is yet another way of using up marrow.

1 lb. marrow	flour
oil for frying	salt and black pepper

Peel marrow and scoop out the seeds. Cut into large matchsticks or chips and plunge them into boiling salted water. Leave for 1 minute over a strong heat, then drain and rinse with cold water. Dry on a towel in the oven for a few minutes. Meanwhile heat the oil, remembering that it shouldn't be *too* hot. Toss the marrow allumettes, a few at a time, in well seasoned flour and fry them until golden brown. Keep hot while you coat the next batch with seasoned flour and fry. Be careful not to have too many in the pan at once. Serve on heated plates immediately.

EGG FRITTERS FROM BUDAPEST

6 hard-boiled large eggs	breadcrumbs
1 raw egg	oil for frying
chopped chives for garnish	toast as required
salt and black pepper	

Cut the eggs into halves lengthways, brush with the raw egg beaten with salt and pepper, and roll in breadcrumbs. Fry in very deep hot oil until golden. Serve on hot buttered toast. Garnish with chopped chives.

India

Although cheese is not part of the staple diet of Indians, Europeans living in India and Indians who have adopted western dietary habits do consume a considerable amount. Both for religious and climatic reasons India does not produce cheeses of any great quality and some are even unpalatable to cheese devotees in other countries. Here are one or two Indian cheeses which are obtainable in other countries.

Dacca is a dry, smoked cheese which is very much an acquired taste.

Surti cheese is a type of cottage cheese with an acid taste. It should be eaten when young because it does not improve with keeping.

Bandal is a soft cream cheese which is smoked. Made entirely from cream it has a softer texture than Surti though the method of making is similar.

INDIAN SANDWICH FILLING

2 cups grated cheese	2 tsp. curry powder
1 cup butter or margarine	mustard (made)
dark rye bread	

Toast the rye bread and butter it hot. Mix together the cheese, curry powder and the rest of the butter until well blended. Spread a thin layer of mustard over each slice of buttered toast, spread thickly with the cheese mixture and brown under the grill.

EGGS DURKHA

6 hard-boiled eggs	1 pint milk
6 tsp. cornflour	1 lb. mashed potatoes
chopped parsley or chives	2 oz. butter
salt and black pepper	

Melt the butter and blend in the cornflour until smooth. Gradually add the hot milk stirring with a wooden spoon. Cook for 3 minutes over a gentle heat. Remove from heat and season with salt and pepper. Add the chopped hard-boiled eggs and stir. Pour the mixture into a well greased small casserole and pile seasoned mashed potatoes round the edge. Brown gently under the grill and serve garnished with parsley or chopped chives.

HIGH PROTEIN SANDWICH

I am grateful to an Indian friend, Shaila, for this recipe.

Cut a very dark rye loaf into thick slices and butter them liberally. Sprinkle with plenty of wheatgerm, pressing it well into the butter, then add a layer of lemon marmalade (the sort with thick peel). Take a very ripe banana and cut it into thin slices along its length. Add this to the sandwich, sprinkle with desiccated coconut and press the sandwich together.

INDIAN CHEESE SANDWICH

Cut a rye loaf into thin slices and butter thickly. Add slices of sharp cheese, hard sweet tomatoes, and a pineapple ring. Sprinkle with caraway seeds and curry powder.

BOMBAY PIE

For this recipe use some of the crispy topping which is described in the chapter from the Netherlands. (*See* p. 129-30)

½ lb. cooked tomatoes with sweet basil leaves	1 tblsp. tomato juice
6 oz. cheese	2 tsp. curry powder
1 oz. butter	1 tsp. home-made mustard
1 oz. oatmeal	a touch of ginger
crispy topping as required	radishes to garnish
salt and black pepper	

Melt the butter, blend in the oatmeal, tomatoes, cheese and seasonings. Cook slowly, stirring all the time with a wooden spoon until the cheese has melted. Pour into a greased casserole, sprinkle with crispy topping and bake in a hot oven until golden brown. Serve at once garnished with radishes.

CURRY AND RICE

4 tsp. curry powder	1 medium-sized onion
2 cloves garlic, minced	1 bay leaf
2 pinches cayenne	plain boiled rice
2 oz. preserved ginger, sliced	

Stew together the garlic, curry powder, cayenne, ginger, the minced onion and the bay leaf. If the onion is a juicy one you won't need any liquid. If you do then use hot water. When the sauce is cooked and well blended pour it over plain boiled long grain (Patna) rice.

VEGETABLE CURRY

3 large strong onions, finely chopped	3 oz. butter
¾ lb. cooked potatoes, diced	2 cloves garlic
¾ lb. ripe tomatoes, sliced	1 heaped tblsp. preserved ginger
½ lb. green beans, sliced	1 heaped tblsp. curry powder
a touch of chilli powder	salt and black pepper

Peel and dice the onions and brown them in the hot fat, then add the garlic and curry powder and fry gently for a further 3 minutes. Add the tomatoes and if necessary some hot water. There should be a thick gravy. Add the beans and simmer for 8 minutes, then add the chopped ginger, the chilli powder, and the bay leaf. Lastly add the potatoes and make sure they are well heated (about 5 or 6 minutes). Season with salt and pepper and serve with plain boiled long grain rice.

ANOTHER VEGETABLE CURRY

This curry is as different from the above as two recipes with the same name can be. It is high in protein because it contains soya beans.

1 lb. carrots	1 oz. flour
½ lb. haricot beans	2 tblsp. butter
¼ lb. soya beans	3 tsp. hot curry powder
1 oz. sultanas	3 tsp. mango chutney
1 oz. currants	1 tsp. raw sugar
1 medium-sized onion, chopped	

Soak the haricot and soya beans overnight before cooking. Then cover them with cold water, bring to the boil and simmer until tender, at least 2 hours. During the last 30 minutes add the scraped and diced carrots. When the carrots are cooked make sure that there is exactly ¾ pint of liquid in the pan. While the beans are cooking prepare the rest of the curry. Peel and chop the onion and fry until brown in the butter. Add the flour, curry powder and cook for 1 minute. Stir in the liquid which is in the pan (¾ pint). Bring to the boil and add chutney, sultanas, beans and carrots and season with salt if necessary. Simmer for 5 more minutes and serve on plain boiled rice.

CURRY SOUP

You can curry almost anything, but you may possibly never have tried curry soup. It is exotic and very filling so make sure the course to follow is a light one.

½ lb. lentils, washed	2 tblsp. butter
2 pints vegetable water	1 tblsp. flour
2 large onions	2 tsp. curry powder
1 kohl-rabi or turnip	2 tsp. chutney
salt and black pepper	

Fry the peeled and sliced onions and kohl-rabi (diced) in the butter until brown. Add the lentils and the vegetable water. Simmer over a very low heat for 1¼ hours, then rub through a sieve. Return to saucepan, add the flour mixed with a little cold water, the curry and the other seasonings, simmer for 2 minutes longer and serve with plain crackers.

CURRIED MARROW SOUP

1 small marrow (about 2 lb.)	1 oz. flour
2 large strong onions	2 oz. butter
½ lb. tomatoes, fried	1½ tsp. curry powder
2 pints vegetable water	a touch of ground ginger
salt and black pepper	

Peel the marrow and the onions, dice and fry until brown in the butter. Add the vegetable water and cook for 20 minutes. Rub through a sieve, return to saucepan, add the fried tomatoes and bring to the boil. Mix the flour with a little water, add the curry powder and stir into the pan. Season with salt and black pepper, simmer for another 6 minutes and serve.

PUNJAB TOMATOES

6 very large tomatoes (not over-ripe)	mango chutney as required
2 large sweet onions	curry powder as required
oil for frying	hot fried bread as required
salt and black pepper	

Peel and slice the onions and brown in the oil. Place them in a greased casserole, add a layer of thickly sliced tomatoes, and sprinkle with salt, black pepper and curry powder. Bake in a moderate oven for 10 minutes. Meanwhile have the fried bread ready, spread with mango chutney and pile the tomatoes and onions on the bread. Two slices for each serving.

CURRIED CHESTNUTS

This is a sweet curry and very filling.

1¼ lb. chestnuts, roasted and peeled	2 tblsp. butter
1½ oz. sultanas and currants mixed	2 tblsp. vinegar
1 carrot	2 tblsp. mango chutney
1 medium-sized Spanish onion	1 tblsp. curry powder
2 large cups vegetable water	1 tblsp. flour
plain boiled rice	

Peel and chop the onion and carrot and brown in the butter. Stir the flour into the pan together with the curry powder and cook for 2 minutes. Very gradually add the vegetable water stirring all the time with a wooden spoon. Heat to boiling, reduce heat and add the fruit, vinegar, chutney and the chestnuts. Simmer for 25 minutes and serve on a bed of plain boiled rice.

STUFFED SWEET PEPPERS

sweet peppers as required	1½ tblsp. flour
1 small onion	1 tblsp. apple purée
½ teacup vegetable water	2 tsp. curry powder
½ oz. butter	1 tsp. chutney
oil for baking	½ tsp. lime juice
boiled rice	salt

Peel and chop onion and brown in the butter. Add the apple purée, the flour and curry powder and cook for 2 minutes. Gradually add the heated vegetable water, heat to boiling point, then add the chutney, lime juice (vinegar can be used instead of lime juice, but is not recommended), salt if necessary. Put a lid on the pan and simmer for 25 minutes. While the sauce is cooking prepare the peppers by taking out the seeds and the pips, place them in boiling water for 3 minutes then drain well. When the sauce is ready add enough cooked rice to make a fairly stiff mixture, stuff the peppers with this, put a knob of butter on each one and bake in a dish containing a little oil for 45 minutes.

CURRY OMELETTE

6 eggs (2 each serving)	a little milk
1 hard-boiled egg	boiled rice
1 teacup curry sauce (see recipe above)	oil for frying

Beat the 6 eggs together with a little milk, approximately ½ a teacupful. Add a touch of salt. Make the curry sauce and when ready mix with enough plain boiled rice to make a mixture suitable for filling the omelettes, that is not too stiff but not runny either. Make the omelettes in the usual way, 6 eggs will make 3, and fill with the hot mixture. Serve on heated plates, garnish with slices of hard-boiled eggs sprinkled with a little curry powder.

INDIAN CROQUETTES

6 hard-boiled eggs	5 tblsp. cooked rice
2 raw eggs	4 or 5 tblsp. fresh breadcrumbs
¼ lb. grated sharp cheese	1 tsp. (or more) curry powder
salt and pepper	toasted crumbs for coating

Chop the hard-boiled eggs and mix well with the cooked rice, the 4 or 5 tablespoonfuls of breadcrumbs, curry and cheese. Add the beaten raw egg yolks and season with black pepper and a little salt if necessary. Some Indians don't use salt at all in curries, but it is a matter of taste. Westerners as a rule prefer a little. In this recipe remember that most cheese is salty to some extent so do taste the mixture to make sure. Form the mixture into flat rounds or triangles and brush with the beaten egg whites. Coat well with toasted breadcrumbs and fry in deep fat until golden.

EGG CURRY

Take the following quantities per serving.

½ cup curry sauce (described above)   2 hard-boiled eggs
2 slices toasted bread, buttered

Have the toast really hot, also the eggs. Slice them lengthways and pour the sauce over the eggs. Garnish with chopped watercress.

Variation 1
Instead of the toast you may use fried bread.
Variation 2
Instead of bread serve the eggs on plain boiled rice and pour the sauce over. Serve garnished with watercress.

DEVILLED ALMONDS

1 lb. blanched almonds	½ cup salad oil
a touch of chilli powder	1 tsp. curry powder
salt as required	

Put the oil in a shallow baking tin and add the nuts, seeing that each one is well coated. Bake at moderate heat until biscuit-coloured. Stir them often for an even colour and when they are ready, sprinkle them with salt, curry powder and a touch of chilli. Leave to cool and dry. Store in airtight jars.

MADRAS CUTLETS

6 hard-boiled eggs	½ cup breadcrumbs
2 raw eggs	½ cup grated sharp cheese
1 tsp. curry powder	½ cup cooked rice
salt and black pepper	

Chop the eggs and mix with the rice, cheese and curry powder. Add 1 well beaten egg and season with salt and pepper. Add sufficient breadcrumbs to make a firm mixture. Shape into balls, then flatten with the palm of the hand. Dip in the other beaten egg, and then in breadcrumbs and fry in oil until golden on both sides.

BAKED CURRY

1 large apple	½ lb. chopped nuts
1 large carrot, sliced	½ lb. ripe tomatoes
2 large onions	¼ pint vegetable water
oil as required	1 tblsp. curry powder
boiled rice	2 tblsp. chutney
turmeric	salt and black pepper

Peel and thinly slice the onions and the carrot and sauté in hot oil until tender. Put this mixture into an oiled oven dish and sprinkle with the chopped nuts. Season with the curry powder, salt and pepper. Add the chutney, then a layer of sliced tomatoes, then the peeled and chopped apple. Add the vegetable water and then another layer of tomatoes. Sprinkle again with curry powder, salt and pepper. Bake in a slow oven for at least 3 hours (300° approximately). Serve with rice boiled in water to which you have added 1 teaspoonful of turmeric to every 3 ounces raw rice. Serve with additional chutney.

Italy

With the exception of France, Italy has a greater variety of cheeses than any other country in the world. Obviously I cannot mention them all here, so I will be content to describe only the best known and most easily obtainable, together with one or two of my own personal favourites of which you may not have heard.

Parmesan Other cheeses may be more delectable, yet others may have a more interesting texture and bouquet, nevertheless Parmesan is one of the truly great cheeses and is a perfect grating cheese. Haute cuisine cooks claim that it is indispensable, especially in the preparation of certain Italian dishes which I shall presently describe.

Bel Paese This was made for the first time about 1920. A delicious, creamy-sweet, mild and soft cheese it has rapidly gained in popularity both in Italy and abroad.

Bitto is a firm, holey cheese which is made from either ewe's, cow's or goat's milk. It can be used either as a table cheese or when fully cured it makes an excellent grater.

Caciocavallo This too is a good table cheese when young and a good grater when fully matured. It is a dark straw colour, rather mild but at the same time spicy and piquant. Quite a distinctive taste which is difficult to describe. Should please the connoisseur.

Fontina This is one of the most popular cheeses in Italy. Made of whole milk it is medium textured, mild and nutty in flavour, and pale yellow in colour. It is much prized as a cooking cheese, as well as a table cheese, because it melts easily and is easy to work with when making, for instance, a dish of polenta which I shall presently describe.

Gorgonzola This cheese is either liked or violently disliked. Good Gorgonzola should be ripe and moist and strong smelling, veined throughout with mould, and on no account should there be dry patches. If there are, then do not buy it. Once having tasted good Gorgonzola, you will never again be satisfied with less than the best.

Mascarpone is a cross between cheese and cream, marvellous clotted cream for which the people of Devonshire are so renowned. Italian Mascarpone is made from fresh cream from cow's milk, is butter coloured and very buttery in taste. A little later I will give you an incomparable recipe for using this clotted cream-cum-cheese as a sweet.

Pepato is a rather unusual Sicilian cheese which is spiced with pepper. Unique in taste, you will have to go to Italy or Sicily to find it for it is rarely seen elsewhere.

Ricotta Romana I said at the beginning of this book that there would be only a few desserts due to the fact that most of them can be obtained from ordinary cookery books. However, on page 104 you will find a recipe which you may not have heard of before, in which Ricotta Romana can be used to very good effect.

Taleggio is a cow's milk cheese which is distinguished by its rose coloured, rough textured crust. Inside it is a buttery yellow, smooth and full flavoured and with a delicate bouquet.

MASCARPONE WHIP

To a ¼ pound of Mascarpone add 1 tablespoonful of natural raw cane sugar or if you cannot obtain this use Barbados sugar, and 2 tablespoonfuls of brandy. Whip up with a fork, or better still in an electric blender, and serve in individual dishes. A good substitute for Mascarpone would be double cream cheese or Devonshire clotted cream.

Mascarpone is also delightful when whipped up with a small quantity of Creme de Menthe or Green Chartreuse and finely ground, but uncooked coffee. Those of you who use instant coffee can use a small quantity of this.

MUSHROOMS MARINARA

Marinara in Italian means in the manner of sailors, or more appropriately in this case, sailors' wives and mothers.

¾ lb. mushrooms	1 tblsp. olive oil
½ lb. ripe tomatoes	½ tsp. brown sugar
1 small sweet onion	¼ tsp. thyme
1 small clove garlic	plain boiled spaghetti
salt and paprika	

Heat the oil in a pan and fry the onions and garlic very slowly until slightly golden. Add tomatoes, thickly sliced, the salt and paprika and the thyme. Add the thinly sliced mushrooms and cook slowly with the lid on the pan for 15 minutes. Serve with plain boiled spaghetti.

STRACCIATELLA

This is a soup, and the name means ragged, because of what happens to the eggs and cheese and breadcrumbs at the end. It is one of Italy's most popular soups and can be made in exactly 12 minutes.

3 small eggs, beaten	¼ lb. grated Parmesan
2 pints vegetable water	paprika to garnish
1 cup breadcrumbs	salt and black pepper

Mix together the beaten eggs, the breadcrumbs, and the cheese. Boil the vegetable water and gently stir in the egg and cheese mixture. Season with black pepper and a little salt, remembering that there is salt in the cheese. Simmer with the lid on the pan for 8 minutes, stirring frequently with a wooden spoon. Now you will see why the soup is called ragged. Serve very hot, garnished with paprika. Pass around dark rye bread separately.

RICOTTA ROMANA DESSERT

Whip up ½ a pound Ricotta Romana with 3 or 4 egg yolks and 2 tablespoonfuls of melted butter. Add confectioner's sugar to sweeten to taste and stir in 2 tablespoonfuls of cognac. Serve with wafers.

MINESTRONE

A chapter on Italian cooking isn't complete without at least one recipe for this soup. There are as many different kinds of minestrone as there are cooks to make it, and I have never made it exactly the same way twice. So in giving you the following recipe I hope you will regard it as a sort of general guide to quantities, the ingredients being as flexible as you choose, provided that three ingredients are never, on any account, left out—these being tomato pulp or purée, onions and macaroni.

4 sticks celery	2 oz. cooked macaroni
3 leeks	2 pints vegetable water
2 carrots	2 tblsp. chopped parsley
1 large onion	Parmesan
½ lb. tomatoes, skinned	rye toast
½ lb. cooked peas	salt and black pepper

Chop the vegetables and put them into the boiling vegetable water, with the exception of the peas. Simmer with the lid on for 30 to 40 minutes, add the peas and season with salt and black pepper. Stir in the chopped parsley and bring to boiling point. Add the cooked macaroni, simmer for 2 minutes, then put a slice of toasted rye bread in the bottom of each plate, pour over the soup and sprinkle liberally with Parmesan.

You can vary your vegetables and use whatever you happen to have in the house—turnips, spinach, cabbage, marrow, broad beans and of course, you can use tinned tomato purée instead of fresh skinned tomatoes if you wish.

CHEESE AND AUBERGINES

2 large aubergines	1 teacup milk
2 eggs	sweet basil leaves
½ lb. peeled tomatoes	butter as required
¼ lb. grated Parmesan	breadcrumbs
salt and black pepper	

Wash, peel and slice the aubergines, sprinkle with salt and leave it for at least 1 hour, then drain well. Mix together the milk, the beaten eggs, and flavour with salt and black pepper. Dip each aubergine slice into the egg mixture, then into breadcrumbs and fry in plenty of butter until golden brown. Butter a casserole and lay in the browned aubergine slices. Add a layer of cheese and the tomatoes and then cheese again. Top with breadcrumbs, dot with plenty of butter and bake until golden on top.

In the Dictionary of Vegetables I mention Calabrese as being Italian sprouting broccoli. This delicious vegetable is good to eat, cold as well as hot, and makes a welcome addition to any meal. The following is a typical Italian method of preparing it.

CALABRESE WITH PARMESAN

4 hard-boiled eggs	½ pint white sauce
2 heads of calabrese	¼ lb. grated Parmesan
butter as required	paprika

Cook the calabrese in butter until tender. Lay the heads in a buttered casserole and arrange a layer of sliced hard-boiled eggs on top. Mix the cheese into the white sauce, pour over the eggs and brown in a moderate oven. This dish can be served with plain boiled rice sprinkled with paprika.

CALABRESE SALAD

1 cup calabrese tips or shoots	mayonnaise
1 head of lettuce	chives
2 hard-boiled eggs	paprika
½ lb. cold boiled potatoes	salt

The potatoes should be of the waxy variety so that they will easily dice. Mix the diced potatoes with the calabrese tips and the chopped chives. Toss in mayonnaise and sprinkle with the chopped eggs. Garnish with paprika and add a shake of salt. Arrange in the centre of a plate of crisp lettuce leaves.

ITALIAN CHEESE SOUFFLÉ

3 large eggs	1 teacup spinach purée
¼ lb. grated Parmesan	5 dessertsp. flour
1 large cup milk (or milk and cream mixed)	3½ tblsp. butter
salt and black pepper	

Melt the butter over a very low heat, blend in the flour and then very gradually the heated milk or milk and cream. Stir with a wooden spoon all the time until well blended. Season with salt and black pepper. Cook very gently until it begins to thicken and then add the spinach purée and the Parmesan. Cook for a few minutes longer and then remove the pan from the heat and allow the mixture to cool. Separate the eggs and add the beaten yolks to the mixture. Beat the egg white until just stiff and fold into the mixture. Butter a straight-sided soufflé tin and pour in the mixture. Bake in a slow oven for 1 hour and serve immediately. If you like you can garnish it with paprika.

ROMAN EGGS

4 large eggs	2 dessertspoon butter
½ lb. cooked spaghetti	1 tblsp. flour
1 teacup tomato sauce	water as required
1 teacup grated Parmesan	salt and black pepper

Make a roux of the butter and flour, cook for 1 minute and gradually stir in the warmed tomato sauce and enough water, about 4 tablespoonfuls, to make a thick and smooth mixture. Add the cheese and season with black pepper and a little salt. Butter a casserole, put in the spaghetti and pour the sauce over it. In this dish I like to add a teaspoonful of raw sugar but this is purely a matter of taste. Break the eggs carefully and lay them, well apart, in the sauce, sprinkle with salt and pepper and if you have any cheese left over sprinkle that over the eggs and heat through in a moderate oven, about 15 to 20 minutes. Eggs should not be overcooked.

SPAGHETTI BOLOGNESE

8 oz. cooked spaghetti	1 teacup tomato purée
4 oz. mushrooms	1 teacup chopped nuts
1 large sweet onion	½ teacup white wine
½ tsp. vegetable extract	oil for cooking
½ tsp. honey	sweet basil leaves
1 clove garlic (optional)	salt and black pepper

Finely chop the onion and the mushrooms and fry them in the oil until golden. Add the tomato purée, the wine, the vegetable extract diluted in a little hot water, the basil leaves (about ½ a teaspoonful) and the honey and cook for 2 minutes until well blended. Season with crushed clove of garlic, salt and black pepper, and cook for a further 3 minutes. Have ready the hot and buttered spaghetti and pour the sauce over. Sprinkle with chopped nuts and serve hot.

VENETIAN RISOTTO

1½ pints vegetable water	1 tblsp. Parmesan, grated
1½ lb. peas	1 tblsp. olive oil
½ lb. rice	1 tblsp. chopped parsley
chopped chives	1 dessertsp. butter
	salt and black pepper

Heat the oil and butter and brown the chives and the parsley gently. Add peas and cook until all the fat is absorbed, then add heated vegetable water to cover, bring to the boil, and add the rice and the rest of the vegetable water. Cook over a low heat for 30 minutes after which time, test to see if rice is cooked. Stir in another tablespoonful of butter and the grated Parmesan and serve hot after seasoning with salt and freshly grated black pepper.

GENOVESE RISOTTO

1 lb. rice	3 pints vegetable stock
¾ lb. grated white cabbage	1 tblsp. tomato paste
½ teacup chopped nuts	salt and black pepper

Cook the cabbage in the hot vegetable water for 6 minutes, add the rice and cook very gently for 20 minutes or until the rice is soft outside and slightly firm on the inside. Rice should *never* be cooked beyond this stage. Dilute the tomato paste in a little hot stock and stir this into the risotto. Lastly add the chopped nuts and season with salt and pepper.

PARMESAN CUSTARD PUDDING

7 small eggs	2 tblsp. flour
6 oz. grated Parmesan	1 breakfast cup milk
boiled rice	1 teacup chopped chives
salt and black pepper	

Separate the eggs. Beat the yolks and mix with flour. Add slightly warmed milk and cook gently until thick. Season, add the cheese and cook until it is melted, then pour into the greased top of a double boiler. Put the lid on and steam gently for 45 minutes but do not let the water in the bottom half of the pan boil. Unmould and serve on a bed of plain boiled noodles, and garnish with chopped chives.

UOVO COL RISO

This egg dish with rice is a delicious way to use up left-over rice. It is also the perfect dish for the housewife in a hurry for it takes very little time to prepare.

6 eggs	¾ lb. cooked rice
3 oz. grated cheese	½ cup chopped chives
2 tblsp. butter	½ cup thick cream
salt and black pepper	

Beat the eggs, add the cream, and cook this mixture in the melted butter until lightly set. Stir all the time with a wooden spoon and do not allow the eggs to get hard. Have the rice hot, and heap it on to a heated serving plate. Just before serving add the grated cheese to the egg mixture and also the chopped chives. Season with grated black pepper and a little salt and pile on to the rice. Serve immediately.

SPAGHETTI ALLA TOSCANA

1 medium cauliflower	1 lb. green peas, cooked
6 oz. cooked spaghetti	1 pint white sauce
1 teacup grated cheese	chopped chives
salt and pepper	

Steam cauliflower in a very little water until tender, and drain well. Put in a serving dish and surround with peas, then the hot spaghetti. Pour over the white sauce, salted and peppered and with the cheese stirred into it, and sprinkle with chopped chives.

NEAPOLITAN NOODLES

1 lb. broad flat noodles, cooked and kept hot	1 cup tomato purée
½ lb. shaved or diced sharp cheese	½ cup grated Parmesan
¼ lb. curd cheese	chopped chives
sweet basil leaves	salt and black pepper

Dilute the tomato purée or paste with a little hot water, stir in 1 teaspoonful of sweet basil leaves and pour this mixture into the bottom of a greased casserole. Add the noodles, then the cheese (diced or shaved), and sprinkle with salt and black pepper. Add the curd cheese, and then the Parmesan, and lastly season with grated black pepper. Bake in a moderate oven for 30 minutes when it will be firm. Serve sprinkled with chopped chives.

MUSHROOM AND TOMATO BAKE

1 lb. mashed potatoes	2 tsp. chopped parsley
½ lb. large tomatoes	2 oz. butter
½ lb. mushrooms	1 small onion
½ cup breadcrumbs	salt and black pepper

Fry the minced onion in the butter until golden, add the sliced tomatoes and the minced mushrooms and cook for a further 10 minutes over a very gentle heat. Add the chopped parsley and season with salt and black pepper. Put the mashed potatoes into a greased baking dish, add the mushrooms and tomato mixture, sprinkle with the breadcrumbs, dot with butter and bake until golden on top.

ROMAN ONIONS

4 large onions	chopped parsley
4 hard-boiled eggs	breadcrumbs
1 cup white sauce	butter as required
1 cup grated sharp cheese	salt and black pepper

Sauté the peeled and thinly sliced onions in butter until golden, mix with the mashed eggs, the white sauce and 1 tablespoonful of chopped parsley. Season with salt and black pepper and place in a greased baking dish. Sprinkle with the grated cheese and then a layer of breadcrumbs, dot with plenty of butter and bake in a moderate oven for 25 minutes.

POLENTA

This is a finely ground yellow cornmeal which is the basis of many popular Italian dishes. It can be obtained very easily in most food stores and sometimes in health-food shops. In cooking, allow at least 2 ounces per serving. The following two recipes are typical Italian dishes incorporating this useful flour.

CHEESE POLENTA

7 oz. finely ground polenta	butter as required
1 cup grated Parmesan	parsley sprigs
1 pint boiling water	additional grated cheese
salt and black pepper	

Add the polenta to the boiling water and cook for 15-20 minutes until thick and smooth. It should be cooked slowly and stirred frequently with a wooden spoon. Spread on to a moistened flat surface to cool. Cut the polenta into slabs and place them in a well buttered casserole. Sprinkle with the Parmesan and season with salt and black pepper. Top with additional grated cheese, then a layer of breadcrumbs. Dot with butter and brown in a hot oven. Serve garnished with sprigs of parsley.

TOMATO POLENTA

This delicious Neapolitan Polenta is the perfect supper dish and is very economical.

1 lb. tomatoes	1 walnut of butter
3 stalks celery	sweet basil leaves
1 medium onion	olive oil as required
salt and pepper	

Cut up the tomatoes and celery and cook in the hot oil until tender. Add 1 teaspoonful of sweet basil leaves and sieve. Season with grated black pepper and salt and add the butter. Keep the sauce hot while you prepare the rest of the dish.

1¼ pints milk and water mixed	2 small eggs
1 cup grated Parmesan	toasted breadcrumbs
½ lb. polenta	olive oil
salt and pepper	

Cook the Polenta in the boiling milk and water for 20 minutes until thick and smooth. Stir in the cheese and the seasonings and blend. Spread on a moistened flat surface to cool, then cut into slices. Dip each slice in beaten egg and breadcrumbs and fry in hot olive oil until a dark golden brown. Serve very hot with the tomato sauce poured over.

MILANESE RICE WITH BEANS

2 lb. string beans	3 egg yolks
½ cup lemon juice	2 cloves garlic
½ cup grated Parmesan	2 tblsp. chopped parsley
¼ lb. butter	salt and black pepper

Prepare the string beans and cook them in butter with the lid on the pan until tender. Season with salt and black pepper and add the parsley and the crushed garlic. Take the pan off the heat and stir in the egg yolks which have been beaten up with a ½ teacupful of water. Add lemon juice and the cheese, taste for seasoning and serve on a bed of white long grain rice.

SICILIAN AUBERGINES

8 aubergines	½ lb. ripe tomatoes
3 eggs	olive oil
2 large onions	plain boiled noodles
salt and black pepper	

Chop the onions finely and brown in olive oil. Add the sliced aubergines and cook for a further 4 minutes. Slice the tomatoes, add to the aubergines and cook until the aubergines are just tender. Beat the eggs and after taking the pan off the heat stir them into the vegetables. Serve on a bed of plain boiled noodles.

ZABAGLIONE

I include this famous Italian dessert because so many people have asked me to and also because it is too good to leave out.

6 egg yolks	6 tblsp. confectioner's sugar	6 tblsp. Marsala or sherry

Beat the egg yolks with the sugar until very pale then add, a little at a time, the Marsala or sherry. Place the mixture in the top half of a double boiler and put hot water in the bottom half. Cook very gently, stirring all the time, until it thickens. Pour it immediately into warm serving dishes and serve hot.

Jewish Cookery

Jewish cooking can truly be described as international in style, for it incorporates the best of Polish, Russian, Spanish, Middle Eastern and Mediterranean cooking. I will include in this section some of the most famous of the typically Jewish dishes served both by the average housewife and first-class chefs.

The first is one of the most commonly served first courses.

CHOPPED EGGS AND ONIONS

12 hard-boiled eggs	2 large sweet Spanish onions
salt and black pepper	½ cup melted butter or margarine
	parsley

Chop the onions and the eggs together until very fine. Season with salt and freshly grated black pepper and mix in the melted butter or margarine. Serve flattened rounds of this mixture garnished with sprigs of parsley.

EGG HORS D'OEUVRES

1 large sweet Spanish onion	4 hard-boiled eggs
¾ cup butter	4 tblsp. tomato sauce
½ cup chopped mixed nuts	salt and black pepper

Finely chop the onion and fry in the butter until golden. Add the eggs, nuts and seasoning, chopping everything very finely. Mix in the tomato sauce and serve piled on to pumpernickel or dark rye bread.

BARLEY SOUP

This well known soup is so filling that if you are going to eat anything after it, I suggest not more than a ½ pint per serving, and even a little less for small appetites.

1 cup pearl barley	3½ pints water
1 small turnip	¾ cup butter
2 large sweet Spanish onions	chopped parsley
4 medium sized carrots	salt and black pepper

Sauté the chopped onions, carrots and turnip in butter, with the lid on the pan, for 15 minutes, stirring occasionally. Add the heated water, bring to boiling point and then add the barley. Cover the pan again and cook over a low heat until barley is tender, about 1½ to 2 hours. At half time add salt and black pepper. At the end of the cooking time check to see that the soup isn't too thick. If it is stir in a little heated milk. Serve garnished with chopped parsley.

CREAM OF TOMATO SOUP

1½ lb. ripe tomatoes	2 tsp. brown sugar
1 large sweet onion	1 tsp. sweet basil leaves
½ pint heated milk	butter as required
1 teacup cooked long grain rice	salt and black pepper

Cook the sliced tomatoes in butter until soft. Put through a sieve, then return to pan and cook with the onion for 5 minutes, adding more butter. Add the sweet basil leaves, the sugar and the salt and pepper, and then stir in the heated milk and the rice. Reheat and serve with dark rye bread.

VEGETABLE SOUP

2 large Spanish onions	3½ pints water
3 carrots	2 cups raw green peas
4 large potatoes, cubed	2 cups French beans
½ lb. tomatoes	1 cup haricot beans, cooked
grated cheese	1 cup soya beans, cooked
celery salt	butter as required
salt and black pepper	

Peel and dice all vegetables and sauté them in butter for 20 minutes. Add the heated water, the green peas and the celery salt and cook until the vegetables are tender. Season with salt and pepper and add the pre-cooked soya and haricot beans. Reboil and serve sprinkled with grated cheese.

COLD BORSHT (1)

This is one of the most delicious soups I know. Though I place it in this chapter on Jewish cooking, it is to be found in any country in Central or Eastern Europe. It makes a spectacular and very easy first course when entertaining guests you wish to impress. The first version is the simplest of all the Borsht recipes. I follow it with a slightly more elaborate one.

1 lb. raw beetroots	2 eggs
1 fresh lemon	2 hard-boiled eggs
fresh cucumber	2 pints water
sour or cultured cream as required	sugar as required
salt and black pepper	

Peel and grate the beetroots and boil in the salted water until tender. Add freshly grated black pepper, then lemon juice and sugar to give a sweet sour taste. This is very much a matter of individual preference. Some like it more sour than sweet, and some like a perfect balance between the two. Taste the soup at this stage to see if there is enough salt, then leave it in the fridge to cool. Beat the eggs in a large bowl, pour on the borsht, return it to the pan and heat very gradually, stirring all the time until slightly thickened. On no account let it reach boiling point. Chill well before serving, top each plate with a spoonful of sour cream, and garnish with slices of egg and cucumber.

COLD BORSHT (2)

2 very large beetroots	1½ pints water
2 large tomatoes	½ bay leaf
2 hard-boiled eggs	fresh lemon juice
2 eggs	yoghourt
2 tblsp. butter	sugar as required
1 tsp. dill	paprika
1 Spanish onion, minced	salt and black pepper

Peel and grate onions and beets and sauté in the butter for 10 minutes. Add lemon juice to your taste and then the sliced tomatoes and seasonings, including the sugar. Cook very slowly for a further 10 minutes, then check your seasonings to make sure you have a distinct sweet and sour taste well pointed up with salt. Add the water and simmer for 20 minutes. Beat the eggs in a large bowl, pour on the cooled borsht and then return to the pan and cook over a gentle heat until thickened. Chill well before serving and add a large spoonful of yoghourt to each plate. Serve garnished with sliced hard-boiled egg.

QUICK CORN SOUP

1 tin creamed sweet corn	1 pint water
1 cup milk	1 onion
1 oz. flour	salt and black pepper

Peel and chop the onion and put it, and the corn, in a saucepan with the water. Simmer until the onion is tender, then blend the flour with a little cold milk and add to the soup, together with the rest of the milk. Bring to the boil and simmer for 4 minutes. Season with salt and black pepper, and garnish with paprika and chopped parsley.

SWEET AND SOUR CABBAGE SOUP

There are several different methods of preparing this soup and this one is a compromise between them all.

1 medium-sized white cabbage	2½ pints vegetable water
1 Spanish onion	1 teacup tomato juice or ½ teacup tomato purée
2 large cooking apples	1 lemon
3 pimentos (allspice)	sugar as required (brown is best)
	salt and black pepper

Shred the cabbage finely and discard the thick stalk. Peel and slice apple and onion and put them, with the cabbage, into the heated vegetable water. Add tomato juice or diluted tomato purée and the pimentos or allspice and simmer gently for 30 minutes. Season with salt and black pepper and add lemon juice and brown sugar to give a sweet and sour taste.

POTATO CAKES (1)

This is a good way to serve left-over mashed potatoes. You can turn a rather depressing sight into a mouth-watering meal with no trouble at all.

½ lb. mashed potatoes	1 dessertsp. butter
1 egg, beaten	corn oil for frying
flour as required	salt and black pepper

Mash the potatoes with the egg and the softened butter and blend well. Season with salt and black pepper. Add sufficient flour to make a fairly stiff paste and roll this out on a floured board. Cut into triangles or any other shape you like and fry in very hot fat until golden on both sides. Serve hot, split open and buttered.

Variations:
1. Serve buttered and with a slice of sharp cheese inside.
2. Instead of frying, you can brush the potato cakes with beaten egg· and bake in a hot oven until golden. About 15 to 20 minutes.

POTATO CAKES (2)

This version of potato cake requires raw instead of cooked potatoes.

3 lb. raw potatoes	oil for frying
2 tblsp. grated onion	salt and black pepper

Peel and grate the potatoes, and season with salt and pepper. Heat the oil until a blue smoke rises and put in spoonfuls of the potatoes and onion. Cook until brown on both sides and then turn down the heat and cook for a further 15 minutes with the lid on the pan. Serve very hot.

POTATO LATKES

This is perhaps the most famous of all the potato dishes in the Jewish repertoire.

1 tblsp. grated onion	2 large cups grated raw potato
2 tblsp. flour	2 large eggs
oil for frying	salt and black pepper

Mix the flour with the grated potato, then add the well beaten eggs, the grated onion and the salt and pepper. The mixture should be sufficiently soft to drop from a spoon. If necessary add another egg if the mixture is too dry or stiff. Heat the oil in a frying pan and drop in spoonfuls of the mixture and brown on both sides. Serve hot.

SWEET PEPPERS AND RICE

4 large sweet peppers (red or green)	4 oz. butter
3 cups cooked rice	4 oz. chopped nuts
2 cups white sauce	4 oz. grated sharp cheese
salt and black pepper	

Seed and shred the peppers and fry in the butter until tender. Add the sauce and cook gently for 10 to 12 minutes. Mix the rice, cheese, nuts, salt and black pepper all together and pour the sauce and pepper mixture over this. Serve very hot.

PEPPER AND TOMATO PIE

4 sweet peppers	¼ lb. tomatoes
2 eggs	vegetable water as required
3 oz. butter	breadcrumbs as required
1 cup green peas	salt and grated black pepper

Seed and shred the peppers and place in a greased casserole. Add a layer of breadcrumbs and sprinkle with salt and black pepper, add a layer of peas, sprinkle with some more breadcrumbs and then add a layer of sliced tomatoes. Season again. Beat the eggs and add about ½ a cup of vegetable water and pour over the tomatoes. Add a final thin layer of breadcrumbs and dot with plenty of butter. Bake in a hot oven for about 30 minutes until nicely browned on top.

BLINTZES

This is another world famous Jewish recipe which requires some preparation but which needs only the simplest ingredients. It is time in the kitchen more than well spent and you will probably be asked to make them again and again.

1 cup flour	2 eggs
1 cup water	salt and black pepper
corn oil	filling (*see* below)

Make a smooth batter with the flour, egg and water and season with salt and grated black pepper. Melt a little corn oil in a frying pan and fry a ¼ cupful of the batter at a time, to make a very thin pancake. Fry on one side only, then turn it out of the pan on to a flat surface, cooked side up, and keep hot. Fry the rest of the batter in the same way, keeping the pancakes hot. Put a good heaped spoonful of your filling into the centre of each pancake and fold over like a little parcel or envelope, sealing the edges well together. Fry in hot fat until golden on each side. Serve at once, with sour cream.

FILLINGS FOR BLINTZES

1. The best known of the blintzes is the cheese blintz and there are several different ways of making this type of filling. Here are three typical ones. 1 pound of cottage cheese mixed with an egg, 2 tablespoonfuls of melted butter, salt and black pepper and cinnamon. Stir in some sultanas and the grated rind of a lemon, and 1 tablespoonful of caster sugar.

2. One pound of cottage or curd cheese mixed with 1 tablespoonful of sugar, salt and pepper and paprika, and 3 ounces of chopped nuts.

3. One pound of cream cheese mixed with 1 egg, salt and black pepper, 1 tablespoonful of lemon juice, and 1 tablespoonful of sugar.

Blintzes are served with sour cream and make an excellent supper dish or a rather filling first course to a sumptuous meal.

CHEESE KNISHES

The blintz is fried and the knish is baked but the difference doesn't end there, for the knish is made with a dough instead of a pancake. However they occupy about the same place on the menu, either as a supper dish or as a really special first course to a large meal.

DOUGH

2 full breakfast cups flour	1 tsp. baking powder
3 eggs	salt and a touch of pepper
6 tblsp. corn oil	water as required

Sift together flour, baking powder and salt, drop the eggs into a well in the centre, then add the oil and mix well with a little water to make a smooth workable dough. Knead until there are no cracks in the dough and then roll out as thinly as possible. Cut out circles of dough with a teacup and put some filling in the centre of each.

FILLING

1 large cup fried onions	½ lb. cottage or curd cheese
2 eggs	salt and black pepper
¼ cup thick cream	paprika

Beat all ingredients together until smooth.

Make the knishes into little parcels by pinching up the edges together, brush with beaten egg and bake in a moderate oven until brown. Serve hot.

MUSHROOM KNISHES

This is a recipe using the knish dough as above but with a different filling.

1 lb. mushrooms or mushroom stalks	4 tblsp. butter
1 large Spanish onion, chopped	¼ cup thick cream
1 hard-boiled egg	breadcrumbs as required
salt and black pepper	

Thinly slice the mushrooms or stalks and sauté them in butter with the onions until tender. Stir in the chopped egg, the cream and seasoning and add enough breadcrumbs to make a suitable filling, not too dry. Proceed as for cheese knishes.

APPLE SAVOURY BAKE

4 large cooking apples	breadcrumbs as required
4 large Spanish onions	butter as required
4 tb sp. flour	water as required
4 tblsp. brown sugar	nutmeg
4 oz. chopped nuts	salt and black pepper

Mix flour with about a ¼ cup of water to a thin consistency. Add a shake of salt and black pepper. Peel and slice the onions and arrange ingredients in a greased casserole as follows: onions, apples, nuts, liquid, adding a little seasoning over each layer. Top with a thick layer of breadcrumbs, dot with plenty of butter and bake until tender. Check after 15 minutes to see if more water is required. This depends on the juiciness of the onions.

LEMON SORBET

One of the loveliest things I have ever tasted was a lemon sorbet I was served with at a banquet. Here is the simple recipe, but it is the simplicity which hallmarks all fine things.

grated rind of 2 lemons	¼ pint lemon juice
1 pint water	½ lb. loaf sugar
2 egg whites	6 empty lemon shells

Boil together the sugar and the water for 12 minutes, add a touch of the lemon juice and pour the syrup over the grated lemon rind. Leave until quite cold and then add the lemon juice, stir and strain through muslin. Pour into a freezing dish and put it in the ice-box. When half frozen (and you will have to watch), whip up the egg whites until really stiff and mix with the lemon ice. Freeze again until stiff but *not hard* and pack the lemon ice into the empty lemon shells and serve immediately. If you must keep the lemon ice, don't let it go on freezing until you cannot get a spoon into it, pack it into the shells and leave in the ice-box until required. If frozen solid allow it to remain outside the fridge before serving to get the right consistency.

CHOLLA (JEWISH EGG BREAD)

This well known and delicious bread can be bought at any good delicatessen or Jewish shop and the cakey taste makes it much more interesting than plain white commercially made bread.

2 heaped cups flour	2 tblsp. poppy seeds
⅝ cup water	1 tblsp. corn oil
¼ oz. yeast	1 tsp. salt
1 large egg	1 tsp. confectioner's sugar

Mix together the yeast, sugar and 3 tablespoonfuls of the warmed water. Allow to stand while you sift the flour and salt into your mixing bowl. Make a well in the flour and drop in the yeast, egg, oil and the rest of the water. Work all together and knead well until smooth and without cracks. Brush the top with a trace of oil and leave in a warm place to rise for 1 hour. The airing cupboard would be a good place or in front of a fire. After an hour flatten the dough and leave to rise again until twice its original bulk.

Divide the dough into three, and roll into strips of equal length. Plait them together and then leave on a floured tin in a warm place for 15 minutes. Brush with beaten egg and sprinkle with poppy seeds and bake at 375 degrees until browned (approximately 45 minutes but maybe less in some ovens). Cholla is delicious fresh but also makes excellent toast.

Another typical bread recipe is Bagels, also obtainable in any Jewish shop or delicatessen. They are usually eaten buttered and with savoury spread or cheese.

BAGELS

1 lb. flour	3 tblsp. corn oil
½ oz. confectioner's sugar	1 tblsp. yeast
½ pint milk and water mixed	1 tsp. salt
2 egg yolks	

Mix together yeast and sugar. Heat oil, milk, and salt together very gently and when lukewarm, add the yeast mixture. Mix into the flour with the beaten egg yolks and knead until firm. Cover with a cloth and leave in a warm place for 1 hour. Knead once again and then cut off small pieces to make rolls approximately 5 to 6 inches long and about as thick as your thumb. Make into rings pinching the ends together very securely. Leave on a floured board for 15 minutes, then drop them into a pan of gently simmering water. Simmer them very gently until they rise to the top. Remove them with a spatula on to a well greased baking tin, sprinkle very lightly with salt and bake at 400 degrees until golden and crusty (approximately 25 to 30 minutes).

Bagels are best used the same day as they tend to harden with keeping. Should you have any left over dip them into water and bake in a hot oven for 5 or 10 minutes. This will revive them.

TOMATO AND LOCKSHEN SOUP

Lockshen is the Jewish name for vermicelli and it comes in various forms. It is sometimes as thin as fine string or can be broad and flat, or even shaped in the letters of the alphabet. It comes shaped in shells and butterflies and whichever type you choose is a matter of taste. This recipe calls for 2 ounces lockshen, which can be bought in any Jewish shop or delicatessen.

1½ lb. tomatoes	2 oz. lockshen
1 large onion	1 oz. butter
1 clove garlic	2 tblsp. chopped parsley
1¾ pints milk and water mixed	½ tsp. honey
sweet basil leaves	salt and black pepper

Peel and slice onions, mince the garlic and sauté in the butter for 5 minutes. Add milk and water, bring to boiling point and simmer for 20 minutes. Add tomatoes, sweet basil and seasonings, and the cooked lockshen and honey. Simmer for a further 10 minutes and serve with croutons.

FRIED MATZOT

Matzot is the Jewish name for unleavened bread which is very useful in cooking. It can be obtained very easily at Jewish shops or any well-stocked delicatessen and in fact it can also be seen in many ordinary bakers because it is becoming so popular. Matzot can be eaten just as any other crispbread but in the following recipe it is cooked, and is very tasty for a quick and nourishing breakfast or supper dish.

4 or 5 sheets matzot	2 eggs
milk as required	oil for frying
salt and black pepper	

Break the matzot into small pieces and soak them in milk for 5 minutes until very slightly soft but not sodden. Drain in a colander and mix in the beaten eggs which have been seasoned with salt and black pepper. Heat some oil in a frying pan until fairly hot, put in enough of the egg and matzot to cover the bottom of the pan and fry until brown. Turn and brown the other side and fork into pieces before serving.

Variations:
1. Fried matzot can be served with a fried egg on top.
2. Serve it sprinkled over with grated cheese and browned under the grill.
3. Can be served sweet in which case omit salt and pepper and substitute sugar and cinnamon which is sprinkled on just before serving.
4. Add 4 eggs to the soaked matzot and scramble in butter instead of oil to make scrambled eggs with a difference. Season with salt and black pepper.
5. Serve fried matzot with a ¼ pound of fried mushrooms on top.

MATZOT PUDDING

4 sheets matzot	4 oz. butter
4 small eggs	4 oz. mixed dried fruit
4 tblsp. matzot meal	3 oz. brown sugar
½ tsp. mixed spice or cinnamon	

Soak the matzot, broken up into handy pieces, until soft and then squeeze out the moisture. Mix with all other ingredients and put the mixture into a well buttered casserole and sprinkle with brown sugar. Bake in a moderate oven for 50 to 60 minutes.

Middle East

Of the Middle Eastern countries perhaps the most cheese is made in Iraq where the women have been making it down through the ages. Most of it is made from ewe's milk and the best cheese is called **Meira**. A whole milk, cooked cheese, it has a rather salty taste and can be bought quite cheaply.

A cheese which is hardly ever marketed but which I have tasted and found delicious is **Biza**. Made from skimmed milk it is flavoured with wild onion or sometimes garlic. It is usually made by the womenfolk for their own families.

Roose is a hard cheese, eaten more than any other cheese in Iraq. It is a perfectly round cheese, the size of a grapefruit, and its taste and texture make it equally suitable as a table or a cooking cheese.

EGGPLANT AND CHEESE WITH RICE

1 lb. eggplants
¼ lb. butter
1 breakfastcup Meira or other salty cheese (try Dutch Edam)
plain boiled rice

2 green or red peppers
1 large onion
1 pint tomato sauce
½ pint water

salt and black pepper

Peel and slice the onion and green peppers and sauté in the butter until tender. Add the diced aubergines (or egg plants), the sauce and the water and seasoning, then simmer for 10 to 15 minutes. Stir in the cheese and cook the mixture just long enough to melt the cheese, then serve on a bed of plain boiled rice.

CHEESE AND RICE BAKE

A nourishing supper dish which is a good way of using up left-over rice.

2 cups cooked rice
2 cups milk
2 cups grated sharp cheese

breadcrumbs as required
butter as required
salt and black pepper

Heat the milk, stir in the rice and cook slowly until milk is absorbed. Butter a casserole and lay the rice in the bottom, and season. Top with the cheese, then with breadcrumbs, dot with butter and bake in a moderate oven until golden.

CHELOU (CRUSTY RICE)

2 egg yolks
2 tblsp. yoghourt
2 tblsp. butter

½ lb. uncooked rice
water as required
additional butter

salt and black pepper

Wash the rice, then drop it into enough boiling water to cover. Boil fairly quickly for 8 minutes, stirring occasionally with a wooden spoon. Test the rice to see if it is done, then drain it and rinse in warm water. Melt the butter in a very little hot water in a large, heavy-bottomed casserole and make sure the bottom of the pan is coated with the butter and water. Mix the rice with the beaten egg yolks and the yoghourt and pat it down into the casserole, but not too tightly. Bake for 15 minutes, after which time spread a ¼ pound of melted butter over the top of the rice, cover the casserole and bake for a further 30 minutes. There will be a delicious brown crust on the bottom of the casserole. To remove this without breaking it put the casserole in 1 inch of cold water for 10 minutes. Turn the casserole upside down on to a hot serving platter so that the crust is on the top. Serve at once.

SYRIAN RICE WITH FRUIT

1 lb. cooked rice	1 small onion
½ lb. mixed dried fruit	¼ tsp. powdered cloves
4 oz. chopped nuts	butter as required
melted butter	

Peel and chop the onion and sauté, together with the nuts and fruit, until the onion turns golden. Add the cloves and mix well. Butter a casserole and put in the plain boiled rice, making a hole in the centre into which you spoon the nut and fruit mixture. Bake in a moderate oven for 15 to 20 minutes, then mix together with a ½ teacup of melted butter. Serve hot.

TURKISH SALAD

3 large oranges or 2 tins mandarins	3 tblsp. olive oil
2 large sweet Spanish onions	¼ tsp. ground coriander seeds
¼ lb. black and green olives, mixed	paprika
salt and black pepper	

Peel the oranges and slice thinly or, if you are using tinned mandarins, drain them before using. Peel and thinly slice the onions, and stone the olives. Toss all together in the oil for 3 minutes until everything is coated, then sprinkle with salt, black pepper, paprika and the coriander seeds. Toss again and serve chilled.

PERSIAN LENTIL SOUP

1 lb. lentils	3 tblsp. butter
1 large Spanish onion	1 tsp. lime or lemon juice
2¾ pints water	½ lb. cooked green peas
salt and black pepper	

Wash the lentils until the water is clean. Peel and slice the onion and sauté in the butter until pale gold. Add the lentils and the water and season with a little salt and pepper. Bring slowly to the boil and simmer, with the lid on the pan, for 1 to 1½ hours. Test after 1 hour to see if the lentils are tender and then add the peas, heat to boiling point again and taste for seasoning. Just before serving, stir in the lemon juice.

SYRIAN THETCHOUKA

This is a meal which is no trouble to prepare but looks and tastes most professional.

6 eggs	1½ lb. tomatoes
4 green or red peppers	½ cup finely grated sharp cheese
4 Spanish onions	4 tblsp. olive oil
3 cloves garlic, minced	salt and black pepper

Peel and slice the onions and sauté them in the oil until golden. Add the garlic and the other vegetables sliced, put the lid on the pan and cook gently until all the vegetables are tender. Transfer the mixture to a buttered casserole with lid, make 6 hollows in the mixture and carefully drop an egg into each one. Sprinkle with the grated cheese and bake for 10 minutes, or until the eggs are set.

APPLES WITH SAVOURY STUFFING (Saudi Arabian)

6 large cooking apples	1 tsp. brown sugar	oil for frying
1 large onion	⅛ tsp. powdered cloves	sour cream
1 cup chopped nuts	breadcrumbs as required	salt and black pepper

Peel and slice the onion and fry in the butter until a dark golden brown. Add the cloves, nuts, and the hollowed-out centres of the apples (discarding the cores), and chop finely. Season with salt and pepper and add enough breadcrumbs to make a firm stuffing. Pack into hollowed-out apples, sprinkle with sugar and bake in a moderate oven for 1 hour. Serve with sour cream.

MUSHROOM KEBABS (Turkish)

1 lb. button mushrooms	1 small tin pineapple cubes (or fresh)
1 lb. very firm tomatoes	plain boiled rice
1 sweet Spanish onion	oil as required
2 large green or red peppers	salt and black pepper

Seed the peppers and cut into 1¼-inch squares approximately. Cut up tomatoes into dice, and peel and dice the onion. Then arrange ingredients on skewers thus—a piece of onion, then a piece of tomato, a mushroom, a piece of pineapple and a piece of pepper. Repeat until skewers are filled. Allow from 2 to 4 skewers per serving. Make sure that the very end piece on the skewer is that of onion or pepper as this will hold firmer than the pineapple or the tomato. Sprinkle the kebabs with salt and pepper and grill them on both sides until brown and tender, after dipping each kebab into oil quickly beforehand. Serve very hot on plain boiled rice.

SWEET POTATO WITH BANANAS

1 large sweet potato, cut into serving slices ½ in. thick	oil as required
2 tsp. grated orange rind	golden syrup or brown sugar
4 to 6 bananas	salt and paprika

Toss the sweet potato (or yam) slices in the oil until well coated. Sprinkle with paprika, then place them on an oiled baking tin and put into a hot oven for 8 to 10 minutes. Take them out of the oven, sprinkle lightly with salt and the grated orange rind. Peel and slice the bananas lengthways, and then slice each half in two, and lay the pieces on the potato slices. Brush with a little golden syrup or sprinkle with a little brown sugar and put back into oven, a moderate one this time, and bake until dark brown and succulent.

BANANAS AND RICE (Persian)

6 eggs	1 lb. cooked long grain rice
6 bananas	¼ lb. butter
2 large Spanish onions	salt and black pepper

Keep the rice hot while you prepare the rest of the dish. Peel and slice the onions and sauté in the butter until brown. Peel and cut the bananas in halves lengthways and then cut across them. Fry these pieces with the onions for a few minutes until brown, adding more butter when necessary. Fry the eggs until the whites are just set and the yolks still liquid. Heap up the rice on a serving plate, top with the onions and the bananas, and crown with the fried eggs. Sprinkle with salt and black pepper.

SYRIAN BAKED ONIONS AND BEETROOTS

4 Spanish onions	breadcrumbs
4 round beets, cooked	butter as required
¾ lb. grated sharp cheese	plain boiled rice
¼ pint yoghourt	salt and black pepper

Peel the onions and scoop out the insides leaving a thick shell. Scoop out the beets likewise. Chop the onion and beet insides and fry them in butter until the onion is brown. Mix with the cheese and the yoghourt, season and add enough breadcrumbs to make a suitable stuffing. Pack this into the onions and beets, put a piece of butter on each, and bake in a moderate oven until golden. Serve on a bed of rice.

EGG AND VEGETABLE KUKU

6 eggs	2 tblsp. chopped parsley
2 eggplants	1½ tblsp. flour
2 stalks celery	1 tblsp. raisins
1 large onion	oil for cooking
saffron	salt and black pepper

Peel and thinly slice the onion, and slice the eggplants and celery. Sauté in oil for 10 minutes. Beat the eggs thoroughly and add the vegetables which have been mixed with the flour. Add the saffron, parsley, raisins, salt and pepper and mix well. Pour into a greased casserole and bake in a moderate preheated oven for 30 minutes. Check to see if the kuku is browned underneath in which case turn it over and bake until the other side is brown—a further 10 to 15 minutes. Serve either hot or cold.

SPICY LEBANESE COFFEE

The subject of drinks is not within the scope of this book but I cannot resist including this delicious iced coffee which I first tasted on a Lebanese boat heading out for Cyprus.

1 pint very strong coffee	2 tsp. grated orange peel
1 cup thick whipped cream	nutmeg or mace
cinnamon	dark brown sugar, or honey

Make your coffee by grinding your own beans and making *real* coffee and not the coffee-flavoured drink that comes in powder form. Make it at least twice as strong as you usually do, then sweeten it with plenty of dark brown (raw) sugar or honey. While the coffee is still hot stir in the grated orange peel and allow to cool. Stir in ¾ of the thick whipped cream and a little nutmeg or mace and a ½ teaspoonful of cinnamon. Chill well, then pour into individual glasses and serve topped with a spoonful of thick cream.

TURKISH CUCUMBER SALAD

1 medium-sized cucumber	¼ lb. sultanas
1 small sweet onion	2 oz. chopped nuts
2 hard-boiled eggs, chopped	½ pint yoghourt
salt and black pepper	

Dice the cucumber, mince the onion, then mix all ingredients and season with salt and black pepper. Chill before serving.

YOGHOURT POLOU

A polou is the Persian name for a risotto or rice dish. It is very nutritious and some of the Middle Eastern rice dishes are very rich and exotic. Here is a basic recipe and you can try out your own variations.

1 cup yoghourt	1 egg
6 oz. chopped nuts	¼ tsp. saffron
½ lb. long grain rice	butter as required
salt and black pepper	

Rinse the rice for 1 minute in boiling water and then drain. Drop it into fast boiling salted water and cook for 10 minutes. Rinse again, but this time in cold water, and drain. Beat the egg and mix it with the yoghourt and half of the cooked rice. Grease a casserole and put in the yoghourt and rice mixture. Sprinkle with the chopped nuts, then a layer of the remaining rice. Repeat layers until all is used up. Sprinkle with saffron, salt and black pepper and bake in a moderate oven for 40 to 50 minutes. There should be a crust on the bottom of the casserole so serve the rice turned upside down with the crust on top.

Variations:

1. Add a layer of grated carrot and chopped celery after the nuts.
2. Add a layer of cooked lentils mixed with yoghourt.
3. Add a layer of dried mixed fruit.
4. Add a layer of string beans.
5. Add a layer of tomatoes sprinkled with sweet basil leaves.

EGYPTIAN AUBERGINES WITH RICE

6 large aubergines	2 cups yoghourt
2 cloves garlic	1 cup olive oil
1 large onion	1 tsp. sugar
plain boiled rice	salt and black pepper

Thickly slice the unpeeled aubergines, sprinkle with salt and leave for 30 minutes after which time thoroughly wash and dry them. Heat the oil and fry the aubergine slices, together with the sliced onion, until tender. Season with salt and black pepper, the minced garlic and the sugar. Mix in the yoghourt and stir well. Serve on a bed of plain boiled rice.

The Netherlands

The policy of Dutch cheesemakers has always been to perfect a limited number of varieties rather than to branch out in a dozen different directions. The result is the comparatively small number of ten varieties. I shall mention the best known and most easily obtainable outside their own country.

Gouda is a creamy cheese, firm textured and flavoursome. Made from cow's milk it is straw coloured but darkens slightly with age, and the rind is more or less the same colour.

Edam is another favourite, though saltier and harder in texture than the creamy Gouda. It is distinguished by its deep yellow inside and the pillar-box red of its rind. Edam is also made from cow's milk.

Leyden cheese is regarded by many as the Netherland's best cheese. It is a spiced cow's milk cheese, primrose yellow laced with green and flavoured with exotic cummin seeds.

Friesian cheese is similar to Leyden but has the added attraction of cloves as well as cummin.

LIGHTNING SUPPER DISH

1 large tin celery hearts	4 oz. Edam cheese
1 cup milk	tarragon vinegar
2 tblsp. flour	butter as required

Heat the celery in a little of its juice. Melt about 1 tablespoonful of butter, mix in 2 tablespoonfuls of flour, and add warm milk stirring until smooth. Add grated cheese and a dash of tarragon vinegar. Drain celery, pour over the cheese mixture, brown under grill and serve at once with toasted bread.

CHEESE FLAN

This makes an original picnic or cold supper dish. Use Edam cheese for best results as it is much saltier than the Gouda.

¼ lb. grated Edam cheese	1 flan case
2½ oz. butter	½ cup milk
½ oz. cornstarch	salt and black pepper

Mix the cornstarch with a little cold milk. Boil the remainder of the milk and mix with the cornstarch. Return it to the pan and, stirring with a wooden spoon over a gentle heat, bring to boiling point and simmer for 3 minutes. Add the grated cheese and season with a good grate of black pepper and a touch of salt if necessary. Leave it to get cold while you cream the butter. Add both together and whisk well until very fluffy. Pour into the flan case and serve cold.

The English are not the only ones who can make a superb bread and butter pudding. You may not have come across one like this before, because instead of being sweet and fruity it is strongly flavoured with *cheese*.

DUTCH BREAD AND BUTTER PUDDING

½ stale loaf (brown or black)	1 pint milk
3 eggs	½ tsp. French mustard
3 oz. grated cheese	butter as required
1 small grated onion	salt and black pepper

Grease a deep pie dish and put in the layers of ingredients as follows. Bread and butter, cheese, onion, pepper and a little salt. Repeat the layers until all is used up. Warm the milk, add to the beaten eggs, season lightly and pour over the layers. Leave aside to soak for 1 hour. Stand the baking dish in another one containing 1 inch of water and bake in a very slow oven for 45 minutes. My own variation of this recipe is to add a thick layer of sliced tomatoes sprinkled with sweet basil leaves.

LENTIL SOUP

2 pints vegetable water	1 kohl-rabi or small white turnip
1 dessertsp. flour	1 large sweet onion
½ head celery	1 carrot
2 oz. lentils	salt and black pepper

Lentils need careful washing so use plenty of water and a fine sieve. Prepare and chop all the vegetables and put them with the lentils in a saucepan. Bring to the boil with the lid on the pan, and simmer for 1¾ hours. Rub through a sieve, return to saucepan and heat to boiling again. Mix the flour with a little cold water and stir it into the soup. Simmer gently for 6 minutes, then season with salt and black pepper.

DUTCH ONION SOUP

I have already given you a recipe for French onion soup. This is the Dutch version, not so sophisticated as the French perhaps but a good solid soup.

2 large sweet onions	1 pint milk
3 oz. butter	½ pint boiling water
3 tblsp. flour	8 oz. mashed potatoes
1 tblsp. fresh parsley	chopped spring onions for garnishing
salt and black pepper	

Peel, slice and sauté the onions in the butter until tender and golden brown. Blend in the flour and very slowly stir in the boiling water, using a wooden spoon. Stir until the soup begins to thicken, then let it simmer over a very low heat while you prepare the next stage. Heat the milk to just under boiling point and mash it into the potatoes. Beat it until it is really creamy and then add it to the golden onions. Season with salt and black pepper and serve very hot, garnished with finely chopped spring onions.

COLD MARROW SOUP

Here is yet another way of using up a marrow in the form of an unusual summer soup.

2 lb. vegetable marrow	½ pint vegetable water
2 large sweet Spanish onions	chopped parsley or chives
4 tblsp. butter	paprika
1 carton single cream	a touch of sugar
salt and black pepper	

Peel the marrow and the onions and sauté them, finely sliced, in the butter until tender. Add the vegetable water and simmer until very soft. Pass through a sieve and add seasoning. Allow to cool before adding the cream. Chill well and serve garnished with chopped parsley or chives.

DUTCH STEAMED PUDDING

½ lb. grated Edam cheese	1 cup wholewheat flour
2 tblsp. butter	parsley and chives
4 separated eggs	salt and black pepper

Cream the butter, add the egg yolks and beat well for several minutes. An electric blender or even a rotary whisk would reduce the labour. Add the cheese, flour and the stiffly beaten egg whites and season with salt and black pepper. Be careful with the salt as Edam is salty itself. Mix well together and pour into a well buttered pudding basin. Cover with grease-proof paper and stand the basin in a pan containing enough water to come half-way up the sides of the pudding basin. Steam for 45 minutes, being careful *never* to let the water boil. Unmould the pudding and surround with chopped chives. Put a sprig of parsley on the top.

DUTCH RED CABBAGE

This marvellous vegetable is as good to look at as to eat. We like it the Dutch way, that is sweet and sour with rice added to make a very substantial meal.

1½ to 2 lb. red cabbage	1 oz. butter
1 lb. apples	2 oz. dark brown sugar
1½ pints water	3 oz. uncooked rice
½ teacup vinegar	salt and black pepper

Remove any coarse outer leaves of the cabbage, cut in half, take out the thick white stem and shred the rest coarsely. I have a wonderful French shredder which will reduce this task to a minimum and there is a choice of five different cutting discs from very fine to very coarse. Peel, core and slice the apples, and put the ingredients in a casserole in the following layers: cabbage, apples, rice, sugar, salt and pepper. Repeat the layers until all is used up. Pour over the water and the vinegar and the melted butter. Cover and leave it in a very slow oven for about 3 hours. This dish is even more delicious if left until the following day.

BROCCOLI AU GRATIN

Broccoli is seasonal and so is all the more welcome when it does put in an appearance. Here is the Dutch way to serve it.

1½ lb. broccoli	2 tblsp. thick cream
1 cup grated sharp cheese	black pepper
½ cup melted butter	paprika

Steam the broccoli until just tender in plenty of butter. Over a slow heat and with a tight lid on the pan it will steam in its own juice without the addition of any water. When ready put it in a buttered casserole, sprinkle with the grated cheese and pour over it the melted butter. Season with paprika and grated black pepper. Sprinkle on more cheese and bake for 10 minutes in a hot oven.

ONIONS IN SOUR CREAM

1 lb. sweet Spanish onions	melted butter as required
1 breakfast cup sour or cultured cream	a touch of mace
salt and black pepper	

Peel and slice the onions and sauté them in the butter until a deep golden brown. Season with salt and black pepper and a touch of mace. Add the cream, stir and serve on a bed of noodles, or cooked greens.

GROUND RICE PUDDING

1½ oz. ground rice	1 pint milk
1 oz. brown sugar	2 tblsp. rum or brandy

Blend the ground rice with a little of the milk. Bring the remainder of the milk to the boil and pour it on to the blended ground rice. Return to saucepan, add sugar and rum or brandy. Simmer very gently for 20 minutes and serve with a touch of grated nutmeg, either hot or cold.

CRISPY APPLE PIE

This is a good recipe for making pastry if you are in a hurry. The big advantage about this Dutch method is that you don't need the rolling pin and there is no mess of flour and dough to clean up afterwards.

4 oz. porridge oats	3 tblsp. melted butter
2 oz. dark brown sugar	3 tblsp. jam
1 pint sweetened apple purée	½ tsp. cinnamon
a pinch of powdered cloves	

Mix together the oats, brown sugar and melted butter, spread over a shallow baking tin and toast in a moderate oven or under a slow grill for 10 minutes. Stir with a fork once or twice. Cool for a few minutes before using. Mix the cloves and cinnamon into the apple purée. Grease a casserole, and put the jam into the bottom, then add the apple purée. Fork the topping into crumbs and scatter these over the apple. Bake in a very moderate oven for 20 to 30 minutes.

My own labour-saving advice is to make lots of topping and store it in a jar with a tightly fitting lid.

New Zealand

Both in New Zealand and Australia, Cheddar cheese is the most popular. The Cheddar of both countries is similar, and has a close texture, weighs heavily for its bulk, and has a peculiarly nutty taste. In colour it is similar to the English Cheddar though somewhat darker.

This is a simple and time-saving way of providing a nice comforting soup on a really cold night.

SOUTH ISLAND SOUP

1 sweet Spanish onion	½ pint water
2 heaped tblsp. flour	½ pint milk
3 dessertsp. butter	¾ cup grated cheese
parsley	¼ teacup thick cream
salt and black pepper	

Peel and slice the onion and sauté in butter until tender. Blend in the flour and cook for 1 minute, then add the heated milk and water, a little at a time, stirring with a wooden spoon. Season, then simmer over a very low heat, stirring frequently, until thick and creamy. Stir in the cheese and cook until just melted, then stir in the cream. Garnish with a sprig of parsley.

VEGETABLE BAKE

1 lb. string beans	¼ pint white sauce
2 egg yolks	½ cup grated sharp cheese
2 stalks celery	breadcrumbs as required
3 large sweet onions	butter as required
3 tblsp. chopped parsley	paprika
salt and black pepper	

String the beans and celery and cut into short pieces. Peel and slice the onions and sauté all vegetables in butter until tender. Lay them in a buttered casserole and season. Stir the cheese into the white sauce together with the parsley, and pour over the vegetables. Season again, top with breadcrumbs, dot with plenty of butter and bake for 20 minutes or until golden brown.

CREAMED MUSHROOMS WITH GREEN PEPPERS

1½ lb. mushrooms	2 tblsp. butter
4 green or red peppers	1 tblsp. flour
½ pint hot milk	1 tsp. French mustard
½ pint thick cream (sweet or sour)	breadcrumbs
salt and black pepper	

Make a roux with the flour and the butter, cook for 1 minute, then blend in the hot milk stirring until thick. Add sliced mushrooms and peppers, season and cook in the top of a double boiler for 20 minutes. Season with mustard, salt and pepper and stir well. Place in a buttered casserole, top with breadcrumbs, dot with butter and bake for 15 minutes.

GARDEN PEA CHOWDER

3½ pints vegetable water	1 tblsp. parsley
2 pints fresh garden peas (shelled)	1 tblsp. butter
1 large sweet onion	1 tblsp. mint
salt and black pepper	

Cook the peas in water with the mint, parsley, onion (chopped) and the seasoning. Not too much seasoning or you will impair the delicate taste of the peas. Cook until tender, pass through a sieve, reheat, stir in the butter and serve with croutons or toast.

For those who may wonder what *is* the difference between croutons and toast, toast is simply toast and croutons are pieces of fried bread cut into triangles or squares.

MUSHROOM AND RICE CROQUETTES

This is an economy recipe which makes an excellent breakfast dish or supper-time snack. It can be prepared in advance.

½ lb. mushroom stalks	2 eggs
1 small onion, minced	1 tsp. chopped parsley
1 breakfast cup cooked rice	butter as required
½ teacup water	breadcrumbs as required
1 oz. flour	oil for frying
salt and black pepper	

Chop the mushroom stalks and sauté them, with the onion, in butter for 10 minutes. Stir in the flour and gradually add the heated water, stirring until boiling. Simmer for 2 minutes, then add the rice, parsley and seasoning and one of the beaten eggs. Cook for 1 minute more, then spread on to a flat surface to get quite cold. Cut into triangles, dip in the other egg (beaten), coat with breadcrumbs and fry in deep hot oil until golden on both sides.

NEW ZEALAND RICE

2 large Spanish onions	1 tblsp. chopped parsley
½ lb. cooked rice	1 tblsp. butter
½ cup cooked green peas	1 tsp. vegetable extract
oil for frying	salt and black pepper

Dilute the vegetable extract in a very little hot water and stir this into the rice, and keep it hot while you continue. Peel and slice the onions and fry in hot oil until golden brown. Heat the peas in the butter and stir in the chopped parsley.

Heap up the rice in your serving dish, smother with the seasoned golden onions, scatter the peas over the onions and serve at once.

COLD SAVOURY PEAS

2 cups cooked peas	2 eggs
2 cups mashed potatoes	2 tblsp. parsley
1 cup white sauce	breadcrumbs as required
1 large onion, minced	butter

Mix all ingredients using enough breadcrumbs to get a fairly thick consistency, sprinkle with more breadcrumbs, dot with plenty of butter and bake until golden. Serve cold with lettuce and cucumber.

SOUTH ISLAND PIE

1 lb. lentils	1 large onion
4 oz. grated cheese	water as required
3 oz. butter	salt and black pepper

Use the red lentils if possible. If you use the green ones you must remember to soak them overnight before cooking them. Cover with water, bring very slowly to the boil, stirring frequently, and cook until soft. This takes 1 hour approximately. Keep them well stirred as they are liable to stick. Meanwhile peel and slice the onion and fry in the butter until brown, then beat them into the lentils with a fork, and stir in half the grated cheese. Put the mixture into a well buttered casserole, sprinkle with remaining cheese, dot with more butter and bake until brown (about 20 minutes) in a hot oven. This is delicious and very filling.

OUT-OF-DOORS SUPPER DISH

1 lb. cooked rice	1 clove garlic, chopped
¼ lb. grated sharp cheese	1 cup cooked peas
¼ lb. butter	salt and black pepper

When the rice is cooked mix in all other ingredients and serve hot.

VEGETABLE CASSEROLE

1 lb. tomatoes	1 large onion
¼ lb. cooked rice	1 medium-sized vegetable marrow
1 cup grated Cheddar cheese	1 tblsp. butter
½ cup milk	sweet basil
	salt and black pepper

Butter a casserole and lay the sliced tomatoes in the bottom. Sprinkle with sweet basil and salt and black pepper. Peel and slice the onions and lay them on the tomatoes. Season, then add the peeled and diced marrow and season again. Mix together the rice, the cheese and the butter and make this the top layer. Pour over the milk and cover with a greased lid. Bake in a moderate oven for 1 hour. If you like you can vary the crust by uncovering the casserole for the last 15 minutes and sprinkling the top with buttered breadcrumbs.

EGGS AND NOODLES

1 lb. cooked noodles	6 eggs
1 cup grated Cheddar cheese	breadcrumbs
oil as required	

Mix the noodles with a little oil and place in a well oiled casserole. Make 6 hollows in the noodles and drop an egg carefully into each. Sprinkle with the grated cheese, then the breadcrumbs, dot with butter and bake in a moderate oven for 15 minutes.

SAUERKRAUT WITH A DIFFERENCE

½ lb. sauerkraut (or 1 large tin)	1 teacup chopped fresh or tinned pineapple
½ lb. red cabbage	1 cup chopped tomatoes
2 tblsp. olive oil	salt and black pepper

The sauerkraut comes in its own juice which you use for cooking. Shred the red cabbage and simmer all ingredients except oil together for 30 minutes. Allow to cool, then reheat and add the oil. Serve very hot.

RASPBERRY PANCAKES

2 cups raspberries	2 eggs
2 cups flour	¼ lb. butter
2 cups milk	¼ lb. confectioner's sugar
whipped cream	

Beat the egg yolks with the sugar, then beat in the flour and the fruit. Melt 1 tablespoonful butter and add that too and lastly fold in the stiffly beaten egg whites. Drop spoonfuls of this mixture into hot butter and fry on both sides. Serve very hot with whipped cream. These are mouth watering and spectacular enough to stun the most fastidious guest.

LEMON TART

This is a good tart to make in a hurry for that unexpected tea-time guest.

8 oz. shortcrust pastry	2 oz. brown sugar
3 oz. butter	2 lemons
3 oz. cake or breadcrumbs	2 eggs

Line a greased pie-plate with the pastry. For the filling, cream the butter and sugar, add the well beaten eggs, crumbs and the juice of the lemons. Lastly grate in the rinds as well and beat all together. Spread over the pastry and bake in a moderate oven until golden, approximately 30 minutes. Serve with whipped cream.

Poland

In Poland the bulk of the cheese manufactured is not native to the country. The Poles enjoy many of the fine cheeses from other European countries, principally Emmental and Gruyère, Tilsit, Edam, Gouda and Cheddar. By far the most popular cheese eaten in Poland is the German Tilsiter.

Poland is a country of considerable output of dairy products and Polish cooks have devised many original ways of preparing and serving cheese. Many of the processed cheeses made in Poland are excellent for cooking.

WARSAW MUSHROOMS AND CHEESE

1 lb. button mushrooms	1 teacup sour cream
1 small sweet onion	½ cup stoned dates
1 heaped tblsp. flour	½ cup grated cheese
butter as required	breadcrumbs
salt and black pepper	

Sauté the mushrooms, whole, in plenty of butter until just tender. Add the chopped onion and simmer for a further 5 minutes. Grease a casserole and put in the mushrooms and onion with the butter left in the pan. Take 1 tablespoonful of the sour cream and mix with the flour. Add the rest of the sour cream and season well. Pour over the mushrooms, then sprinkle with the grated cheese. Top with breadcrumbs, dot with butter and stoned olives and brown in a hot oven for 10 minutes.

POLISH CHEESE SPREAD

This is Poland's answer to Liptauer spread and it is just as delicious.

½ lb. cottage (or curd) cheese	2 pickled gherkins, chopped
½ lb. chopped chives (or spring onions)	2 tblsp. sour cream
8 small radishes, chopped	salt and black pepper to taste

Combine all ingredients and mix well. Serve on dark rye bread or pumpernickel.

POLISH BORSHCH

Here is yet another of those succulent beetroot soups.

½ lb. cooked and peeled beets	sour cream as required
1 small onion, chopped	a touch of sugar
1 tblsp. flour	chopped parsley
2 tblsp. butter	salt and black pepper

Put the beets through a ricer or sieve and add the finely chopped onion. Cook the flour in the butter for 2 minutes, add the beets and onion and stir. Heat enough sour cream to make a thick soup when added to the mixture. Stir again, season and serve garnished with chopped parsley.

CABBAGE BORSHCH

I was given this recipe by an elderly Polish lady whom I met on top of a Kensington-bound London bus, and have since made it many times. If the donor of the recipe should pick up this book do please accept my thanks once again.

1 lb. raw beets	1 small tin tomato purée or paste
½ lb. white cabbage	2 tsp. vinegar
2 large onions	a touch of brown sugar
2 cups vegetable water	butter as required
salt and black pepper	

Peel and slice the onions and sauté in butter until golden, add the finely shredded cabbage and cook for a further 10 minutes, stirring frequently. Put the beets through a julienne or shred into matchsticks and add to the cabbage and onions. Cook all together for 5 minutes, then add the vegetable water, the tomato paste diluted with a little of the liquid, the sugar, vinegar salt and pepper. Simmer for 50 minutes, check seasoning and if necessary add a further cupful of vegetable water. Serve with dark rye bread.

HONEY SHALLOTS

Polish cooking has a distinctly dual personality with the aristocrat and the peasant living happily together in the same kitchen, and so I follow a big and beautiful peasant soup with the fine delicacy of honeyed shallots.

1 lb. shallots	3 tblsp. butter
1 cup vegetable stock	2 tblsp. thick honey
salt and black pepper	

Blanch the shallots and cool slightly. Peel and brown them in the butter. Heat a little of the water in a heavy saucepan and add the honey, stirring well. Add the shallots, the rest of the water, and a touch of salt and black pepper. Cover with a well fitting lid and simmer for 30 minutes, stirring from time to time. If liquid reduces add a few tablespoonfuls more vegetable water. Check your seasoning at the end of the cooking time to make sure you have a sweet taste with the bite of salt in it.

STUFFED CABBAGE

This is another peasant dish which to most non-Polish cooks is a very unusual way of preparing and cooking cabbage.

1 medium-sized firm cabbage	2 cups cooked rice
1 large Spanish onion	½ pint thick tomato sauce
1 tsp. mixed herbs	sweet basil leaves
2 tblsp. butter	salt and black pepper

Either keep the sauce hot while you prepare the rest of the dish, or make the sauce as the dish is cooking. Remove any coarse outer leaves from the cabbage and steam it whole, in a very little salted water, for 1 hour. When cool enough to handle, remove the central stem and some of the inside and chop finely. Now make your stuffing by mixing together the rice, chopped cabbage, well fried onion, herbs, butter and seasonings, but not the basil—that is stirred into the tomato sauce. Stuff the cabbage with the mixture, put in a baking tin with plenty of oil and bake for a further 40 minutes, basting frequently. Serve with the sauce and basil poured over it.

SWEET AND SOUR STRING BEANS

2 lb. string beans	sugar as required
½ cup wine vinegar	butter as required
plain boiled noodles	salt to taste

String the beans and cut into convenient lengths. Cook in plenty of butter until tender in a pan with a close-fitting lid. Do not add water and cook them over a *low* heat. When the beans are done add the vinegar and a touch of salt and enough sugar to give a distinctly sweet-sour taste. Serve heaped up on plain boiled noodles.

POLISH MASHED POTATOES

1 lb. potatoes	1 tblsp. butter
2 large sweet onions	a touch of nutmeg
2 or 3 tblsp. thick cream	salt and black pepper

Wash the potatoes and boil them in their skins until tender. Meanwhile peel and slice the onions and brown them well in some butter. Chop finely. When the potatoes are done and cool enough to handle, peel them and mash them with the butter, then with the cream and whip them until really light and fluffy. Fold in the fried and chopped onions and season with salt and black pepper.

Variation:
For a full meal sprinkle the above potatoes with a breakfast-cupful of grated sharp cheese and brown in a hot oven for a few minutes.

COUNTRY VEGETABLE STEW

2 lb. cabbage	2 cloves garlic
6 large plump tomatoes	2 sticks celery
4 hard-boiled eggs	4 oz. melted butter
4 large Spanish onions	½ tsp. dill
salt and black pepper	

Shred the cabbage finely and cook in butter until tender. Add the well fried onions, chopped celery and sliced tomatoes. Mince the garlic, and mix into the vegetables. Add the melted butter, the dill and seasoning and cook in a casserole in a slow oven for 40 to 50 minutes. Serve with the eggs sliced on top.

WARSAW RED CABBAGE

2 lb. red cabbage	4 tblsp. sour cream
1½ lb. chestnuts	2 tblsp. vinegar
4 oz. sultanas and currants mixed	1 tblsp. brown sugar
3 oz. butter	½ pint vegetable water
1 oz. flour	salt and black pepper

Prepare and shred the cabbage and blanch in boiling water for 5 minutes. Drain, then cook in the butter for 10 minutes with the lid on the pan. Stir well, then add the vegetable water, sugar and vinegar, replace the lid and cook until tender. Meanwhile roast the chestnuts until tender in a hot oven, peel and chop them and add them to the cabbage together with the dried fruit. Mix the flour with a little cold water, blend in the sour cream and add to the cabbage. Season to your taste, adding more vinegar or sugar if you wish, and cook for a further 5 minutes.

ASPARAGUS POLONAISE

1 large bundle asparagus	1 tblsp. lemon juice
8 oz. butter	1 tsp. sugar
2 egg yolks, uncooked	1 tsp. salt
water as required	a dash of cayenne
salt to taste	

Keep the asparagus tied in a bundle and steam it in a large pan with the lid on. The bundle should be standing upright in about 5 inches of water to which you have added 1 teaspoonful of salt. Do not let the water touch the tips of the asparagus but let them cook in the steam. Now make the Hollandaise sauce by the following method. Take a double boiler and simmer about a ½ teacupful of water in the bottom half. Before assembling the boiler put the butter, chopped up, into the top half, mash it well with a fork until it is creamy, then add the lemon juice a drop at a time, beating well all the time. Next add the egg yolks carefully and beat the entire mixture vigorously. Add a touch of cayenne and a sprinkle of salt and then assemble the boiler and cook the sauce, beating all the time with a fork. Immediately it is thick and creamy remove it from the hot water and serve it in a sauce boat. Give each person a pile of asparagus to dip into the Hollandaise. If you like you can add, just before serving, 2 large spoonfuls of thick cream.

BEETROOTS IN SOUR CREAM

2 lb. cooked beets	sugar to taste
1 tblsp. butter	vinegar as required
2 level tsp. flour	plain boiled rice
½ teacup sour cream	salt and black pepper

Peel the beets and chop. Make a roux with the flour and the butter and cook for 2 minutes. Add the sour cream and seasoning and then the chopped beetroots. Add a little sugar and vinegar to taste, and serve on plain boiled rice.

MUSHROOMS AND SHALLOTS ON SKEWERS

1 lb. shallots	butter as required
1 lb. button mushrooms	sweet basil leaves
½ lb. hard tomatoes	salt and black pepper

Peel the shallots and sauté in butter with the whole mushrooms for 10 minutes over a gentle heat. When cool enough to handle, place the shallots, mushrooms and cut-up tomatoes alternately on skewers. Sprinkle a little sweet basil over the tomatoes and a little salt and pepper over the shallots and mushrooms. Grill under a medium heat, basting frequently with butter, for 10 minutes. The shallots should be crisp, and done this way they taste quite delicious.

SOUR CREAM SALAD

1 very large fresh cucumber	2 tblsp. wine vinegar
1 breakfast cup sour cream	1 tblsp. crushed dill seeds or fresh dill
1 endive	salt and black pepper

Do not peel cucumber, but cut it into rather thin slices. Season with pepper and add the sour cream and vinegar, mixing well. Chill and add the dill, then serve on a bed of endive which has been sprinkled with salt. Chill again before serving.

TOMATO SALAD

1 lb. firm tomatoes	fresh dill or dill seeds
½ cup minced onions or shallots	white vinegar to taste
½ cup corn oil	sweet basil leaves
salt and black pepper	

Thickly slice the tomatoes and mix with the minced onion, dill and sweet basil. Toss in the oil until well coated, then toss in the vinegar, about 2 tablespoonfuls. Season with salt and black pepper, toss again and chill slightly before serving.

The above salad is especially good when served with sour cream into which you have stirred plenty of real Hungarian paprika.

NO-COOK CHOCOLATE CAKES

No matter how much one enjoys cooking, the occasional no-cook recipe can brighten up a flagging housewife like magic. These are little petit fours and they will earn you compliments without really trying.

½ lb. chocolate buds	2 cups cornflakes or toasted breadcrumbs
½ cup seeded raisins	2 tblsp. hot water

Assemble a double boiler and have a little water simmering in the bottom half. Grate the chocolate into the top half and stir until melted. (Plain chocolate buds melt quickly with no grating.) Stir in the hot water, then the flakes or breadcrumbs, and keep stirring all the time. Finally add the fruit and mix well. Take out small spoonfuls of the mixture, shape into balls and set aside to cool before placing them before your admiring family or guests.

Russia

Cottage cheese being very popular in the U.S.S.R. there are many fine recipes using this and other Russian soft cheeses. The Russian version of cottage cheese is often called **Smetana** and can easily be obtained in delicatessens all over the world.

FRIED CHEESE CAKES

¾ lb. cottage cheese	paprika
½ breakfast cup plain flour	a little water
1 tblsp. sugar	butter as required
1 large egg	salt and black pepper

Scrape and thinly slice the carrots and cook in butter, very slowly with a well fitting lid on the pan, until tender. When ready, mash them well with the cottage cheese adding the flour, beaten egg, sugar and seasoning. Mix well, then with floured hands roll the mixture into flat cakes and fry in plenty of butter until golden on both sides.

CHEESE PUDDING WITH NUTS

1 lb. cottage cheese	6 small eggs
4 heaped tblsp. sugar	3½ tblsp. butter
4 oz. mixed dried fruit	1 tsp. grated lemon peel
2 oz. chopped mixed nuts	1 teacup breadcrumbs
a touch of salt	

If the dried fruit is large, such as figs or dates or prunes, then chop it up small before using. Mix together the nuts, sugar, well mashed cheese, melted butter, egg yolks and the lemon peel and beat really well with a wooden spoon. Add the chopped fruit, breadcrumbs and stiffly beaten egg whites. Add a touch of salt and beat well once more. Butter a pudding basin and put in the mixture. Cover and steam for 1 hour with water reaching half-way up the side of the basin. You can tell if this pudding is quite ready because it will leave the sides of the basin and will have risen slightly if you have beaten it really well. Serve at once with sour cream, or just as it is.

BORSHCH

This is the famous beetroot soup and there are many different ways of making it, two of which you will find in the chapter on Jewish cooking. The following is a typical Russian method of making Borshch.

1 lb. baby beetroots, uncooked	1 large onion
¼ lb. ripe tomatoes	1 bay leaf
4 potatoes	vegetable water as required
2 small carrots	sour cream as required
2 stalks celery	salt and black pepper

Peel and slice the beetroots thinly and cook in boiling vegetable water, or plain water, for 15 minutes. Peel and slice the potatoes, slice the celery, the onion and the carrots and add them to the beetroots, pouring on more boiling vegetable water. Cook for a further 15 minutes, then add the bay leaf, tomatoes and seasoning. Cook until the vegetables are tender and serve hot with a spoonful of sour cream in each plate.

MUSHROOM AND POTATO SOUP

1 lb. potatoes	1 bay leaf
½ lb. mushrooms	chopped chives to garnish
1 large Spanish onion	butter as required
1 large carrot	sour cream as required
salt and black pepper	

Slice the mushrooms and sauté them in butter until tender, add the thinly sliced onion and brown it. Add the peeled and thinly sliced potato and bay leaf and continue cooking in butter, adding more butter when necessary. Peel and cut the carrot into matchsticks and add it to the vegetables, at the same time adding a ½ pint of boiling vegetable stock to the pan. Cook until the vegetables are tender, season to your taste and serve with a heaped spoonful of sour cream in each plate.

UKRAINIAN CAULIFLOWER SOUP

½ lb. cauliflower sprigs	½ cup thin cream
½ lb. potatoes	½ cup milk
2 tblsp. butter	toasted rye bread
salt and black pepper	

Cook the cauliflower sprigs and the peeled and diced potatoes until tender, in a very little salted water. Pass through a sieve, return to the pan and add the heated milk, the cream and seasoning. Put a slice of toasted rye bread in each plate, pour on the soup and add a knob of butter to each plate.

GEORGIAN FRUIT SOUP

½ lb. dried mixed fruit	1 oz. potato flour
2 tblsp. honey	3 oz. boiled rice
a touch of mace	

Any dried fruit can be used for this soup—raisins, sultanas, apricots, currants, prunes, dried apples or figs. Soak them for 2 hours in cold water, rinse well and then stew in water until tender. Add the honey and a touch of mace (or cinnamon if you prefer it), and simmer for a further 5 minutes. Mix the flour with a little water and add it to the soup. Bring to the boil once more, add the rice and serve. If you like you may add, to good effect, 1 tablespoonful of fresh lemon juice.

POTATO AND ONION CASSEROLE (ZAPEKANKA)

1 lb. potatoes	butter as required
2 oz. chopped nuts	sour cream as required
2 medium-sized onions, fried	paprika
2 eggs	breadcrumbs
1 cup milk	salt and black pepper

Peel, dice and cook the potatoes until tender. Mash with plenty of butter, then add the hot milk and whip until creamy. Add seasoning. Grease a casserole, put a layer of the potato purée in the bottom, add a layer of fried onions, then chopped nuts, and rest of potatoes. Pour over about half a cup of sour cream, sprinkle with seasonings, add layer of buttered breadcrumbs and bake in a hot oven until browned—about 20 minutes.

MUSHROOM BAKE

1 lb. mushrooms	1 bay leaf
1 lb. potatoes	butter as required
2 large Spanish onions, fried	paprika
1 teacup sour cream	salt and black pepper

Slice the mushrooms and sauté the butter until tender. Meanwhile thinly slice the potatoes and sauté them until tender. Combine the two and add all other ingredients and seasonings, cover with *just* enough water and simmer for 30 minutes. Sprinkle with paprika and serve at once.

FRIED POTATO CAKES WITH SAUCE

1½ lb. potatoes	butter as required
¼ lb. mushrooms	breadcrumbs as required
½ pint white sauce	parsley
2 eggs	salt and black pepper

Slice the mushrooms and sauté in plenty of butter until tender. Season and combine with the white sauce. Keep the sauce hot and boil the potatoes in their jackets until tender. When cool enough to handle, peel and mash them with butter and the beaten eggs. Season and make into flat cakes about 4 inches in diameter and ½ an inch thick. Coat with breadcrumbs and fry in hot butter until golden on both sides. Serve at once with the sauce poured over them. Garnish with parsley.

VEGETABLE CASSEROLE

2 lb. mixed fresh vegetables (onions, mushrooms, cabbage, potatoes, turnips, carrots)	2 cups vegetable water
¼ lb. ripe tomatoes	2 dried pimentos
1 tblsp. flour	2 cloves
1 bay leaf	butter as required
	salt and black pepper

Prepare your vegetables and either dice or slice them according to which is appropriate, and sauté them in plenty of butter in a heavy pan with a close fitting lid. When tender pour a little of the liquid from the vegetables into a cup, allow to cool a little and mix with the flour, which has been cooked in butter for 2 minutes. Stir well and add to the cooked vegetables, then add the sliced tomatoes, bay leaf, pimentos, cloves, seasoning and the vegetable water. Cover and simmer very slowly for a further 20 minutes. Serve hot.

MIXED NUTS AND BEANS

4 oz. chopped mixed nuts	½ cup cooked butter beans
2 tblsp. cooked soya beans	½ cup cooked haricot beans
1 large Spanish onion	½ cup sour cream
butter as required	a touch of sugar
salt and black pepper	

Peel and slice the onion and sauté in butter until golden. Add the beans and the nuts, stir in the cream and season well, adding a touch of sugar. Serve either as it is or on plain boiled noodles.

BUTTON MUSHROOMS IN SOUR CREAM

This is one of the most delectable ways of cooking mushrooms.

2 lb. button mushrooms	butter as required
2 tblsp. grated cheese	parsley sprigs
2 tblsp. flour	plain boiled rice
1 large cup sour cream	salt and black pepper

Slice the mushrooms in half and sauté them in plenty of butter until tender. Add the flour and blend well. Stir in the sour cream and heat to boiling. Stir in the grated cheese and seasoning, and simmer until the cheese is just melting. Serve on plain boiled rice.

SOLYANKA

1½ lb. mushrooms	2 tsp. brown sugar
1 lb. white cabbage	butter as required
¼ lb. tomatoes	sweet basil leaves
1 large onion, fried	breadcrumbs
1 bay leaf	salt and black pepper

Shred the cabbage and sauté in butter until tender. Slice the mushrooms and sauté in butter likewise. Butter a casserole and put a layer of the cabbage in the bottom, sprinkle with a little sugar and add a layer of fried onion. Lay the mushrooms on the onion, then add the sliced tomatoes, sprinkle with sweet basil leaves and grated black pepper and salt. Top with the rest of the cabbage and sprinkle with breadcrumbs. Dot with at least 3 ounces of butter and bake until golden.

MUSHROOM SPREAD

1 lb. mushrooms	rye bread, toasted
1 large Spanish onion	butter as required
salt and black pepper	

Slice the mushrooms and the onions and sauté together in butter until quite tender. Mash well with a fork, season to taste and spread on hot buttered rye toast.

SAUERKRAUT WITH CREAM AND MUSHROOMS

½ lb. sauerkraut, drained	1 teacup sour cream
¼ lb. mushrooms	butter as required
salt and black pepper	

Slice the mushrooms and sauté in butter until tender. Add the sauerkraut and cook for 55 minutes over a gentle heat with the lid on the pan. When tender add the cream, season and serve hot.

RUSSIAN SALAD

4 hard-boiled eggs, chopped	4 tblsp. salad oil
3 pickled gherkins, chopped	1 tblsp. wine vinegar
2 cups cold potatoes, diced	2 oz. black olives, stoned
1 large beetroot, cooked and diced	¼ lb. chopped mixed nuts
¼ cup sour cream	salt and black pepper

Combine all ingredients and season well. Chill before serving and hand dark rye bread separately.

PASHKA

This traditional Russian dish is eaten at Easter time. I was lucky enough to be in Russia at the appropriate time, otherwise I would never have tasted it. It is very easy to make and is a matter of simple assembly.

1 cup each of the following ingredients: double cream cheese, sour cream, chopped mixed candied peel, sultanas and currants mixed, confectioner's sugar, softened and unsalted margarine or butter, chopped mixed nuts and 2 tablespoonfuls of chopped dates. Mix well together and press into a rinsed flat tin so that the pashka is about 1 inch thick. Place in the fridge overnight and serve with plaver (plain sponge cake) or plain biscuits.

POPPY SEED TOFFEE

For this recipe you must have poppy seeds. I suggest you try a delicacies shop, and failing that try any Jewish shop. It isn't impossible to get them but you might have to wait until the right season.

¾ cup poppy seeds	3 tblsp. chopped mixed nuts
½ breakfast cup dark molasses	¼ tsp. unsalted butter

Heat the molasses, add the poppy seeds, butter and nuts and mix with a wooden spoon. Cook over a very gentle heat and stir frequently. Turn the toffee out of the pan on to a flat wet surface, smooth it flat with a moistened rolling pin until it is about as thick as your little finger. Cut it into shapes, small enough to pop into your mouth.

Scandinavia

NORWAY

There are two distinct kinds of Norwegian cheeses, those made from curds and those made from whey. Of the former one of the most pleasant is the national soft cheese, named **Pultost**. It is made of sour, skimmed milk, with sometimes buttermilk added. Caraway seeds, and sometimes very heavy cream are added to the Pultost which is primrose yellow in colour but which gradually darkens with age. It keeps well and is useful for cooking.

Gammelost is also made from sour skimmed milk and is quite unusually veined in shades of blue, green and brown. An uncommon looking cheese, it is also sometimes given a most unusual flavour with a touch of juniper extract.

Nokkelost is a cheese similar to the well known Dutch Leyden which is a spicy, salty, rather hard cheese whose flavour is enriched with cloves and cummin seeds.

The cheeses made from whey are all called **Myost** cheeses. The texture varies from the semi-hard to the consistency of paste, and in flavour it can be anything from pungent to slightly sweet.

Jarlsberg cheese is comparatively new to me. In fact I tasted it for the first time only a few months ago when it first became available at my local supermarket. Liking the taste and texture I wrote to the importers and received the following information. It has been made in Norway for some time but only recently was made in sufficient quantities to warrant export. A hard pressed, cow's milk cheese, it is cooked to produce its characteristic smooth, close textured paste.

In appearance, texture and flavour I found it similar to Swiss Gruyère but it is very much cheaper to buy. It has the familiar round holes or eyes of the Gruyère but the paste is rather softer, and the rind also rather less hard than that of the Gruyère.

The importers tell me that Jarlsberg is of the same family as Swiss Emmenthal (often called Gruyère in other countries) but is not intended to be a copy of it. It is a younger cheese than Emmenthal and therefore has not quite the strength of flavour. However, I found it delightful as a table cheese, and also produced a very creditable fondue from it. If you cannot obtain it at your local grocers, it is worth inquiring about it.

DENMARK

There are two types of Danish cheese which stand out above all others in popularity. Of these perhaps the two best are the golden **Samsoe** and the well known **Danish Blue**.

146

The former is an indispensable experience in cheese eating. When young it has a nutty flavour with a succulent texture and bouquet. In appearance it has rather large holes like Gruyère, and in taste it is buttery and rich and sweet. When left to mature Samsoe is even more worthy of praise for it gains in richness and pungency and altogether is a cheese for the discerning.

Danish Blue is of two kinds, the Danblu and the Mycella. The former is a chalk white cheese with veining of green and blue. It has a very creamy consistency and a rich look about it but is razor-sharp in flavour. Indeed it must be eaten a little at a time or it can make the skin inside the mouth distinctly uncomfortable. It is best to eat Danish Blue sparingly when the full enjoyment may be obtained from its unique quality. It goes particularly well with dark rye bread or digestive biscuits.

Mycella has a veining which is rather more green than blue and the cheese itself is a creamy yellow instead of the chalky white of Danblu. In flavour it is not nearly so fierce and also it has a more aromatic bouquet.

SWEDEN

The most popular of the Swedish cheeses is the delightfully flavoured **Herrgard**. Rather like the Swiss Emmenthal in flavour and appearance when made from whole cow's milk, it is quite a hard cheese, equally useful both as a table cheese and as a cooking cheese. A very passable Fondue can be made with a Swedish Herrgard. There is also a Herrgard made from partly skimmed milk and this tastes similar to the Dutch Gouda. This makes a good toasting cheese, especially when a little mustard is added.

A really pungent cheese from Sweden is the **Vasterbotton**. Strongly flavoured, hard in texture, with a peculiarly mature flavour and bouquet, this is a connoisseur's cheese.

The last cheese from Scandinavia I want to mention is the aromatic and spicy flavoured **Vastgota**. Made of cow's milk, it is a rather hard textured cheese and makes a wonderful cooker as well as a first-class table cheese.

CREAM CHEESE OMELETTE

6 eggs	½ cup thick cream
4 oz. double cream cheese	butter as required
4 tblsp. chopped chives	a dash of Worcester sauce
¼ lb. fried tomatoes	sweet basil
salt and black pepper	

Beat together the cheese and the cream until quite smooth and well blended. Add the chives, Worcester sauce, salt and black pepper. Separate the eggs and beat the yolks, and mix these into the cheese and cream. Whip the whites until they stand up in peaks, and fold into the mixture. Heat plenty of butter in a frying pan and pour in the mixture, then cook over a gentle heat until set on the bottom. Finish off under the grill or broiler and brown on top. Serve the omelette opened out flat and spread with fried tomatoes sprinkled with salt and sweet basil.

SWEDISH MUESLI

4 tblsp. rolled oats	2 bananas
4 tblsp. lemon juice	2 large eating apples
¼ lb. chopped nuts	2 oz. brown sugar

1 small bottle yoghourt

Peel, core and chop the apples. Peel and slice the bananas which should be ripe but not brown. Mix with all the other ingredients and serve as a first-class nourishing breakfast. Some people like to soak the rolled oats overnight before adding to the other ingredients, but personally I prefer not to as I think they make a more interesting textured muesli the way they are.

BRUSSELS SPROUTS SOUP

1¾ lb. sprouts	2½ pints vegetable water
2 Spanish onions	1 tsp. butter
1 oz. butter	½ tsp. savoury

salt and black pepper

Wash and prepare sprouts, peel and chop the onions and sprouts together and boil in the stock until quite tender. Season with salt and black pepper and the savoury. Rub through a fine sieve. Make a roux with the flour and butter and cook for 2 minutes. Gradually add the hot soup stirring well, cook for a further 3 minutes and serve with croutons.

NORWEGIAN GRAPEFRUIT

Take a large grapefruit and cut it in half. Spread it with a mixture of thick honey and powdered ginger. Bake in a hot oven for 5 minutes.

SWEDISH CABBAGE SOUP

2 lb. firm cabbage	1 tblsp. brown sugar
3½ pints vegetable water	caraway seeds
3 oz. butter	salt and black pepper

Dissolve the sugar in the butter, add the finely shredded cabbage and cook for 50 minutes, stirring from time to time but otherwise keeping the lid on tightly. Pour over the boiling vegetable water, season with salt and black pepper and stir in about a teaspoonful of caraway seeds if liked.

DANISH FRUIT AND VEGETABLE SALAD

2 carrots	½ tin mandarin oranges, drained
2 large sweet unpeeled apples	½ bottle yoghourt
2 stalks celery	½ small tin chopped pineapple
watercress or lettuce	½ tsp. grated orange peel

salt and black pepper

Prepare and slice or dice all vegetables, and fruit where appropriate. Mix with the yoghourt and orange peel, season and serve on a bed of watercress or lettuce, whichever is in season.

NORWEGIAN PANCAKES

1 cup fresh milk	5 small eggs
¼ cup flour	4 tblsp. powdered milk
grated sharp cheese	2 tblsp. butter
butter for frying	salt to taste

Sift the powdered milk and salt and flour together and then beat in the fresh milk and the beaten eggs. Leave aside for 30 minutes before cooking. Melt a little butter in a frying pan and pour in a little of the batter at a time to make thin pancakes. Keep hot in the oven until all the mixture is used up. Heap on to a hot serving dish. Sprinkle with grated cheese before serving.

SWEDISH BUTTERMILK SOUP

2¾ pints buttermilk	2 cups blackberries
2½ oz. flour	2 egg yolks
honey as required	2 tblsp. confectioner's sugar
	thick cream

Mix together the flour and a ½ pint of the buttermilk and blend well. Boil the rest of the milk, then pour the hot liquid into the cold, stirring all the time. Stew the blackberries in a little water and sweeten with whichever honey you like. I find that inexpensive clover honey is very suitable, in fact I find it very useful and economical for cooking and always have a jar of it in the house. Simmer the buttermilk mixture for a few minutes, then add the egg yolks beaten with the sugar with the pan off the heat. Stir in the stewed blackberries, chill well before serving. Add a heaped spoonful of thick cream to each plate just before serving.

DANISH ALE SOUP

1 pint mild ale	1 tblsp. ground rice
1 pint milk	1 tsp. grated lemon rind
sugar as required	rye toast as required
	a touch of salt

Mix the ground rice with a little milk and then add the rest of the milk. Put into a saucepan and heat to boiling point, gradually stirring in the ale and the lemon rind. Add sugar and salt to taste and serve with a thick slice of brown rye toast in the bottom of each plate.

NORWEGIAN TOAST

4 large eggs	butter as required
2 cups milk	thick slices rye bread
2 tblsp. tomato paste	salt and black pepper

Beat the milk, salt, and eggs together and stir in the tomato purée which has been diluted in a little water. Beat again, then add a touch of freshly grated black pepper. Heat plenty of butter in a heavy frying pan, dip your thick slices of bread in the egg mixture, coating both sides well, and fry in the hot butter until golden brown. An excellent breakfast or supper dish which tastes more impressive than these simple instructions would suggest.

CHESTNUT SUPPER DISH

1 lb. roasted chestnuts	butter as required
1 lb. sprouts	breadcrumbs
1 cup grated sharp cheese	salt and black pepper

Prepare the sprouts and cook in salted butter until tender but not very soft. You can cut each sprout in half if you wish; they will cook more quickly this way and it won't spoil the look of the finished dish. Grease an oven-to-table dish and put a layer of the buttery sprouts in the bottom. Add a layer of the peeled and chopped roasted chestnuts, then another layer of sprouts, and so on until all is used up. Top with a layer of breadcrumbs, sprinkle with salt and black pepper, then add the grated cheese, and finally another layer of breadcrumbs. Dot with butter and bake in a hot oven for 15 minutes until golden on top.

Variation:
I have used broccoli in this recipe with complete success. Cook it in butter until tender and proceed as above.

CUCUMBER SALAD WITH DILL

Fresh dill is best for this salad but if you cannot get it, try using crushed dill seeds. You will find a small seed grinder a good investment for it will release the fragrant oils from seeds and culinary herbs.

1 large cucumber	oil
lettuce or endive	dill
tarragon vinegar	salt as required and black pepper

Do not peel your cucumber, but cut it into fairly thin slices. Sprinkle with salt and leave aside for an hour or so, then drain. Toss in corn or sunflower seed oil, then in vinegar to your taste, and sprinkle with salt and freshly grated black pepper and dill, whether fresh or seeds. Chill well and serve on a bed of lettuce or endive, according to season.

SWEDISH BAKED LEEKS

Clean and cut some leeks into convenient lengths and parboil them in a little salted water for 5 minutes. Grease a casserole and lay the leeks in it. Sprinkle with Vastgota or other sharp cheese, grated finely, then top with breadcrumbs. Dot with plenty of butter and brown in a medium oven.

DANISH BLUE SALAD

3 oz. Danish Blue cheese	tarragon vinegar as required
2 green or red peppers	oil as required
1 medium-sized onion, minced	½ cup thick cream
lettuce or endive	

Dice the cheese and toss it in the cream until well coated. Seed and thinly slice the peppers and mix with the onion, then toss in salad oil and then in a little vinegar. Line a salad bowl with lettuce or endive, pile up the cheese in the centre and surround with the peppers and onions.

SCANDINAVIAN BREAKFAST DISH

I ate several versions of this wholesome porridge-type dish while I was in Norway but I understand that it is widely eaten both in Denmark and in Sweden.

1 pkt. Danish rye slices or pumpernickel	1 tsp. grated lemon peel
1 small wholemeal or rye loaf	sugar as required (brown is best)
2 pints brown ale	thick cream as required
2 egg yolks	powdered cinnamon to taste
salt to taste	

Soak the pumpernickel or Danish rye slices and the bread in cold water overnight. I find it best to thinly slice the bread before soaking. Bring everything to the boil, just as it is, then turn down the heat and cook, stirring all the time, until a thick paste results. Add the warmed ale and the lemon peel and flavour to your taste with brown sugar, salt and powdered cinnamon. Bring to boiling point again, still stirring, and just before serving, blend in the beaten egg yolks. Serve with a spoonful of thick cream in each plate.

SWEDISH DUNKS AND DIPS

These are party ideas, and very simple too. All you need is a big bowl of some thick savoury sauce, a jar of toothpicks and some tasty bits to spear with the toothpicks and dip in the dunk, or dunk in the dip.

1. Cream cheese whipped with salad cream, and sprinkled with paprika. Thin with whipped cream to required consistency. Dip large potato crisps into this dunk.
2. Curd cheese with chopped nuts, gherkins and olives. Season with paprika and salt, and thin slightly with thick cream. Spear small cauliflower sprigs (uncooked) to dunk in this one.
3. A plain dunk with an elaborate dip—just mayonnaise and thick cream beaten together and sprinkled with freshly grated black pepper. For the dips take some dates and stone them, and where the stone was put a chunk of preserved ginger. Spear with toothpicks.

NORWEGIAN MACARONI SALAD WITH EGGS

4 hard-boiled eggs	¼ lb. firm tomatoes
2 tblsp. chopped olives	lettuce or endive
1 large apple	tarragon vinegar
1 cup cooked macaroni	marjoram
½ cup diced beetroot	oil as required
salt and black pepper	

Cut up the macaroni into ½-inch pieces. Dice the tomatoes, apple and beetroot and mix with the chopped eggs, olives and seasonings. Toss in plenty of corn oil until everything is well coated, then toss again in tarragon vinegar to your taste. Chill and serve on a bed of lettuce or endive.

KALE IN SOUR CREAM

Kale, at least the only variety I am able to buy, is rather a tough vegetable. It has dark green curly leaves of a leathery texture, and stalks as thick and tough as young saplings. Nevertheless it can, with careful cooking, be made not only palatable but very delicious, though it needs patience. I have tried kale a dozen different ways but have never discovered a better way to cook it than this Danish one.

2 lb. bunch kale	butter as required
1 cup sour cream	a touch of sugar
1 large sweet Spanish onion	salt and black pepper

Take the kale leaves off the stems and chop the leaves or else shred them. Cook them in butter in a pan with a well fitting lid for at least 30 minutes (it may take longer). Season, then add the well fried onion and chop all together. Add a little sugar, brown preferably, and stir in the cream. Heat once again and serve.

RUTABAGAS

These are turnips with a fancy name and you can cook them any way you would cook turnips. This is the unusual Swedish way with them. Take small rutabagas, no bigger than billiard balls, and scrub them well. Brush with a little oil and bake in a hot oven until tender. Cut off a lid from each rutabaga, insert a good wedge of any well flavoured Scandinavian cheese, put the lid back on and serve hot.

WINTER EGGS

6 hard-boiled eggs	¾ pint milk
3 oz. flour	2 tblsp. grated sharp cheese
3 oz. butter	2 tsp. French mustard
salt and grated black pepper	

Butter a shallow oven-to-table dish or casserole lid and arrange the eggs, which have been sliced lengthways, in it. Sprinkle with the grated cheese and put into a warm oven until the cheese melts. Meanwhile make the sauce as follows. Cook the flour in the butter for 3 minutes, then gradually add the hot milk, stirring with a wooden spoon. Stir in the mustard and season to your taste. Add even more mustard if you like a really hot sauce for a cold winter's night. Cook the sauce over a gentle heat and stir until thickened. Pour over the eggs and cheese and serve hot.

ASPARAGUS OMELETTE

5 eggs	1 cup thick white sauce
1 large tin asparagus tips	1 cup milk
2 tblsp. grated cheese	1 cup cream
salt and black pepper	

Beat the eggs, add the milk and cream and season. Butter an oven dish and pour in the egg mixture. Bake for 15 minutes. Meanwhile stir the drained asparagus tips into the white sauce, season to your taste and when the omelette is baked, pour over the asparagus mixture. Top with grated cheese and serve at once.

DANISH POTATO BALLS

2 teacups mashed potatoes	butter as required
2 teacups flour	oil for frying
1 large onion, fried	salt and pepper

Mash the potatoes with plenty of butter and a touch of milk, and beat until creamy. Stir in the fried onion, together with any butter left in the pan, and season to taste. Add enough flour to make a fairly stiff dough, shape into balls and fry in deep hot oil until golden.

MUSHROOM AND ONION SOUP

A good thick mug of this soup is a feast, especially if someone hands you one while you are on a boat sailing round Norway's complicated, and often chilly, coast.

¼ lb. mushrooms	butter as required
1 large onion	milk as required
2 tblsp. corn meal	a little sugar
salt and pepper	

Slice the mushrooms and peel and thinly slice the onions. Sauté in plenty of butter until quite tender and the onions are turning golden. Stir in the cornmeal (the yellow cornmeal is the one to use), then gradually add sufficient milk to make about ¾ a pint altogether. Cook very gently, stirring frequently, for about 20 minutes, then season with a teaspoonful of sugar and salt and pepper to your taste. Put the sugar in *first*, then balance it up with the salt and pepper. Just before serving add a knob of butter to each serving.

I have often been asked what waffles are and how to make them. Well, you need a waffle iron to start with but after that it is all very easy.

SWEDISH WAFFLES

8 oz. flour	3 tblsp. sugar
4 eggs	1 pint sour cream or yoghourt
	honey as required

Sift flour with the sugar, add the well beaten eggs, then the cream or yoghourt. Leave aside for at least 1 hour, then bake in a waffle iron. Serve with melted honey.

South America

ARGENTINA

One of the most unusual of all cheeses is the **Reggiano** cheese from Argentina. It is a black rinded cheese, pale buttercup yellow inside, and with a rather grainy texture. Mild in flavour and bouquet it makes a very good cooking cheese and can be grated very easily for sprinkling on soups and vegetables.

Another colourful cheese, this time with an olive green rind, is the **Sardo** cheese. This is a very tasty cheese, with a distinct bite to its flavour and a bouquet to match. It is made from full cream cow's milk.

Canestrato is a favourite of mine, as unusual in colouring in its own way as the two previously mentioned. It is white rinded but not, as you might expect, white inside but very decidedly yellow. When it is in the house you know about it for it has a pungent bouquet. This is not a cooking cheese but goes with dark black bread as strawberries go with cream.

CUBA

A whole cow's milk cheese which I enjoy is the Cuban **Pantagras**. A close textured hard cheese, it looks and tastes like the Dutch Edam with the Edam's pillar-box red outer coat, but without, however, the Edam's saltiness. It is a good toaster, and can be grated when old.

VENEZUELA

A good all-purpose cheese from this country is the **Llanero**. A very dry cheese, and a very hard one, it has the grating qualities of a first-class Parmesan. Delightful and rare in taste, it is a joy to cook with and grated on to toast and popped under the grill it makes a tasty meal.

De Mano is a very delicious cheese. Though many people would question my reverence for the sublime Gorgonzola and the French Brie, I doubt if they would not come back for more if they tasted Venezuelan de Mano cheese. I was told, when visiting the country, that de Mano gets its delicate and distinct flavour from being wrapped in banana leaves.

ARGENTINE VEGETABLE SOUP

1 lb. ripe tomatoes	2 pints vegetable water
1 large Spanish onion	2 oz. grated sharp cheese
1 cup cooked vermicelli	2 tblsp. chopped parsley
a touch of chilli powder	3 tblsp. butter
salt and black pepper	

Peel and chop the onion finely and fry in the butter with the parsley for a few minutes, until turning golden. Add sliced tomatoes and cook for a further 5 or 6 minutes, stirring frequently. Pour on the vegetable water, bring to the boil and simmer for 20 minutes. Season with salt and black pepper and a touch of chilli powder. The latter is very fiery and you can leave it out if you prefer to. Add the cooked vermicelli and heat to boiling point once more. Just before serving, sprinkle with the grated cheese.

COLOMBIAN SQUASH SOUP

The word squash doesn't mean to be sat on, it comes from an Indian word meaning eaten uncooked. Perhaps the Indians preferred their squash uncooked but most of us enjoy it in soups or chowders and stews. The following unusual soup is very easy to prepare and also very economical when squash is in season.

2 lb. squash	1 pint milk
2 egg yolks	½ pint sour cream
2 tblsp. butter	additional butter if required
2 tblsp. flour	salt and black pepper

Peel and slice the squash and sauté in the butter until tender. Melt 2 tablespoonfuls of butter and cook the flour in it for 2 minutes. Gradually add the heated milk stirring all the time. Mash the squash well with a fork and add it to the soup. Heat the sour cream and stir that in, then season well. Take the pan off the heat and stir in the beaten egg yolks. Serve at once with croutons or toasted dark bread.

SQUASH BAKE

2 lb. squash	1 cup grated cheese
2 tsp. chopped parsley	1 cup breadcrumbs
butter as required	salt and black pepper

Peel and slice the squash and sauté in butter until tender. Grease a casserole or oven-to-table dish and lay in the slices of squash. Remember to discard the seeds. Cover with the cheese, then the chopped parsley, and then the breadcrumbs. Dot very thickly with butter and bake until golden.

COSTA RICAN TOMATO SOUP

I think that this is one of the most unusual tomato soups ever invented. There is nothing unusual about the ingredients, of which there are comparatively few, it is the ingenious way they are combined.

6 breakfast cups tomato juice	1 small green pepper, chopped
4 tblsp. shredded carrot	1 cup thick mayonnaise
4 tblsp. finely chopped celery	½ cup thick cream
4 tblsp. chopped chives or spring onions	½ tsp. brown sugar
1 large sweet Spanish onion	½ tsp. sweet basil leaves

salt and black pepper

Combine all ingredients, except the mayonnaise and cream, and season. Simmer very gently with the lid on the pan for 15 minutes. Blend a little of the hot soup with the mayonnaise and then stir into the soup. Serve with a heaped spoonful of thick cream in each plate. Garnish with chopped chives or spring onions.

SALVADOR LETTUCE SALAD

For this salad one must have a very hard head of lettuce, a lettuce that is as tightly packed as a cabbage. Simply wash the lettuce, or 2 lettuces according to the number of servings required, and then put it in the fridge for 2 hours, wrapped in a teacloth. Cut into wedge-shaped pieces and toss them in plenty of corn or olive oil. When well coated sprinkle with salt and black pepper and crushed dill seeds, and then toss again in a little tarragon vinegar. Serve on a bed of cooked and buttered sweet corn.

BRAZILIAN FIESTA

12 green or red peppers	½ pint white sauce
5 eggs	olive oil as required
2 cups soft cheese	sweet basil leaves
1 cup tomato purée	salt and black pepper

Cut a lid from each pepper and carefully remove the seeds and pith with a small spoon. Dust inside the peppers with salt and pepper, pack them with soft cheese, and place a knob of butter on top of the cheese. Replace lid on each pepper (this is not eaten but it adds to the appearance of the dish). Now beat the egg yolks separately until creamy and whip up the whites until they stand up in peaks. Combine yolks and whites, then coat the peppers with the seasoned eggs and drop into deep hot oil and fry until brown. The peppers will still be crisp by the time they are the right shade of brown, and this way they are at their best. Serve with the white sauce into which you have stirred the tomato purée and sprinkled a teaspoonful of sweet basil leaves. Plain boiled rice can be passed around separately.

AVOCADO SALAD

This is not a luxury dish in South America because avocados are cheap there. However in the right season, in other countries, they can be bought reasonably cheaply. This method makes them go a long way.

3 avocados (large and ripe)	2 oz. chopped mixed nuts
1 head endive or lettuce	½ teacup mayonnaise
1 hard-boiled egg	salt and black pepper

Halve the avocados and take out the stone. Arrange the endive or lettuce on a serving plate and reserve a few leaves to mix, shredded, with the chopped nuts and mayonnaise. Season lightly, then pile the mixture into the avocados. Serve on the bed of lettuce or endive and garnish with the sliced egg. More than 1 egg can be used if you wish. These quantities will serve 6 people.

EMPANADAS

These are delicious fried turnovers, and are useful in three ways—for a hot and filling meal, for a cold packed lunch or picnic, and for using up tasty left-overs.

½ lb. rough puff pastry	1 large Spanish onion
¼ lb. sliced tomatoes	1 green pepper
½ cup sliced peaches	2 tblsp. chopped chives
6 oz. chopped nuts	2 tblsp. dry wine
butter as required	breadcrumbs
salt and black pepper	

Peel and chop the onion, seed and chop the pepper, and sauté in plenty of butter until tender. Add the sliced tomatoes and continue cooking until they begin to disintegrate. Add the chopped peaches and chives and stir well. Add the chopped nuts, then the wine and season to your taste. Add sufficient breadcrumbs to make a fairly stiff mixture and then roll out the rough puff pastry and cut into large rounds, about the size of a saucer. Place some of the filling on the pastry and fold over into half moon shapes. Press the edges well together and fry in deep hot fat until golden on both sides. This can be eaten hot or cold.

BOLIVIAN BAKED POTATOES

1½ cups diced cooked potatoes	1 cup sour cream
1½ tblsp. flour	watercress or mustard and cress
1½ tblsp. butter	butter as required
1 tblsp. chopped parsley	breadcrumbs
3 tblsp. grated sharp cheese	a touch of brown sugar
salt and black pepper	

Make a roux with the butter and flour and cook for 2 minutes. Gradually add the sour cream and seasoning. Toss together the potatoes, parsley, cheese and a little more seasoning, and place this mixture in a well buttered oven-to-table dish. Pour the cream mixture over the potatoes and sprinkle liberally with breadcrumbs and a little more grated cheese. Bake in a moderate oven until golden on top. Serve garnished with watercress or mustard and cress.

MEXICAN KEBABS

4 slices stale dark bread	½ cup sour cream
1 or 2 egg yolks	flour as required
½ lb. sharp cheese	olive oil for deep frying
¼ lb. firm tomatoes	salt and black pepper

Cut up the cheese into small cubes, each side about 1 inch long. Cut up the bread in roughly the same sized pieces, and also the tomatoes. Skewer the cheese, tomato and bread pieces alternately until all is used up. Blend the beaten egg yolks with the cream, and season. Dip each kebab into this mixture, sprinkle generously with flour and fry in hot olive oil until pale golden brown. Drain well before serving.

COSTA RICAN GRAPE SALAD

½ lb. seedless grapes	1 head lettuce or endive
½ cup olive oil	1 clove garlic
2 sweet apples	lemon juice as required
2 egg yolks	salt and black pepper

Make the salad dressing first, so that you can leave it aside for a little while to marry the flavours. Mince the garlic and blend with the egg yolks. Gradually add the oil, a little at a time, beating well. Season with salt and black pepper and then gradually beat in the lemon juice, not more than 1 tablespoonful. Beat until creamy and then put the dressing in the fridge until you need it.

Wash the apples, quarter and core them, and chop coarsely. Mix immediately with a little lemon juice to stop them turning brown. Halve the grapes and mix them with the apples. Arrange your lettuce or endive leaves on your serving dish, pile the fruit in the centre and pour the dressing over.

BRAZILIAN SWEET POTATOES

This is a dish I make for guests when I want to serve something really different but haven't the time to spend hours in the kitchen. I always accompany these potato balls with a heaped platter of mixed vegetables cooked in butter, and smothered with grated sharp cheese.

2 lb. sweet potatoes	3 egg yolks
2 egg whites	cubed pineapple
2 tblsp. milk	flour
½ cup finely chopped mixed nuts	oil for frying
salt and black pepper	

Scrub the sweet potatoes, then cook in boiling salted water until quite tender. Peel and mash them with the beaten egg yolks, the milk and the seasoning. Let the mixture go quite cold before proceeding. Beat the egg whites until frothy and fairly stiff. When the potato mixture has cooled form into balls around cubes of pineapple. Make sure that there are no cracks, otherwise you will spoil the appearance of the dish. Roll the balls in flour and then refrigerate for 30 minutes. Roll them in the beaten egg whites and then in the chopped nuts and fry in deep hot oil until golden. Serve hot with mixed vegetables or any kind of sauce you wish.

FRIED ONIONS AND RICE

4 large Spanish onions	½ cup milk
2 eggs	plain boiled rice
1 cup flour	butter as required
salt and black pepper	

Cook the rice in the usual way and keep hot. Peel and thinly slice one of the onions and cook in butter until well browned. Chop it, together with any butter left in the pan and season well. Mix with the rice. Meanwhile peel the other 3 onions and slice them fairly thickly. Separate into rings and pour over the milk, mixing well. Now sift the flour and season with salt and black pepper. Mix with the milk which you poured over the onion rings and add the beaten eggs together with 2 tablespoonfuls of the melted butter. Beat well, then dip the onion rings in the batter and fry until a deep golden brown. Serve hot on a bed of onions and rice mixed. If you are an onionophile as I am, you will appreciate the succulence and simplicity of this dish.

BRAZIL CASSEROLE

2 cups chopped Brazil nuts	3 tblsp. flour
2 cups milk	½ tsp. brown sugar
½ lb. cooked noodles	butter as required
¼ lb. olives	breadcrumbs
a dash of chilli or tabasco sauce	salt and black pepper

Make a sauce by cooking the flour in 3 or 4 tablespoonsful of butter for 3 minutes. Gradually add the heated milk and cook until thick and creamy. Season with salt, black pepper, a dash of sauce, and the sugar. Keep warm. Butter an oven-to-table dish and put in a layer of the cooked noodles. Add a few dots of butter, then add a layer of the Brazil nuts, then one of chopped olives. Repeat the layers until all is used up, topping with a layer of noodles. Pour the sauce over the noodles and sprinkle thickly with breadcrumbs. Scatter a few sliced Brazils over the breadcrumbs if you have any left and dot liberally with butter. Bake for 30 minutes in a moderate oven.

CUBAN NUTS AND BEANS

1 cup chopped mixed nuts	plain boiled rice
½ lb. string beans	butter as required
salt and black pepper	

Prepare the beans and cut into convenient pieces. I always cut them lengthways into 3 or 4 strips, then I cut them across 3 times and the result is a pile of matchsticks. Some cooks, though, do not slice them lengthways but simply string them and then cut them diagonally into 2 inch long pieces. Sauté the string beans in plenty of butter until just tender (there should be a slight bite to all cooked vegetables, they should never be sloppy). Season them well. While they are cooking, sauté the nuts in another pan in plenty of butter for about 6 minutes, then add the cooked beans and mix well together. Heat the serving dish, put in the boiled rice and stir in a few dots of butter. Pile beans and nuts on the top and serve at once.

TWENTY-MINUTE BANANA PIE

This sounds too good to be true as pies usually take time. You don't *have* to make this one in a great hurry, but you can if you must.

11 or 12 digestive biscuits	1 large cup thick cream
4 or 5 tblsp. melted butter	1 tblsp. brown sugar
4 bananas, ripe but not brown	2 tsp. rum or cognac
3 tblsp. icing sugar	½ cup desiccated coconut

Put the digestive, or other suitable biscuits, between layers of paper and crush with a rolling pin. Mix with the icing sugar and sufficient melted butter to make a firm mixture. Pack this into a well buttered pie dish, and pat it down flat. Put it in the fridge to become firm (about 12 to 15 minutes). Meanwhile peel and slice the bananas and beat the brown sugar into the thick cream. Mix with the banana slices and rum and pile on top of the biscuit mixture. Sprinkle with desiccated coconut and the pie is ready to serve.

VENEZUELA VEGETABLE PIE

1 lb. hot mashed potatoes	1 egg yolk
1 lb. small potatoes, new or diced old ones	2 tblsp. chopped chives
½ lb. freshly cooked peas	3 tblsp. butter
½ lb. shallots	mustard and cress or watercress
salt and black pepper	

Steam the potatoes until tender. Ten minutes before they are done add the peeled shallots. After 10 minutes the potatoes should be tender and the shallots still crisp. Melt plenty of butter in a heavy skillet and sauté the potatoes, shallots, and peas until golden. As the peas are pre-cooked, this should take only a few minutes. Now beat the chopped chives into the mashed potatoes and arrange them around the edge of your serving dish which should be heat-proof. Brush the potatoes with the egg yolk, using it all to make a heavy coating of egg. Heap the sauté vegetables in the centre and place under a medium grill until the potatoes are beginning to brown. Serve garnished with cress.

COLOMBIAN SPINACH BAKE

½ lb. spinach purée	butter as required
1 cup thick whipped cream	breadcrumbs
1 cup grated sharp cheese	chopped chives
salt and black pepper	

Mix the spinach purée with the cream and season well. You may use sour cream if you wish. Butter a shallow oven dish and put in the spinach mixture. Top with the grated cheese, then add a thick layer of breadcrumbs. Dot with butter and bake in a hot oven until golden, about 15 minutes. Serve hot, garnished with chopped chives.

EGG CASSEROLE WITH CHILLI

6 fried eggs	½ lb. mushrooms, sauté in butter
2 egg yolks, uncooked	½ lb. cooked rice
1 cup white sauce	½ cup thick cream
½ tsp. chilli powder	½ cup grated sharp cheese
salt and black pepper	

Mix together rice, cooked mushrooms, and season. Butter an oven-to-table dish and place the rice and mushrooms in it. Fry the eggs and place on top. Mix the egg yolks, beaten, the cream and the chilli into the white sauce and blend well. Pour over the eggs, top with the grated cheese and brown in a hot oven for 10 to 15 minutes.

CHEESE DUMPLINGS

This is another dish you can make very quickly though time taken over it is well spent.

6 eggs, separated	2½ tblsp. flour
1½ lb. curd cheese	2 tblsp. butter
melted butter as required	2 tsp. minced onion
salt and black pepper	

Cream the egg yolks and the slightly softened butter, then blend with the cheese. Add the flour and season well. Add the minced onion and fold in the stiffly beaten egg whites. Roll into balls with floured hands and drop them into boiling salted water. Simmer for 15 minutes, then take out with a perforated spoon and drain well. Serve with plenty of melted salty butter.

CHICORY SALAD

I am indebted to my friend, and fellow chicory enthusiast, Carmela Arriaz, for this recipe which I think is highly unusual.

½ lb. chicory	3 ripe pears
½ cup dried apricots, soaked	2 tblsp. tarragon vinegar
½ cup chopped mixed nuts	salad oil
½ cup currants and sultanas, soaked	a touch of marjoram
salt and black pepper	

Peel and dice the pears and mix with the dried fruit which has soaked for at least 6 hours. Cut the heads of chicory in half lengthways and then into pieces about 2 inches long. Mix with the pears, and also add the chopped nuts. Toss in plenty of salad oil (olive oil, corn oil or sunflower seed oil can be used), and then season with salt and black pepper and a little marjoram. Add the vinegar and toss again. Chill slightly before serving.

BRAISED CHICORY

Those who dislike the slightly bitter taste of chicory so beloved of chicory-philes, will find this way of preparing it more to their liking.

6 heads chicory	1 tsp. honey
2 oz. butter	milk as required
1 large sweet onion	salt and black pepper

Plunge the chicory heads into boiling salted water and leave for 5 minutes with the lid on the pan. Peel and slice the onions and brown in the butter. Transfer to an oven dish and add a touch of salt and pepper and a little sugar. Slice the chicory heads lengthways and lay them on the onions. Melt the honey in about a ½ teacupful of milk and mix before pouring over the chicory. Cook in a low oven, with the lid on, until the chicory is tender. Baste from time to time, and sprinkle with a little more seasoning before serving.

HONEY FRITTERS

This is a protein rich dessert and so economical that you can feast on these Honey Fritters for next to no money. The following quantities will be sufficient for at least 4 or 5 hungry people.

6 slices of wholewheat bread (stale)	1½ pints single cream
1 cup milk	2 tblsp. thick honey
½ cup thin honey	cinnamon as required
¼ tsp. mace	butter as required

Melt the thick honey in the milk and beat with the cream. Add the mace and about 1 teaspoonful of cinnamon. Leave aside while you cut the bread into fingers. Soak the bread in the cream mixture for 3 minutes. Drain and drop them into really hot butter and fry until golden on both sides. Heat the thin honey and pour it over the fritters. Serve at once.

Spain

Think of Spanish cheese and you think of **Manchego**. It has been made and enjoyed for literally centuries. A ewe's milk cheese, it is hard to describe once you get under the yellow rind. It can be any colour from chalky white to buttercup. It also comes with a plain smooth texture or with many little holes. But two other things, with the rind, are consistent: one is the texture which is hard, and the other is its flavour which is delightful.

Roncal cheese is a good grater made from full cream cow's milk. It is a salty cheese which has been smoked, yellow inside and a deep brown outside. It *tastes* smoked very decidedly and is pungent. Spain's famous soft cheese is the **Villalon**. Made of ewe's milk, it can be eaten fresh or used in cooking.

Spain has an answer to the sublime Roquefort and its name is **Cabrales**. This name covers a multitude of goat's milk cheeses which are veined with blue and have a very assertive bouquet.

SPANISH FRIED CHEESE

Spanish Roncal cheese is best for this recipe but any fairly hard and strong tasting cheese will do.

½ lb. cheese, sliced	toasted breadcrumbs as required
6 tblsp. milk	olive oil for frying
2 small eggs	salt and black pepper

Slice the cheese fairly thinly into convenient serving pieces. Beat the eggs and the milk together and season. Dip the cheese (using a fork) in the egg, then coat well with the toasted breadcrumbs. Drop into hot oil and brown on both sides. Serve at once, with dark bread.

GRANADA EGG SOUP

6 or 7 eggs	2½ pints water
6 or 7 slices dark bread cut into squares	2½ tblsp. olive oil
½ lb. tomatoes	1 small onion
3 large cloves garlic	1 small bayleaf
paprika	salt and black pepper

Peel and slice the onion and garlic and brown in the oil. Add the sliced tomatoes and the bay leaf and cook for a further 5 minutes. Add the water (or vegetable water if possible) and simmer for 15 to 20 minutes. Season with salt and black pepper and paprika. Place the slices of bread in an oven-proof tureen and break the eggs on to them very carefully. Pour the soup gently over the eggs and put the tureen in the oven until a crust forms on top of the soup. Serve at once.

CHEESE AND WATERCRESS SOUP

4 egg yolks	½ cup cream
4 large potatoes	½ cup grated cheese
2 bundles watercress	butter as required
2 pints vegetable water	salt and black pepper

Boil the potatoes in the vegetable water until soft, lift them out with a perforated spoon and mash them with butter, salt and pepper. Mix them with the chopped watercress and stir into the stock. Beat the egg yolks into the warm cream and stir into the stock. Bring to just below boiling point but do not boil or you will curdle the soup. Taste for seasoning, pour the soup into a hot tureen and sprinkle with the grated cheese.

ICED TOMATO SOUP

1 lb. ripe tomatoes	1 clove garlic
1 large Spanish onion	chopped parsley
2 tblsp. red wine	chopped green and black olives
1½ tblsp. olive oil	sweet basil leaves
1 tsp. sugar	paprika
salt and black pepper	

Slice the onion very thinly and sauté in the hot oil until tender. Add the tomatoes and cook until tender, adding more oil if necessary. Season with salt, pepper, paprika, sugar and sweet basil leaves to your taste, then add the minced garlic and the wine. If soup is too thick, add a little water. Chill well and serve garnished with chopped olives and parsley.

SPANISH GRAPE SOUP

1 lb. grapes	1 pint water
¼ lb. ground almonds	1 tblsp. vinegar
¼ cup olive oil	3 cloves garlic
2 oz. dark brown breadcrumbs	salt and black pepper

Mix together the almonds, breadcrumbs, garlic and salt and pepper and if you have a mortar and pestle, pound them well. If not, mince the garlic and mash all together with a fork. Add the oil very gradually, then the vinegar and then the water, mixing well. Lastly add the skinned and seeded grapes and chill well before serving. You will have to be light-handed with the seasoning in this soup lest the delicate flavour be impaired. Serve with buttered crackers.

ALMOND SOUP

This unusual soup is very easy to make and the result is spectacular.

¼ lb. whole almonds	1¾ pints water
1 green pepper	1 dessertsp. minced onion
3 pimentos (the herb)	1 dessertsp. chopped parsley
2 cloves garlic	2 tblsp. olive oil
2 slices rye or dark brown bread	salt and black pepper

Peel the almonds and fry them with the minced onion in the oil for a few minutes, then drain them well. Seed and chop the green pepper, cube the bread very small, and fry with the minced garlic, parsley and pimentos until the green pepper is tender. Pound in a mortar or mash well with a fork. Stir the boiling water into the mixture, cook very gently for a few minutes, stirring with a wooden spoon, season with salt and a touch of black pepper and serve very hot.

CUCUMBER SOUP

1 large or 2 small cucumbers	chopped mint
1 small onion	chopped parsley
4 tsp. fresh lemon juice	water as required
½ oz. gelatine	salt and black pepper

Grate the onion and cucumber and mix with the juice, the mint and the parsley. Melt the gelatine in a little hot water, add to the cucumber mixture and add 1 pint of water, or slightly less. Season with salt and black pepper and chill before serving.

GREEN AND RED PEPPER OMELETTE

1 green pepper	¼ lb. tomatoes
1 red pepper	sprigs of parsley
5 small eggs	olive oil as required
salt and black pepper	

Beat the eggs well and leave aside while you seed and slice the peppers and peel and slice the tomatoes. Fry these in the olive oil until the peppers are tender, season with salt and pepper and mix well. Now pour on the beaten eggs and cook slowly, with the lid on the frying pan, until the omelette is solid. Garnish with parsley sprigs and serve on a heated plate. These quantities will serve 2.

SPANISH OMELETTE

Don't confuse the French omelette with the Spanish, as they are quite different. The French omelette, which is barely cooked in the middle, and should in fact be quite runny, is folded over and tipped on to a hot plate like an envelope. The Spanish omelette requires the filling to be cooked *with* the eggs, something like the Chinese Egg Foo Yong, while in the French one the filling is added just before serving. Below is a typical Spanish omelette which you can vary according to what you have in the house at the time. Almost any vegetable will do, provided it is fried in oil before you pour on the eggs.

6 eggs	1 large potato
1 green pepper	oil for frying
1 medium-sized onion	salt and black pepper

Either julienne the peeled potatoes, seeded pepper and peeled onion or else slice then very finely into matchsticks. Fry them in the oil, very slowly, until tender but try not to brown the onion. Beat the eggs until frothy and add to the vegetables. Cook very slowly until the underside of the omelette (or tortilla) is done. You can either finish it off under the grill, or else turn it over very carefully and do the other side in the frying pan. This makes a savoury and sustaining meal for at least 3 hungry people. The variations are endless of course but we like Spanish omelette with fried mushrooms and thickly sliced tomatoes.

STUFFED GREEN PEPPERS

6 green peppers	½ lb. grated sharp cheese
2 eggs	hot water as required
1 large tin sweet corn, drained	salt and black pepper

Seed the peppers carefully without damaging the outer shells. Plunge them into boiling salted water for 2 minutes then, drain in a colander. Mix all remaining ingredients and season to your taste. Stuff the mixture into the peppers and place them in a pan containing ¼ to ½ a cup of boiling water, or sufficient to just cover the bottoms of the peppers and bake in a very moderate oven for 30 minutes. This is a delicious dish, and you can of course use corn on the cob as well as the tinned corn. With the fresh cobs boil them in salted water until tender, scrape off the corn and use as directed.

CADIZ EGGS WITH RICE

6 large eggs	breadcrumbs as required
1 beaten egg	flour as required
plain boiled rice	olive oil for frying
	salt and black pepper

Poach the eggs until firm. If possible use a poacher which has oval shaped cups which make the eggs more unusual. Remove the eggs carefully from the poacher and dip them in seasoned flour. Shake off the surplus, then dip them in the beaten egg, then in the breadcrumbs and fry in deep hot oil until golden. Serve with plain boiled rice.

SPANISH EGG AND VEGETABLE BAKE

6-8 eggs	½ lb. string beans
3 red or green peppers	¼ cup fresh peas
2 large Spanish onions	½ cup grated sharp cheese
1 cup thick tomato sauce	butter as required
	salt and black pepper

Prepare your vegetables and cut into small pieces. Cook them in butter for 15 minutes, stirring from time to time. Then add the tomato sauce and cook until the vegetables are just tender, then season. Transfer everything to a well greased large casserole and break the eggs carefully over the top. Sprinkle with a very little salt, then with the grated cheese and bake in a moderate oven until the eggs are set.

SPANISH CARROTS

1 lb. carrots	2 eggs
1 medium-sized Spanish onion	butter as required
1 pint milk	olive oil
1 tsp. flour	salt and black pepper

Scrape and thinly slice the carrots and sauté them in butter until just tender. Fry the peeled and thinly sliced onion separately and then combine it with the carrots. Stir in the flour and cook for 2 minutes. Gradually add the boiling milk, or you can use milk and water if you wish, and stir all the time with a wooden spoon. Cook until thick over a very gentle heat and just before serving add the beaten eggs and season to taste.

SPANISH CAULIFLOWER WITH NOODLES

1 cauliflower	toasted breadcrumbs
1 lb. cooked noodles	butter as required
2 eggs, beaten	olive oil for frying
salt and black pepper	

When the noodles are cooked put a good sized knob of butter through them using two forks, and keep them hot. Meanwhile cut up the cauliflower into small sprigs and sauté them in butter for 5 or 6 minutes. Drain, then dip the sprigs into the well beaten and seasoned eggs, then into the breadcrumbs and drop into deep hot oil. Fry until golden and serve at once on a bed of noodles.

POTATOES WITH ALMONDS

1 lb. potatoes	1 bay leaf
¼ lb. ground almonds	1 tsp. saffron
2 slices bread	a touch of powdered cloves
2 cloves garlic	buttered breadcrumbs
2 tblsp. minced onion	olive oil for frying
salt and black pepper	

Fry the cubed bread in the oil with the minced garlic, bay leaf and minced onion. When fried, mix with the ground almonds and mix all together with the saffron, seasoning well. Peel and thinly slice the potatoes, place them in a well greased casserole and pour over them the almond mixture. Moisten with a little milk if necessary. Add sufficient boiling water to cover the potatoes, sprinkle with salt, pepper and cloves and buttered breadcrumbs and bake in a moderate oven until tender and brown.

APPLES WITH SAVOURY STUFFING

6 large cooking apples	2 tsp. vinegar
2 large potatoes (about ½ lb.)	2 tblsp. chopped parsley
3 eggs	juice of ½ lemon
3 stalks celery	butter as required
2 oz. chopped nuts	buttered breadcrumbs
salt and black pepper	

Wash the apples and take out the cores carefully, leaving a thick walled shell. Boil and mash the potatoes with butter. Season with salt and black pepper. Mix in the beaten egg yolks, any of the apple pulp you may have, finely chopped, and the nuts. Finely chop the celery and add that to the mixture. Lastly add the vinegar and lemon juice and season to your taste. Stuff the mixture into the apples, putting a small piece of butter deep into the stuffing. Sprinkle with buttered breadcrumbs, place the apples in a greased casserole and bake in a moderate oven for 20 to 25 minutes until the apples are well heated but not quite soft.

SAVOURY EGGS ON TOAST

6 eggs	1 clove garlic
6 large ripe tomatoes	hot buttered toast as required
1 green or red pepper	olive oil as required
1 medium-sized Spanish onion	salt and black pepper

Peel and slice the onion, seed and thinly slice the pepper and sauté in hot olive oil with the minced garlic until the onion is almost tender. Add the thinly sliced tomatoes and continue cooking for a further 6 or 7 minutes. Beat the eggs and stir them into the mixture over a gentle heat until they are set. Season and serve on hot buttered toast.

RICE WITH NUTS

2 large Spanish onions	2 tblsp. chopped parsley
2 green or red peppers	2 tsp. saffron
½ lb. rice	2 cloves garlic
½ lb. chopped mixed nuts	olive oil as required
salt and black pepper	

Peel and thinly slice the onions and sauté them, with the minced garlic, in the oil. When the onions are nicely browned add the rice and the nuts, and stir well. Cook until the oil is absorbed, then add sufficient boiling water to cover. Bring to boiling point again, cover the pan and cook for 20 to 25 minutes until the rice is just tender. While the rice is cooking, fry the seeded and sliced peppers separately and when the rice is cooked, season to your taste, add the parsley and saffron and sprinkle the peppers on top of the rice. Serve at once.

EGG AND CINNAMON BISCUITS

These are very nourishing biscuits and so deserve a place in this book.

¼ lb. butter	¼ lb. icing sugar
¼ lb. flour	3 large eggs
½ flat tsp. cinnamon	

Cream the butter and sugar until pale, beat in the eggs and very gradually stir in the sifted flour and the cinnamon. Make sure everything is well mixed. Put small spoonfuls in paper cases and bake in a moderate oven for 10 minutes.

The following recipe, with which I end this chapter on Spanish cooking is not only a dessert but also a sweetmeat. It contains a very high percentage of protein.

SPANISH NOUGAT

4 small egg yolks	½ lb. granulated sugar
1 egg white	½ lb. ground almonds

Mix the sugar and almonds, and gradually add the beaten egg yolks. Whip it up well with a wooden spoon and then add the well beaten egg white. Grease some paper and place on a square or oblong cake tin. Spread with the mixture, press down firmly, and put a weight on top. Leave for 3 days and then cut up the nougat into cubes and serve with coffee or chocolate.

Switzerland

Switzerland is distinguished on two counts as far as cheese is concerned. Firstly because per head of the population there is more cheese made, eaten, and exported than in any other country in the world and secondly because of:

Emmentaler and **Gruyère** A cow's milk cheese, centuries old, **Emmentaler** is a delicate creamy golden colour, marked with holes or eyes, and with a flavour hard to describe. But cheese lovers everywhere agree on the superlative quality of the Swiss Emmentaler.

Gruyère This is, in many ways, similar to the Emmentaler, but is rather more salty and often has larger and fewer holes. This is due to the difference in the making of it. Gruyère is rather sweeter in taste than Emmentaler, and, like a really ripe Camembert, has a distinct smell of ammonia. Gruyère is the inspiration behind the famous Swiss dish, Fondue.

The moon may or may not be a piece of green cheese, according to your particular views on the subject, but one thing is agreed by cheese eaters like myself, not only *is* there such a thing as Green Cheese but Switzerland makes one that has no peer. It goes by the rather unwieldy name of **Schabzieger**, and has been made in Switzerland for over five hundred years. Made of skimmed cow's milk, it is mixed with blue melilot which imparts the excellently full bodied and highly pungent flavour. Not a cooking cheese, but when mixed with butter or cream it makes a perfect sandwich filling.

The Swiss are also great lovers of the German Tilsiter and make large quantities of it. The Swiss version is somewhat different though not, to my mind, less excellent. It is slightly sweeter and superb in its own way.

BREAD AND CHEESE SOUP

It sounds an unlikely sort of soup, but after a long, hard day on skis it is really tasty and the Swiss lady who made it for us gave me the following astonishingly simple recipe.

8 slices toasted rye bread or black bread	1 pint milk
½ lb. grated Swiss cheese or Parmesan	a touch of mace or nutmeg
¼ cup butter	chopped chives to garnish
salt and black pepper	

Put the milk on to boil and meanwhile put a slice of toast in each soup plate (these ingredients make soup for 4). Cover the bread with a thick layer of the grated cheese and place another slice on top. Now pour the boiling milk, seasoned with salt, pepper and mace or nutmeg, over the toasted bread and add a good-sized knob of butter to each plate. Serve garnished with chopped chives.

SWISS CUCUMBER SOUP

1 large cucumber	4 tblsp. chopped chives or parsley
1 medium-sized onion	2 tblsp. butter
1¾ pints vegetable water	1 tblsp. cornflour
2 cups milk	salt and black pepper

Peel and slice onion and cucumber and sauté them in butter for 6 minutes, then add the heated vegetable water and simmer until vegetables are tender. Sieve and season. Mix the cornflour with a little cold milk and add it to the soup, at the same time adding the rest of the milk. Simmer very gently for a few minutes until it starts to thicken. Check your seasoning, then serve garnished with chopped chives or parsley.

SWISS EGGS WITH ONIONS

6 eggs	½ lb. cheese, sliced
2 large sweet Spanish onions	½ cup thin cream or evaporated milk
1 cup grated Parmesan cheese	salt as required
a touch of cayenne	butter as required

Peel and thinly slice the onions and fry in butter until brown. Line a shallow greased oven dish with them and cover with thin slices of cheese. Break the eggs carefully over the cheese, add a touch of cayenne (but only a touch for cayenne is fiery) and a sprinkle of salt, then pour the cream over the eggs. Sprinkle with the Parmesan, dot with plenty of butter, and bake in a moderate oven for about 10 to 15 minutes until eggs are set.

SWISS PIE

shortcrust pastry	4 small eggs
½ lb. grated Gruyère	1 tblsp. flour
½ cup milk	breadcrumbs
½ cup thin cream	butter as required
salt and black pepper	

Line a fairly large oven-proof plate with shortcrust pastry, put the grated cheese on the pastry and sprinkle with the flour. Mix together the beaten eggs, the milk and the cream, season and pour the egg mixture over the cheese. Scatter with plenty of toasted breadcrumbs, dot with butter, and bake for 30 minutes, the first 15 minutes in a hot oven and the second in a slow oven. Test with a silver knife to see if the pie is cooked through. If it comes out clean, serve at once.

SWISS BREAD PUDDING

4 eggs	½ cup chopped mixed nuts
4 slices brown bread	½ cup chopped dried fruit (dates, figs,
½ breakfast cup sugar	raisins, apricots)
½ cup cream	cinnamon
½ cup milk	additional milk

Mix together the sugar, cream, milk and eggs and beat well, in a blender if possible. Add the diced bread and about 2 small cups additional milk, together with the fruit and the nuts. Pour into a greased baking dish, sprinkle liberally with cinnamon and bake in a moderate oven for 30 to 40 minutes.

FONDUE

This is the most famous cheese dish in the world and certainly is the best-known dish to come from Switzerland. There are many different ways to make fondue but this is a simple basic one.

6 eggs	1 French loaf (warmed and crisped in the oven)
2 oz. butter	½ cup dry white wine
¼ lb. Gruyère cheese	salt and black pepper

Grate the Gruyère, then beat the eggs well in a saucepan and add the cheese and the butter cut up into dots. Cook the mixture fairly quickly until it begins to thicken. Stir in the wine and serve in the pan. The bread is cut into crusty cubes, speared with a fork and everyone dips. Anyone who loses his bread in the fondue pays a forfeit.

EGGS WITH NOODLES

4 hard-boiled eggs	½ pint tomato sauce or white sauce
¾ lb. cooked noodles	½ pint tomato purée
½ lb. Gruyère cheese	chopped chives

Grate or shave the cheese into thin slivers and add to the heated tomato sauce. Stir until cheese has melted, then add the sliced hard-boiled eggs. Serve on the hot noodles, and garnish with plenty of chopped chives.

SWISS SOUFFLÉ

4 large eggs	½ cup milk
½ lb. hot mashed potatoes	butter as required
¼ lb. grated Gruyère cheese	parsley

The potatoes should be whipped up with butter and milk until creamy. Beat in the hot milk, then the cheese, and some chopped parsley. Separate the eggs and beat the yolks until creamy and pale and then beat the egg whites until stiff, but not too dry. Fold first the yolks and then the whites into the cheese and potato mixture and place in a well buttered soufflé tin. Bake in a hot oven for 25 to 30 minutes. It should be brown on top and should, of course, be served at once.

CREAMY EGGS

6 eggs	½ cup cream
2 tblsp. butter	breadcrumbs as required
¼ lb. Gruyère cheese	additional butter
salt and black pepper	

173

Beat the eggs, season and add the cream. Melt the butter, stir in the egg mixture and cook very slowly until the eggs are *just* set. Place in a well-buttered casserole, add the thinly sliced cheese and top with breadcrumbs. Dot with plenty of butter and bake in a moderate oven until pale gold.

POTATO PUDDING

We used to love this as children. It was everyone's favourite savoury pudding but the best part was definitely the crust.

1 lb. potatoes	2 oz. butter
1 large sweet Spanish onion	2 tblsp. S.R. flour
salt and black pepper	

Grate the potatoes on a very fine grater, and also grate the peeled onion. Add the flour and the melted butter and blend well. Season with plenty of salt and grated black pepper and mix again. Butter an oven-proof pie dish or casserole and put in the mixture. Bake in a pre-heated moderate oven for 30 minutes, then reduce the heat by half and continue baking for a further 35 minutes when there should be a deep brown and crunchy crust on the top. It is delicious either straight out of the oven, heated up the next day, or eaten cold.

SWISS CHEESE SANDWICHES

12 slices rye or dark brown bread	French mustard
Gruyère cheese as required	parsley sprigs
butter as required	

Spread the bread with plenty of butter and then add a thin layer of French mustard. Cover half the slices of bread with a thick layer of sliced Gruyère, cover with the rest of the bread and press down well. Sauté the sandwiches in lots of butter until brown on both sides. Serve hot, garnished with parsley sprigs.

Variations:
1. Add sweet pickles to the sandwiches instead of mustard.
2. Add sliced pickled gherkins instead of the mustard.
3. Add a few drops of garlic oil to the butter before spreading on the bread.

SWISS FRIED ONIONS WITH RICE

6 large sweet Spanish onions	1 bunch watercress
2 tblsp. butter	1 clove garlic
2 tblsp. cooking oil	plain boiled rice
1 tsp. marjoram	salt and black pepper

Melt the butter, add the oil and sauté the peeled and sliced onions and the minced garlic for 3 minutes, then add the marjoram and seasoning. Cook until the onions are golden brown, about 15 minutes, and taste for seasoning. If any moisture has collected in the pan, pour this off into the hot boiled rice and mix well with a fork. Pile the onions on to the rice and serve garnished with chopped watercress.

The United States of America

There are very few cheeses of American origin. Of all the cheeses eaten in the United States, Cheddar, of English origin, is the most widely popular.

Brick Cheese is one of the original cheeses, and is made in great quantities. A cow's milk cheese, rather soft and with a sweetish taste, it has a rather strong flavour, something like a toned-down Limburger. The latter is one of the most aggressively strong tasting cheeses of all, with a bouquet to match, and although American Brick cheese cannot compete with the Limburger's strong personality, it has nevertheless something of its full-blooded charm.

There is a form of Cottage Cheese in almost every country and in the United States it is called **Baker's Cheese.** But while English cottage cheese is rather coarse grained, the American counterpart is finer and somewhat creamier. It is an excellent cheese for baking into pies and fritters and blintzes.

Hand Cheese An unusual cheese made from skim milk and buttermilk and flavoured with caraway seed. It has a very sharp and piquant flavour and bouquet.

Switzerland isn't the only country to produce that rare commodity, green cheese. The United States makes one called **Sage Cheese.** There is something very delightful about the combination of cheese and herbs, and sage flavoured cheese is impressive.

Cornhusker was first introduced in the state of Nebraska about 23 years ago. It is something like a moist Cheddar but rather softer. It has a pleasant nutty flavour like a Cheddar, but is less waxy in texture.

NEW ENGLAND CHEESE RISOTTO

Cornhusker cheese is ideal for this recipe but if you cannot get it, Cheddar will do just as well.

6 oz. grated cheese	$\frac{1}{2}$ lb. rice, almost cooked
6 tblsp. dry white wine	$\frac{1}{2}$ cup chopped mixed nuts
4 tblsp. butter	$\frac{1}{4}$ pint vegetable water
1 large Spanish onion	salt and black pepper

Keep the rice hot while you fry the peeled and sliced onion in butter until brown. Mix with the rice and season well. Add the vegetable water and the wine and simmer for about 10 minutes, stirring all the time. After 5 minutes, stir in the nuts and taste for seasoning. Make sure all the liquid is absorbed before serving the risotto. Pile it into a warmed serving dish and smother with the grated cheese.

AMERICAN FONDUE

3 large eggs	1 cup breadcrumbs
¼ tsp. dry mustard	1 cup milk
salt and black pepper	1 cup Cheddar cheese, grated

Bring the milk to boiling point and take off the heat immediately. Stir in the breadcrumbs, cheese and seasonings. Simmer very gently until the cheese has melted. Separate the eggs and beat the yolks. Pour the milk mixture over the yolks and stir. Leave to cool. Whip up the egg whites until stiff and fold into the mixture. Bake in a buttered casserole for 25 to 30 minutes, at moderate heat. Serve with crusty bread.

CONNECTICUT CAULIFLOWER SOUP

2 large Spanish onions	½ pint milk
1 large cauliflower	½ cup thick cream
3 sticks celery	a touch of sugar
2 tblsp. butter	a touch of mace or nutmeg (optional)
2 tblsp. flour	watercress for garnishing
	salt and black pepper

Prepare the cauliflower and cut into sprigs. Plunge them into boiling salted water, drain and repeat the process. Then steam the cauliflower in a very little salted water until tender, together with the chopped onions and celery. Rub through a sieve and return to the pan. Meanwhile make a roux with the butter and the flour and cook for 2 minutes. Gradually add the heated milk and stir well. Add the vegetables and stir again. Season with salt, pepper, a touch of sugar and a little grated nutmeg or mace. Stir in the cream and if the soup seems a little too thick use additional hot milk until you have achieved the required consistency. Serve at once garnished with sprigs of watercress.

NEBRASKA CELERY SOUP

1 large head of celery	1¾ pints vegetable water
1 large Spanish onion	1½ oz. flour
2 tblsp. butter	½ cup thick cream
salt and black pepper	¼ cup milk

Prepare the celery and chop together with the peeled onion. Reserve a few tiny leaves of the celery for garnishing. Sauté the vegetables in butter for 10 minutes until the onion begins to turn golden. Add the vegetable water and simmer until tender. Rub through a sieve and return to the pan, adding the seasoning. Make a roux with a little more butter and cook for 3 minutes. Meanwhile add sufficient hot vegetable stock from the pan to make up a large cupful when added to the milk. Gradually stir this into the butter/flour mixture, and cook until thickened. Stir this into the soup, taste for seasoning, add the cream and serve garnished with celery leaves.

ROASTED CHESTNUT SOUP

1 lb. chestnuts	2 pints vegetable water
3 or 4 spring onions or chives	2 oz. butter
1 tblsp. flour	2 cups milk
½ cup thick cream	salt and black pepper

Cut an X in the skin of each chestnut with the point of a sharp fruit knife and roast in a hot oven until tender. Test whether they are done by putting a skewer through one of them. If it goes in easily the chestnuts are ready. It takes approximately 15 minutes according to the oven temperature and the size and age of the chestnuts. When they are cool enough to handle, peel off their outer and inner skins, and mill or chop them. Sauté them in 1 tablespoonful of the butter together with the chopped onions for 6 minutes, then put them on to boil with the vegetable water and the milk. Make a roux with the rest of the butter and the flour and cook for 3 minutes. Gradually add some of the hot soup and stir well. Add the flour mixture to the soup and season to your taste. Add the cream, stir, and serve at once. This method gives the chestnuts a delicious nutty bite which I think is more interesting than using the purée method.

DEEP SOUTH CORN SOUP

2 cups sweet corn	1 medium-sized onion, minced
2 tblsp. chopped parsley	1 pint milk
2 tblsp. butter	½ cup thick cream
1 oz. flour	¾ pint water
salt and black pepper	

You can use either tinned sweet corn or fresh corn cobs, cooked, and with the grains then removed. Sauté the corn and the chopped onion in the hot butter until the onion is just turning golden. Stir into the milk and water mixed and bring to the boil. Turn down the heat and simmer for 10 minutes. Make a roux with the flour and some more butter and cook for 3 minutes. Gradually add some of the hot soup and stir until thickened. Stir this into the soup and bring to the boil once more. Turn down the heat and simmer for a further 5 minutes, after which season to your taste. Just before serving stir in the cream and chopped parsley.

CALIFORNIAN ARTICHOKE PIE

2 lb. Jerusalem artichokes	3 oz. grated cheese
2 large Spanish onions	breadcrumbs as required
2 oz. butter	salt and black pepper

Steam the scrubbed artichokes in a very little salted water for 10 minutes. Drain and slice. Meanwhile sauté the chopped onions in the butter until golden brown. Butter an oven dish and put a layer of sliced artichoke in it followed by a layer of onion. Sprinkle with salt and black pepper and then with grated cheese. Repeat the layers until all is used up and top with a thick layer of breadcrumbs. Sprinkle again with a little seasoning and dot with butter. Bake in a hot oven for 20 to 30 minutes until brown on top.

SWEET CORN OMELETTE

6 eggs separated   1 tsp. salt
1 cup sweet corn   paprika
½ cup fresh milk   corn oil for frying
ground black pepper

Beat the egg yolks until creamy, add the milk and the salt and beat again, then grate in some black pepper. Whip the egg whites until stiff and fold into the mixture, and lastly fold in the drained sweet corn. Butter a glass oven-proof baking dish and pour in the mixture. Bake in a slow oven for about 30 minutes or until set. Serve from the dish, after sprinkling with paprika.

CORN PUDDING

2 large eggs   2 tblsp. butter
1 large Spanish onion   2 oz. flour
1 cup creamed tinned corn   a touch of paprika
1 cup milk   salt and black pepper

Peel and chop the onion and sauté in the butter until tender and golden. Beat the egg yolks until creamy, then add the creamed corn, the sauté onion, and seasonings, mixing well. Make a roux of 1 tablespoonful butter and the flour and very gradually add the warmed milk, stirring until creamy. Season and mix with the creamed corn. Fold in the stiffly beaten egg whites and bake in a well buttered casserole at moderate heat until golden.

BOSTON SQUASH PIE

4 cups cooked squash   brown sugar
3 cups stewed apples   ground ginger to taste
3 pieces preserved ginger   butter as required
a touch of mace   thick cream as required
breadcrumbs

Butter a pie-dish and put in a layer of the squash and sprinkle with powdered ginger and a little mace. Add a layer of apples scattered with chopped preserved ginger. Repeat the layers until all is used up, then cover with a thick layer of breadcrumbs, sprinkle with brown sugar and dot with at least 3 ounces butter. Bake until the crust is crisp and golden and buttery. Serve with thick cream into which you have whipped a little brown sugar.

SWEET CORN SALAD

2 cups or 1 small tin cooked sweet corn   1 bunch watercress
2 sticks celery   1 head of endive or lettuce
1 small onion, chopped   French mustard
salad cream as required

If you use tinned corn then drain it well. Add to ½ cup of salad cream or mayonnaise, 1 level teaspoon French mustard. Toss the corn and the chopped celery in this until well coated. Add the chopped onion (or a small bunch of chopped spring onions) and mix again. Serve on a bed of endive or lettuce leaves and hand round a dish of watercress separately.

FLORIDA CHEESE AND VEGETABLE PIE

1 lb. mixed vegetables, diced and cooked	1 cup milk
¼ lb. ripe tomatoes	sweet basil leaves
¼ lb. grated Cheddar cheese	butter as required
3 eggs	breadcrumbs
2 large Spanish onions	salt and black pepper

For this recipe, if you are in a hurry you can use a large tin of Macedoine, or cooked diced mixed vegetables, but it is nicer and there is more variety if you choose and cook your own. Peel and chop the onions and sauté in butter until brown. Add a touch of sugar and a generous grate of black pepper. Combine with the mixed vegetables and mix well, adding salt to taste. Butter a deep but not too large casserole and lay some of the mixed vegetables in the bottom of it. Add a layer of grated cheese and then a few slices of tomato. Sprinkle the tomatoes with sweet basil leaves. Repeat the layers, topping with tomatoes and grated cheese. Add beaten eggs and hot milk mixed, then add a thick layer of breadcrumbs, sprinkle with a little seasoning and dot with plenty of butter. Bake at moderate heat until brown, approximately 30 minutes, but this depends on which oven shelf you use.

CRUNCHY SALAD

4 firm heads of chicory	½ cup grated Parmesan
1 head celery	a bunch of watercress
1 large cooking apple	vinegar
1 medium-sized onion	salad oil
1 baby beet, raw	salt and black pepper

Peel and shred the vegetables and the apple, and separate the chicory into leaves. Season well, then toss in plenty of salad oil and then in a little tarragon or wine vinegar. Chill well, sprinkle with Parmesan and serve on a bed of watercress. *Note.* This is the original recipe but it can be varied by adding 1 small shredded green or red pepper, when they are in season.

MARYLAND ASPARAGUS

1 bunch cooked asparagus or	butter as required
1 large tin	grated cheese as required

If you are using tinned asparagus then drain it well before using. Butter an oven-to-table dish and put a layer of asparagus in the bottom of it. Sprinkle with finely grated cheese, and dot with plenty of butter. Repeat the layers until all is used up, topping with the cheese. Put it into a pre-heated hot oven and leave it for exactly 5 minutes and no longer. Serve it in the dish at once. For a more substantial dish, serve it with savoury rice handed round separately.

AMERICAN SAVOURY RICE

2 cups raw long grain rice	2 oz. currants
½ lb. white cabbage	1 oz. sultanas
¼ lb. ripe tomatoes	¾ pint water
¼ lb. chopped mixed nuts	corn oil as required
1 chopped onion	salt and black pepper

Shred the cabbage finely and sauté in hot corn oil for a few minutes. Use about 1 tablespoonful of oil and then add another tablespoonful when you add the rice and mix well with the cabbage. Cook, stirring frequently, for 5 minutes, then add the heated water, onion, seasonings and dried fruit. Stir well, then cover the pan and simmer for 30 minutes. Ten minutes before time is up add the sliced tomatoes and stir again. Make sure that there is enough liquid to cook the rice. If there is not, then add a little more heated water. The rice is ready when it is soft on the outside of the grain but with a bite in the centre. Never cook rice until it is completely soft right through.

POTATO PIE WITH NUTS

1½ lb. sweet potatoes	1 cup milk
2 large Spanish onions, fried	1½ tblsp. flour
4 oz. chopped mixed nuts	breadcrumbs
2 oz. butter	salt and black pepper

Cook the potatoes, then peel and dice them. Fry the flour in the butter for a few minutes, then gradually add the heated milk, stirring all the time until thick and creamy. Season with salt and black pepper. Butter a casserole and put a layer of fried onions in the bottom. Add a layer of sweet potatoes and then a layer of chopped nuts. Repeat layers until all is used up, then pour over the white sauce. Top with breadcrumbs, dot with butter and bake in a hot oven until the crust is brown.

If you do not like sweet potatoes, or if you cannot get them in your district, then the ordinary kind of potatoes make an equally good pie.

OLD-FASHIONED CALIFORNIA BAKE

1 lb. mushrooms	4 tblsp. chopped parsley
1 Spanish onion	1 tsp. ground cummin seeds
1 green or red pepper	½ tsp. brown sugar
1 clove garlic	breadcrumbs
2 cups sweet corn	butter as required
2 cups grated Cheddar cheese	corn oil as required
salt and black pepper	

Peel and chop onion and garlic and sauté in butter until turning golden. Add the shredded green or red pepper and the sliced mushrooms. Cook with the lid on the pan for 8 minutes. Season with salt and black pepper. Oil an oven-proof dish and lid and lay 1 cup sweet corn in the bottom. Add a layer of sauté vegetables, then a layer of cheese. Sprinkle with half of the parsley and ground cummin, and add a grate of black pepper. Sprinkle with sugar and then repeat the layers until all is used up. Top with bread-crumbs, dot with butter and bake for 1 hour in a fairly slow oven. The top should be golden.

DEEP SOUTH BAKE

1 lb. cooked sweet potatoes	4 oz. chopped nuts
1 tin pineapple slices	black treacle as required
1 tsp. grated lemon peel	cinnamon as required

This is an easy one and can be made while the family are eating their soup. Slice the sweet potatoes and lay them in a well buttered casserole. Pour over them 1 tablespoonful dark treacle thinned with a very little water. Add a layer of the drained pineapple slices and sprinkle with the chopped nuts and grated lemon peel. Dust with cinnamon and heat it in a moderate oven for 5 or 10 minutes.

PICNIC PIE

1 lb. shaved or grated Cheddar cheese	$\frac{1}{2}$ lb. shortcrust pastry
1 lb. mushrooms	butter as required
salt and black pepper	

Butter a pie-plate and line with pastry. Cover the pastry with cheese and dot with butter. Sauté the sliced mushrooms in butter until tender and place them on top of the cheese. Dot again with butter, then add the top crust, sealing well to the bottom crust with a little water round the edges. Go round the edges of the pie with a fork dipped in water to make a pattern, then make 3 deep slits in the top of the crust to let the steam escape. Brush the top with a little milk and bake in a hot oven until the pie is brown—about 25 to 30 minutes. Serve hot or cold.

RICE PUDDING

Rice pudding sounds neither very American nor very exciting but this one is just a little different.

3 cups milk	3 eggs
2 cups unpolished rice, cooked	a few drops of vanilla
$\frac{1}{4}$ cup chopped mixed nuts	a touch of salt
$\frac{1}{2}$ cup brown sugar	grated nutmeg
$\frac{1}{2}$ cup shredded coconut	2 tblsp. currants

Mix together the beaten eggs, milk, vanilla, sugar and the salt and leave them aside while you cook the unpolished rice in the ordinary way, i.e. boil in sufficient salted water to cover until just tender, drain and rinse with hot water. Mix rice with the milk and egg mixture. Add nuts, currants and coconut and stir well. Pour into a well buttered casserole and add a generous sprinkling of nutmeg. Bake in a slow oven for 30 minutes.

HOME-MADE YOGHOURT

This is the simplest way I know of making yoghourt. You can, if you wish, send away for a bottle of yoghourt culture but it may take some time and patience to get it right. The other way is to buy a carton of plain unsweetened yoghourt and eat it, leaving 1 tablespoonful in the bottom to try out my recipe. Take 1 pint of milk, bring it almost to boiling point, then allow it to cool to blood heat. Test this either by using a thermometer or by dipping your finger into it. If you can hardly feel the milk, then it's about right.

When the milk is at blood heat, stir in the 1 tablespoonful of yoghourt and then put the mixture in front of the hottest heater you have. If you have central heating then put it right up against a radiator and just leave it. In a few hours you will have yoghourt. It is difficult to know exactly how long it will take, for yoghourt is very unpredictable but if you are lucky it may be as little as 3 hours, although I have known it to take 5 or 6 hours or even longer. When the yoghourt is finally made don't forget to save 1 tablespoonful of it to start again. You need never buy yoghourt again so long as you have a spoonful of it in the house.

ARTICHOKES WITH ASPARAGUS

This recipe is in the luxury class.

6 large French artichokes	black pepper as required
2 cups asparagus tips	butter as required
a little boiling water	salt

Wash the artichokes, cut off the stems, and remove the tough outer leaves. Steam them in a little boiling salted water until tender (at least 30 to 40 minutes), then drain them well. Meanwhile melt about ½ cup of butter, add a touch of salt and black pepper to it and then stir in the cooked asparagus tips. When the artichokes are ready take out the grasslike choke in the centre and fill them with the asparagus and butter. Serve at once.

FLORIDA EGGS

6 large eggs	a dash of chilli or tabasco sauce
1 green or red pepper	watercress to garnish
½ cup grated cheese	butter as required
½ cup thin cream	plain boiled rice
½ cup chopped chives or spring onions	salt and black pepper

Seed and thinly slice the pepper and sauté, with the chopped chives, in butter until tender. Add a dash of chilli or tabasco sauce and add the cheese. See that there is a very gentle heat under the pan at this stage. Beat the eggs with the milk and season. Cook over a very low heat in plenty of butter, stirring all the time with a wooden spoon. When eggs are just beginning to set, stir in the pepper mixture and mix well. Pile on to plain boiled hot rice and garnish with plenty of watercress.

MUSHROOM RAREBIT

This is very economical wây to serve something really special.

1 small tin evaporated milk	4 slices wholewheat bread
½ lb. mushrooms, sauté in butter	1 tsp. French mustard
½ lb. grated mild cheese	¼ tsp. salt
½ pint thick white sauce	butter as required

Beat together the milk, mustard and salt and put the mixture in the top half of a double boiler. Heat until gently simmering and then add the grated cheese and let it stand, off the heat, until the cheese has melted. Meanwhile mix the sauté mushrooms into the thick white sauce and season to your taste. Butter a shallow oven dish and lay the bread in the bottom. Pour over the cheese mixture and then the mushroom mixture. Top with a thin layer of buttered breadcrumbs and bake in a slow oven until top begins to turn golden. Serve very hot. For further economy you may use sliced mushroom stalks for this recipe.

NO-BAKE CHRISTMAS CAKE

This sounds too good to be true but I have made it and it is *quite* special. Save your time and your energy for a change and see what the family think of this one. My guess is that they'll be back for more.

¼ lb. chopped dates	6 tblsp. raisins (seedless)
1 cup ground almonds	2 heaped tblsp. candied peel
1 cup prunes (soaked overnight)	1 tblsp. walnut halves
3 pieces preserved ginger (chopped)	1 tblsp. glacé cherries
rice paper	1 tsp. sliced angelica
	vanilla icing for the top

Mix together the minced fruits, nuts, candied peel and ginger. Take a flat cake tin and line the bottom with rice paper. Put in the mixture and press it well down. Cover with another layer of rice paper. Leave overnight in a cool place, or for a few hours at least, then ice the top with whichever icing you wish. Decorate with walnuts, glacé cherries and angelica.

NO-BAKE CHRISTMAS PUDDING

4 oz. breadcrumbs	4 pieces preserved ginger
2 oz. ground almonds	3 tblsp. candied peel
2 medium sized apples, minced	3 tblsp. orange juice
2 large carrots	2 or 3 tsp. grated orange rind
2 cups raisins (seedless)	1 tsp. ground coffee
1 cup sultanas or currants or mixed	a touch of cinnamon or mace
¼ cup glacé cherries	butter as required
	custard or whipped cream

Mince together dried fruit and ginger, and mix with the minced apple. Add the finely grated carrots, orange juice and peel, almonds and breadcrumbs. Flavour with cinnamon or mace according to your taste. Put the mixture into a buttered pudding basin and press down firmly. Keep in the fridge overnight with a weight on top. Turn it out on Christmas Day and serve with custard, or whipped cream sprinkled with coffee grains.

INDEX

arco Books
on Health and Nutrition

VITAMIN E
Your Key to a Healthy Heart
Herbert Bailey

WHY IS VITAMIN E therapy for mankind's foremost killing disease still controversial in the United States? This is one of the questions asked and answered in this slashing, fully-documented book. It tells how the efficacy of vitamin E in the treatment of cardiovascular disease was discovered by Dr. Evan Shute of Canada, and of the remarkable cures effected by him and his brother, also a doctor . . . how the author himself suffered a severe heart attack and how in a short time he was restored to normal active life by massive doses of the vitamin . . . how a barrier against vitamin E has been erected in this country by the medical traditionalists of the American Medical Association at the same time that it is being widely used with spectacular results in such medically-advanced countries as England, Germany, France, Italy, and Russia . . . how continuing study indicates that vitamin E may be an effective preventive for diabetes, sterility, arthritis and a variety of other diseases. "Literally worth its weight in gold."
—The Pittsburgh Courier   **$1.65**

GET WELL NATURALLY
Linda Clark

LINDA CLARK believes that relieving human suffering and obtaining optimum health should be mankind's major goal. She insists that it does not matter whether a remedy is orthodox or unorthodox, currently praised or currently scorned in medical circles—as long as it works for you. Miss Clark, who is also the author of **Stay Young Longer**, makes a plea for the natural methods of treating disease—methods which do not rely on either drugs or surgery. Drawing not only from well-known sources but also from folklore and from the more revolutionary modern theories, she presents a wealth of information about diseases ranging from alcoholism to ulcers. Here are frank discussions of such controversial modes of treatment as herbal medicine, auto-therapy, homeopathy, and human electronics, plus some startling facts and theories about nutrition and about the natural ways of treating twenty-two of the most serious illnesses that plague modern man.   **$1.65**

FOOD FACTS AND FALLACIES
Carlton Fredericks and Herbert Bailey

A noted nutritionist and veteran medical reporter present medical evidence based on modern research to prove that a good diet can lessen your effects of coming down with one of today's common health problems, such as heart disease, arthritis, mental illness, and many others. This book gives the unadulterated facts about fad diets, and it presents some startling information about proper diet and the prevention and treatment of alcoholism. To help you be sure that you are getting the balanced meals you need, the authors have included eleven rules for menu selection; tips on buying meats, cereals, and breads; lists of common sources of vitamins, carbohydrates, and fats; and an appendix of suggested menus.   **$1.45**

LOW BLOOD SUGAR AND YOUR HEALTH
Eat Your Way Out of Fatigue
Clement G. Martin, M.D.

In this revolutionary new book, Dr. Martin tells exactly how to determine if hypoglycemia is the cause of fatigue problems, and if so, he outlines a diet that can make anyone feel better after the first week. It's not a starvation diet, not a fad diet. But it is unusual. The Doctor instructs the reader to eat eight times a day rather than three. And for those who don't suffer from hypoglycemia, it is still probable that the cause of the fatigue or mental distress is nutrition. These people will find Dr. Martin's delicious, eight-times-a-day diet pouring new energy into their bodies.

This is not a book of "miracle cures." It is a book about common sense attitudes toward nutrition and exercise—proof positive that a sensible, well-balanced diet is the **real** key to good health. **$1.65**

ORGANIC GARDENING AND FARMING
Joseph A. Cocannouer

A blueprint for soil management designed to enable you to grow better-testing, healthful, fruits, vegetables and other food crops. Here is complete information on **organic** gardening and farming—gardening without poisonous pesticides—where to start, what to do and how to follow through whether in a window box, backyard or on acres of soil. Everything you need to know to make friends with the earth the natural way is included—organic soil conditioners, composts and mulches, pest control without poison, tips on planting and landscaping.
Clothbound: $4.50
Paperbound: $1.45

NATURE'S MIRACLE MEDICINE CHEST
C. Edward Burtis

How to achieve abundant good health through everyday wonder foods—pure natural foods, our gifts from the land and sea. Mr. Burtis covers many of the wonder foods found in nature's miracle medicine chest and explains how to use them for better health—the fantastic papaya melon, digestive disorders and the lime, slipped discs and vitamin C, cabbage juice and ulcers, yogurt and digestive health, calcium and the heart, bone meal and loose teeth, garlic and diarrhea, the bactericidal qualities of honey, the remarkable powers of royal jelly, kelp for the common cold, cod liver oil and arthritis, vitamin E and the heart, brewer's yeast as a protective agent, sesame seeds as a tranquilizer.
Clothbound, $5.95

COMMON AND UNCOMMON USES OF HERBS FOR HEALTHFUL LIVING
Richard Lucas

A fascinating account of the herbal remedies used through the ages. Plant medicine has been used for thousands of years and modern science is now re-evaluating many old-time herbal medicines. Described here are the herbal folk remedies that have been used for centuries by the American Indians, the gypsies, the ancient herbalists, the countryfolk, and the old-time country doctor. The background, history and uses of such healing herbs as dandelion, elder, nettle, sage, kelp, onion, parsley, sassafras, rosemary, camomile, corn silk, celery as cures for rash, hives, urinary disorders, ulcers, gout, and nervous disorders are described. **$1.65**

HEALTH, FITNESS, and MEDICINE BOOKS

All books are available at your bookseller or directly from ARCO PUBLISHING COM-
PANY INC., 219 Park Avenue South, New York, N.Y. 10003. Send price of books plus
25¢ for postage and handling. No C.O.D.